Our Lives Out Loud

In Pursuit of Justice & Equality

ANN LOUISE GILLIGAN, PhD, was appointed to the staff of St Patrick's College, Drumcondra, in 1976 and has worked in the area of teacher education at undergraduate and post-graduate levels for the past thirty years. She established and directed the college's Educational Disadvantage Centre and has lectured and published on the philosophy of the imagination, philosophies of difference and educational equality. In 2001, she was appointed by the Minister for Education to establish and chair the National Education Welfare Board. She loves travel, wine, jazz, her BMW motorbike – and golf, on a good day.

KATHERINE ZAPPONE, PhD, is an independent public policy consultant and educator. Appointed by the Minister for Justice, she has served as a Commissioner on the Irish Human Rights Commission since 2001. She taught Practical Theology in Trinity College Dublin, has lectured widely throughout Europe, Canada, Australia and the United States and has written extensively on matters related to ethics, spirituality, equality and human rights. She learned the art of public policy as Chief Executive of the National Women's Council of Ireland. She loves fast cars, singing and good food, which she walks off in the Dublin hills.

OUR LIVES

OUT LOUD

IN PURSUIT OF JUSTICE & EQUALITY

FOREWORD BY DESMOND TUTU

Ann Louise Gilligan

Katherine Zappone

THE O'BRIEN PRESS
DUBLIN

First published 2008 by The O'Brien Press Ltd,
12 Terenure Road East, Dublin 6, Ireland.
Tel: +353 1 4923333; Fax: +353 1 4922777
E-mail: books@obrien.ie
Website: www.obrien.ie

ISBN: 978-1-84717-066-8

Photographs: most of the photographs are the authors' own;
page viii, bottom, *The Irish Times*. If any infringement has occurred
the authors and publisher ask the holders of copyright to contact them.

British Library Cataloguing-in-Publication Data
Gilligan, Ann Louise
Our lives out loud : in pursuit of justice and equality
1. Gilligan, Ann Louise 2. Zappone, Katherine 3. Lesbian couples - Ireland 4. Gay couples -
Legal status, laws, etc. - Ireland 5. Same-sex marriage
I. Title II. Zappone, Katherine
306.7'663'0922'417

1 2 3 4 5 6 7 8 9
08 09 10 11 12 13 14 15

Editing, typesetting, layout and design: The O'Brien Press Ltd
Printing: MPG Books Ltd.

TO OUR PARENTS
Imelda and Arthur, Kathie and Bob

**Our parents have provided us with exceptional models of love and
married life, and we are inspired by them and grateful to them**

Imelda and Arthur Gilligan
on the day of their wedding
in Dun Laoghaire, Dublin, 1939.

Kathie and Bob Zappone
on their fiftieth
wedding anniversary, 2000.

FOREWORD

ARCHBISHOP EMERITUS
DESMOND TUTU

This book is a story of two lives conjoined in love and the pursuit of justice. Their narrative is placed in dialogue with the social history of the times over the past twenty-seven years and depicts the different social projects they have been part of to contribute to the eradication of poverty in Ireland. More recently, they have engaged in a court case seeking justice for themselves. This book describes their formation as theologians and educators, influenced by the liberation thinkers of both disciplines – South African, feminist and Latin American – and how they used these influences in both their academic and social change work. A community education organisation they co-founded in 1987, The Shanty/An Cosán, thrives to this day.

They outline the place of spirituality in the process of engaging in social change. The book also documents their love story, their reasons for getting married in Vancouver, British Columbia, in 2003 and their search for justice through the legal recognition of that marriage in Ireland. At present, they await the hearing of their appeal in the Supreme Court. The book finishes by including an outline of their method for practising social change which they describe as 'soulwork in the public sphere'.

I recommend this book highly and believe that it will be an inspiration and a resource to many around the world who seek to establish a more just world. The text demonstrates the importance of relationship and attention to the spiritual in order to sustain struggle for societal transformation. The aspiration of this book is clearly to offer an understanding of topics that are not often addressed out loud. I hope that this empowers and sustains those who read it.

CONTENTS

1

ANN LOUISE

My parents married at the beginning of the Second World War, and I was born at the end of it. Perhaps my optimism throughout life can be attributed in part to my arrival into a world that was excavating hope from the rubble of destruction. Although Ireland remained 'neutral' in this war while its neighbours defended their versions of freedom, a canopy of threat still hung like a cloud over the Republic during those six years. In fact, the cloud burst accidentally, at times raining down devastation. The German bombing on the North Strand in May 1941, I was told, was clearly audible from our home across the bay in Nutley Park, South Dublin. There were other bombings too, and I grew up regaled with stories about my parents crouching in the press under the stairs seeking protection during those terrifying episodes.

It is the glance backwards from adulthood that really allows one to assess and evaluate one's childhood. What I experienced then, and what is confirmed by my memories now, is that I had a blissfully happy childhood. My parents simply adored each other. I never once heard an argument or cross word pass between them. My father, Arthur, was a businessman, a confirmed bachelor until, at thirty-three, he unexpectedly met my mother, Imelda, then barely twenty. Marrying my father forced my mother to leave her briefly held job in the Central Bank in Dublin – the marriage ban, which prohibited married women from working in the public service, was not removed until 1973.

I recall as a tiny child asking my mother which of the three of us children she loved the most, and without hesitation she responded, 'I love your father most of all and after that I love each of you equally.' When my mother died of cancer in her early sixties, with little warning, many of her close friends confided that she died of a broken heart. It was true. Try as she did, she never got over my father's death, also of cancer, a few years earlier.

While strongly middle-class, our upbringing was marked by careful expenditure of resources and genuine simplicity. We consumed few goods and services. I have no memory as a child of eating out; however, eating in was delicious as my mother was a wonderful cook and frequently entertained at home. The laughter from their dinner parties and her bridge evenings would ring through the house.

Early on in my life I learned that perceptions of wealth and well-being are relative. At school in Loreto, Foxrock, I had friends who lived in that very affluent suburb of County Dublin. Their fathers were among the industrialists who were reaping the benefit of Ireland's break from the cocoon of protectionism led by Sean Lemass. We often attended parties in homes on Westminster Road where butlers and cooks served us and the chauffeur waited on long, winding driveways. All this led me to conclude that our own comforts were few and sparse.

Class distinctions in the Ireland of my childhood were sharp but unspoken. Apart from my grandmother's discourse at every Sunday lunch which always referred to people's titles and connections, our privilege and others' deprivation was never mentioned. Yet, this was a time of marked differences and harsh poverty. Historians remind us that during this post-war period Taoiseach Éamon De Valera defended the dearth of social services when compared to our northern neighbours on the fact that they paid double the taxes.

Politics were never discussed in our family or within the walls of Loreto, Foxrock, where my sister June and I were educated. My brother Arthur, who also started his schooling in this genteel environment, graduated after his First Communion to the rough and tumble of a Christian Brothers' school. However, after a brief sojourn in this ambiance of Republican idealism, he electrified our Sunday lunch conversation on one occasion by asking my father where our grandfather had died. That the response 'at home, in his bed' was wholly unsatisfactory was evident from my brother's crestfallen face. 'Oh, dear,' he stated, 'I hoped that he died in a ditch fighting for Ireland.'

Shortly thereafter he was transferred to a private boarding school in Newbridge, County Kildare, run by the Dominicans. Any socialisation to patriotic hatred was anathema to my father whose manner was marked by a gracious, good-humoured gentleness. This said, one of the most formative stories of my childhood was told by him of his own experience as a boarder in the Jesuit school, Clongowes Wood. Shortly after his arrival there he became aware that a ritual of new boys being severely bullied by older pupils was practised. When the moment came for his initiation, he was prepared. He took a compass from his pocket and drove it through the leg of the leader of the gang. They fled and never touched him again. He quietly added a codicil to this story: 'Never tolerate an injustice', a phrase that has profoundly influenced my life.

The Catholic Church commanded absolute obedience from its members during this period, and I was among its servants. From my earliest years I had a deep sensibility for the spiritual dimensions of life. I loved solitude, and, reflecting back on my early childhood, I remember thinking a lot about questions related to life and death, and, indeed, pre-life and after-death issues.

My mother had a quiet piety. Her yearly visits to Lough Derg on a penitential pilgrimage involving quite a bit of hardship, our family outings to visit her beloved sister, Mother Dolorosa Gately, in a convent in far-flung Wexford, and her rosary and prayer books beside her bed all had a formative influence. My Dad, on the other side of the bed, muttered, as he smoked his pipe, that she did the praying for all of us. He read from his large pile of history books as she said her rosary. In fact, he offered a perfect antidote, balancing her devotion with scepticism, if not agnosticism, in relation to all dogmatic absolutes.

An abiding memory of my childhood is kneeling beside my mother at

Monday evening devotions in the nearby church on Merrion Road. Her voice soared, incense wafted, candles burned in abundance, and I experienced Heaven. However, no links were ever made between the mystical experience of Marian devotions and the incarceration of unmarried women on the Donnybrook Road less than a mile away, in the Magdalen Laundry. The Sisters of Charity ran this institution on behalf of the same Church. I always experienced a cloud of depression as my mother left me at the huge, wrought-iron gates at the entrance to this grey residence and whispered that she needed to leave in a packet. While alms-giving was part of our family culture, there was no critique of the injustice of poverty nor any engagement to act for its transformation. Furthermore, there was no analysis as to why places such as the Magdalen Laundry existed. I continue now to feel anger and outrage that the lives of many young women, my age, were destroyed as they bore the sins of their fathers, literally and metaphorically, and were incarcerated in the gloom and damp of imposed guilt.

The underside of a child's sensibility towards the spiritual in the period of my youth was the controlling influence and the dogmatic arrogance of the Catholic Church. 'Outside the Church there is no salvation' was a teaching from school that rang in my ears as I tried to fall asleep at night having laughed and played with my Protestant and Jewish friends who lived on our park. At this point, I had not awoken from my 'dogmatic slumber' and simply struggled with the contradiction and confusion that caused me genuine worry and distress.

My home and school shared common factors: they both were places of love, warmth and excitement. I can still feel the hug from Mother Imelda in the cloakroom as I arrived at school, an embrace of love that was extended to each child every morning. This rotund, jolly woman had a profound influence on my life. Although she died in her thirties of cancer while I was still in the junior school, it was her name I chose when I entered religious life some twelve years later. I remember how movingly she spoke of God's love for us as we prepared for First Confession and Holy Communion; this was one of those rare moments when words allow one to experience the reality. While some claim we grow into innocence, that it is not something we are born with, I would disagree; those years were years of pure, untarnished innocence, which was the greatest privilege of all.

My desire to become a teacher was formed during those earliest years. Something in me wanted to ensure that all children could experience their birthright to such openness and know love and joy within an educational setting. Before she died, my mother reminded me that when I was a very small child I used to wander up and down our park gathering up children, large and small, and bring them back for lessons at our dining-room table, where I presided as the teacher!

Growing up, I came to realise that I lacked certain linguistic wirings – the dawning was gradual. Thankfully, this was never termed a 'learning disability' or diagnosed as dyslexia, which is what it was, and so never really blocked my educational journey. Orally, I had no difficulty – one repetition was enough. I remember sitting in Junior Infants saying to myself, If they repeat this one more time I will scream. But spelling was another matter. Week on week my mother and I would sit by the fire in the drawing room on a Thursday night as she 'heard' my spellings in preparation for the Friday test. Neither she nor I was ever too deflated when each Friday revealed that, no matter what I did, I couldn't get them right. She'd always smile and say, 'Well, all that matters is that you did your best.'

These Friday-morning 'failures' quickly evaporated into longing for Friday evening. My father, a publican, always worked late, and so, after our baths, the three of us snuggled into our parents' bed, and my mother read to us. I don't recall what she read, but the emotional warmth remains. Certainly this experience inculcated a love of books, and early on in my childhood I became an avid reader, starting with comics such *The Beano*, then the Noddy books, and quickly graduating to everything I could get my hands on. Then, as now, I was a slow reader, and I have never been able to read for long periods at a time; however, that has never taken away from the enjoyment and love of reading.

Not being able to spell and being incapable of reading aloud never became a major issue. The curriculum in our school was eclectic at best, varied at least, and, in general, ideal for someone with my challenges. The day started with either marching with Major Gollard or ballet lessons, with Miss Doran on piano. My sense of rhythm, love of dance and jazz all had their formation in those early years. By the time I was eleven years of age, Miss Cahill had trained us to be proficient public speakers. Our sessions were early examples of how the Toastmasters conduct their meetings: a pupil was called forward and given a topic to address spontaneously, others then had to speak against them. I found these sessions exhilarating, and they certainly prepared me for the position as leader of the school's debating team in later years. Later still, when I won the All-Ireland Toastmasters' competition, I stated my firm belief that training in oral confidence is imperative for children with dyslexia.

Music formed a large part of our education. We had a school orchestra, in which I played first violin, and a school choir, where we sang and were examined in a large choral repertoire, while at home I learned piano. When I was eight, my sister June and I played duets on Raidio Éireann. Art education also featured strongly, and Mother Peter prepared us each year to enter the Caltex Art Competition where we all won all sorts of prizes. This was an aspect of education that linked my home and school: my father was related to the Irish artist Fr Jack Hanlon, and early on it became evident that my brother Arthur was a gifted artist.

My greatest love in school was sport, a passion that has never faded. During my first year in secondary school I was given a place in goal on the first senior hockey team, a position I held for the following six years. It was utterly unusual that a twelve-year-old would play on a senior team, but I was fearless and adored the rush of adrenalin as girls twice my size charged at the goal. My sister, three years ahead of me, played on the same team, as right wing – unlike me, she could run like lightning. I was happy to flank the goal, and, as a large, heavy child, I would make the occasional dash when the opponent's approach needed to be halted.

As I reflect on my schooling, I think that my engagement with school in general and love for the whole school environment was more important for my future happiness and well-being than academic achievements. Indeed, my attendance in class reflected what the great educationalist John Dewey spoke of as 'double-mindedness'. I never gave more than half my mind to what was going on at the top of the room, some of which I found extremely boring; the rest of my mind was plotting the next adventure or creative prank. I was always a leader in class and recall my fifteen classmates, when faced with a written examination in religious education, pleading with me to think of something to save us. The nun entered the room, settled herself on the raised podium and produced the exam papers. On cue, I 'fainted'. The exam was postponed.

Thankfully, I attended school in an era when there was no points rating for university places. All we needed was to matriculate in six subjects, including Latin and Maths. Indeed, a basic Leaving Certificate, so long as you passed Irish, could be your entrée into medicine or any other field. However, such opportunities were available only to the middle classes and those who could pay for secondary school and university.

There is much evidence that poorer children in Ireland at the time left school after primary, between twelve and fourteen years of age, having suffered their schooling in classrooms of up to, or over, forty-five children. It wasn't until 1967 that the then Minister for Education, Donogh O'Malley, without permission from anyone (the Taoiseach, Jack Lynch, was out of the country) announced free education for all second-level students. This decision rocked the Government and changed the Irish nation. His decision was clearly influenced by the Organisation for Economic Co-operation and Development (OECD)/Irish Government report of 1965, *Investment in Education,* which forewarned that future economic growth would be hindered if an educated workforce were unavailable. I also like to believe that he was moved by an awareness of the injustice of a school system riddled with classism.

It was in my final two years of school that it became clear not simply *that* I wanted to teach but *what* I wanted to teach. Questions of meaning always fascinated me, so the day that a friend of mine asked the nun teaching us religion whether God really existed or not, I snapped out of my day-dream and listened intently for the answer. What happened next really shocked me. With a crushing glare, the nun told the girl to sit down and never ask such a question again. That moment was formative, helping me decide that what I wanted to do was teach religion and to encourage questioning of the given or received truths that shaped our lives.

As I entered my final year at school in the autumn of 1962, the twenty-first Council of the Catholic Church began. It was a time of huge optimism that a new age was dawning, led by a charismatic pope in the twilight of his life. Pope John XXIII's notion of *aggiornamento*, 'to-day-ing', became a household word in Ireland. We had just got television, so we could see images of a sea of bishops, some 23,000 of them, descend on Rome. I do recall being informed, when I boldly asked, that twenty-four women, half of them nuns, would be allowed in as observers!

Two weeks later, the mood changed, and I recall lying awake waiting for the world to end. US President John F Kennedy had confirmed reports that Soviet missile sites were located ninety miles from America, and so we were in the midst of the Cuban missile crisis. Most of us believed this was the beginning of a third World War, the beginning of the end. The fear evaporated but left its mark in relation to the transience and uncertainty of human life.

Change happens in many ways, but, on a few occasions in my own life, I have experienced what I would describe as an intellectual conversion – by this I mean a fundamental shift in my way of understanding the world, caused not by direct experience but by reflecting on new ideas. During our final year at school in 1963, a priest from the Oblate Order was invited to teach us the Social Encyclicals, which, in my opinion, are 'the best kept secret of the Catholic Church'.

The earliest of these was written in 1891 when the Church was perceived by many intellectuals as essentially irrelevant. Each encyclical offered radical insights into Catholic responsibility to engage in social analysis and action, especially on behalf of the poor.

We started our study with Pope Leo XIII's *On the Condition of Labour* (*Rerum Novarum*), and heard the pope rail against the inhuman conditions that many working people were subjected to in industrialised societies. He emphasised the dignity of the worker and the necessity of a just wage that took into account the needs of the individual. To my ears it all sounded remarkably similar to the radical views that had been expressed by the trade-union leader 'Big Jim' Larkin, especially when he addressed workers on O'Connell Street during the 1913 lock-out. The fact that the Church deemed that it had a responsibility to speak out about social issues was new, as was the connection between human rights and the economic order.

Forty years on, Pope Pius XI wrote *The Reconstruction of the Social Order* (*Quadragesimo Anno*, 1931). In it, he addressed a very different world where the First World War had shattered the liberal confidence of the earlier period. In his own words, he sought to 'expose the root of the present social disorder'. We were introduced to a new term, namely, 'social justice', and we critically reflected on how this type of justice demanded recognition of the 'common good'. I recall our discussions about the right to own private property and it being clarified that with this right came a duty. This idea stayed with me and was certainly influential in later years when Katherine and I decided to share our home with the people of Tallaght West, a situation that continues to this day.

We also had extensive discussions on the requirement on Catholics to share superfluous wealth. This was neither communism nor socialism, I had to remind myself, this was the teaching of the Church! There was an anomaly about sitting in a classroom with some of the wealthiest young people in Ireland reflecting on these ideas. Whatever the aim of this course, it utterly changed my life. I have often thought, then and now, that if the institutional Church practised what it taught it might have credibility and meaning in the lives of more people today, including my own.

Throughout our schooling, respect for authority was never questioned, and discipline was never an issue; however, minor misdemeanours assumed an inordinate *gravitas*. In my final term at school it was agreed that I would not be allowed to become a Child of Mary, the final badge of honour for a Catholic schoolgirl, because of my persistent talking in class. In my opinion, this was clearly ridiculous, and so I summoned the Mother Superior to the front parlour for a meeting to discuss the matter. To her credit, she listened, and so I graduated along with the other sixteen with this honour.

Shortly afterwards, my classmates and I took a group of inner-city children on a summer holiday to Sunshine House in Balbriggan, and seeing the injustice of poverty etched in their faces confirmed my commitment to take the next, rather unexpected, step. I entered religious life in Loreto, Rathfarnham, some months later. My personal guiding motto was: What return can I make to the Lord for all that He has given to me?

My parents greeted my decision with shock, if not dismay; my father was especially reserved about the wisdom of the idea. This was a period in Ireland when droves of young people were entering religious communities and few were leaving. In fact, leaving was much more difficult than entering. Like many young people at that time, I was full of enthusiasm and idealism. I was also innocent, if not ignorant, about my sexual identity. Never having any interest in boys could have been attributed to the fact that we all but lived at our all-girls' school. Weekends were as occupied as weekdays, playing inter-school matches or preparing for and performing in school plays. One could say I was completely undeveloped sexually, and none of this would alter as I prepared to take a vow of chastity!

Entering religious life was like stepping into the nineteenth century. Founded in 1821, Loreto, Rathfarnham, had retained all the graciousness and discipline of Victorian living. Being a postulant in 1963 was like living a synthesis of the 'upstairs/downstairs' cultures of that earlier period. Our parents visited us in the glorious, if faded, grandeur of leather-wallpapered parlours with magnificent antique furniture, overlooking manicured lawns. While they sipped tea from fine, bone-china cups, we struggled to make conversation across the divide of different worlds. However, once downstairs in the novitiate, we cleaned, dusted, polished, shone silver and distributed laundry in an endless rotation of housework. The Sub-Mistress of Novices stood over us, ensuring perfection in the execution of each task. For someone who had never dusted or polished anything in my life, this was a shock to the system.

It was a period when the nuns were divided into 'sisters' and 'mothers'. The sisters performed the mundane, menial tasks such as housekeeping and cooking, and the mothers did the professional work of teaching. The sisters sat apart in church, had their own community room, ate separately and slept in the basement quarters. The mothers had cells high above the church, looking down on the 'blessed sacrament'. From the day I entered, this 'apartheid' system deeply disturbed me. One of my fondest memories and greatest achievements was gaining permission, while still in the novitiate, to put on a course in scripture for the sisters, which I taught them in their separate community room.

After an initial year as a postulant, during which I had the chance to teach in a local school which I loved, I made the transition to becoming a novice and entering what was called a spiritual year. This transition was traumatic as it involved having all my hair cut off and wearing a veil of heavily starched white linen. As an older novice cut off my long, thick hair, leaving me in a bald state, I remember thinking, rather irreverently: Well, that's it – none of us will be leaping over the wall anytime soon! On a more serious note, I also silently questioned the gender injustice of this act, knowing for sure that the Jesuit novices across the road in Rathfarnham Castle were not being subjected to the same indignity. This was a time when Vatican II was writing its document on religious life, *Perfectae Caritatis*, and recommending 'that religious dress should meet the style of contemporary fashion'. Donning the habit was a gesture that was both symbolic and real as it also severed all connection with the outside world. Much to my regret, I lost all contact with all my very close school friends. However, this was the culture: friendship was not encouraged, and 'particular friendships' were shunned. I was always perplexed as to why! I was allowed the odd letter, which would be opened, from my parents. My mother later spoke of her alarm when, in response to her correspondence that referred to The Beatles, I wrote back questioning why she was talking about insects!

It was serendipitous that, as I finished three years in the novitiate in Loreto, Mater Dei Institute opened, a college that, for the first time in Ireland, provided a formal training for religion teachers at secondary level. While most newly professed nuns waited passively for their assignment, I wrote to the Provincial and requested that I be sent to Mater Dei. To her credit, while informing me that my petition was inconsistent with my vow of obedience, she let me go. My teaching life began in earnest when I completed the course there.

However, I began to have a growing sense of disconnection between the world in which we lived out our religious commitment and the 'outside' world. Although I loved much about community life, especially the times of stillness, and I relished my teaching, I had the distinct impression that we were living a pre-modern existence, though this was supposed to be an 'active religious order', working within the framework of Vatican II ideas about the Church in the modern world. Furthermore, I had entered religious life with the expressed desire of going to Mauritius, where the Loreto sisters had a strong commitment to the Creole people. When I was informed that I was needed in Ireland, my love affair with convent life began to wane. In my opinion, I could be a good teacher and an effective administrator in any walk of life in Ireland, especially in middle-class schools. I didn't need to be a nun to do that. I was also acutely aware of what I considered to be my lack of faith. To be an excellent religious, one needed, I felt, a faith deeper and less questioning than mine. I decided to leave the religious life.

Leaving the convent happened under a shroud of secrecy. While those in authority didn't resist my decision and respected the echoes of my conscience that told me I must now go, they cautioned me to tell no one, to say no 'goodbyes'. The sadness of this transition was cushioned by the kindness of my sister June, who collected me quietly, bringing the necessary change of clothes, and welcoming me into her home. I had no money but quickly gathered the train fare to Spain where I spent the next three months as an *au pair* to an extremely wealthy family in Seville. My father told me that the day I left was one of the best days of his life! Sadly, he died shortly after.

My fascination with community life persisted, however, and soon after leaving the religious community I set off for a kibbutz in Israel with two close friends. Having read the Jewish philosopher Martin Buber's work *Paths in Utopia*, I wanted to experience this ideal of communal life, rooted in the theory of socialist democracy, and see whether it could be lived in practice. Our kibbutz, of some five hundred *kibbutzim*, followed the usual template. It was a classless, rural collective, striving to live out a social ideal. Here in Givat Hashlosha, a kibbutz of secular Judaism, land and language, not religion, seemed to bind the group. Adults had their own small living quarters, and children lived and were educated apart. This, we were told, contributed in part to the ideal of sexual equality, allowing women and men to work for the collective and to run for public office. After the work day, parents and children came together for what was popularly known as 'the love hour'. Each afternoon, one could observe children gleefully bringing the fruits of their latest project to their parents' home. The volunteers lived in small wooden shacks that were prone to visits from cockroaches and mice, especially at night.

The profits from the cotton industry, the orange groves and the chicken factory were reinvested in the settlement. There was a weekly meeting, and I recall endless wrangling over the use of the four cars the collective owned! Living in the kibbutz made us privy to a level of discontent such as one would never read in the literature describing this movement. During our time there, all families were rewarded with a television set out of the comprehensive budget. As volunteers, we certainly contributed to the profits, working long and arduous hours. I was assigned to the kitchens and peeled so many carrots over the months that my hands turned orange! My co-workers were immigrant Jewish Russian women who spoke Yiddish. We bonded without spoken language, and, when finally it came time to leave, we wept.

I felt I learned a lot about a different form of communal living. Although the kibbutz movement had a strong aspiration to change the order of human social living, and a strong feminist discourse about the need to equalise the status of women and to relativise the authority of men, in my experience women continued to bear the yoke of domestic work and resource the relational aspects of the kibbutz, including roles such as nurses, carers and educators.

I observed their system of 'collective education' that had the aim of fostering in the young *kibbutzim* values of 'labour, equality, collectivism, democracy and voluntarism'. By living together in a 'children's society', the idea was that children were trained for communal life, co-operation and equality from the beginning of their lives. I recall one woman saying to me that they learned the meaning of 'ours' before they understood 'mine'.

Since that time, I have read much of the research about their system of 'communal education', and, while totally different to the individualistic, economically driven, competitive model of secondary education we have grown to accept in Ireland, it too is a biased system of education not without its critics as well as its proponents, serving its own ideology of state and nationhood.

While we were there, Palestine and Israel were enjoying a period of relative peace, yet an unspoken threat always hung in the air. Armed guards used to parade up and down the refectory where we ate our meals, which was not conducive to digestion – but then, neither was the food, as we lived for months on the cooked entrails of chickens!

However, having returned since on a few occasions to work with Palestinian people, I can observe that, comparatively speaking, this was a time of exceptional calm in this complex and troubled land.

I returned to Ireland with many questions buzzing in my head and settled into secondary-school teaching at the Mercy Convent, New Ross, County Wexford. No sooner had I started, though, than another opportunity arose. In 1974, the Director of the Mater Dei Institute, Fr Pat Wallace, offered me a scholarship to do a master's degree in Paris for the following two years. This was a moment of pure gift, made possible by a man who did nothing but good all his life. Pat Wallace was a priest and a poet, who gently nudged all his graduates to image the possible in their lives. In this case, a legacy had been left to the college for a student to do further studies, and I was the chosen recipient. With my parents content that I had landed a permanent and pensionable position, I was now faced with a new set of decisions – but, truthfully, it wasn't hard, and the following September I began two of the happiest years of my life. While I was confident of my standard of oral French, having spent three summers as an *au pair* in France while still at school, the written language would be a different challenge. However, my years in religious life had eased my dyslexia as the Sub-Mistress of Novices had an intuitive talent with difficulties such as mine and had trained me to read aloud and spell more proficiently. So, coinciding with my college registration, I signed up with the Alliance Française in Paris and took French language exams concurrently with my degree courses.

I lived in the Latin Quarter, where the heavy presence of the French police, sitting in huge, black armoured vans at most street corners, offered a warning to all of us students that no repetition of the students' civil-rights protests of 1968 would be tolerated. The 1970s had brought an easing of tensions. 'Demand the impossible', a slogan from the students' riots, had, it seemed, borne fruit, for I arrived in a Paris where contraception and abortion were now legalised, and divorce by mutual consent had been introduced. Simone de Beauvoir was still alive and active, raising consciousness about the sexism and patriarchal behaviour of men who considered themselves part of the leftist movement.

To study theology, philosophy, psychology and education in Paris during the mid-seventies was an extraordinary privilege. Now I had the opportunity to meet my footnotes. Giants in theological and philosophical thinking at the time taught us. Yves Congar was among them; his 'ecumenical passion' never wavered despite an uninterrupted series of denunciations of his work. Lectures from this man were formative. I still recall his words: 'Whatever we have to say, as sublime as it is, it is really not worth much unless it is accompanied by a praxis, by real action, by concrete service and love.' These were European thinkers refreshingly open and creative in their reflection.

There was a practical component to our studies, so each week a young African priest, Lucian, and I used to head off to one of the new 'dormitory cities' to experience life in a new, multicultural parish miles from Paris. Few of these new immigrants spoke French, and almost none had any interest in the Catholic Church. However, the local 'worker priest', Fr Philippe, who had a factory job alongside his parish duties, put out a plea for help to paint and decorate his church, located in the basement of a huge, concrete block of flats. Gradually, while working together to create a space of beauty in a place of desolation, a community was formed and a parish was born. It was a privilege to be part of such an undertaking. Working with Fr Philippe on this project gave me an insight into the radical worker-priest movement. Founded by a Dominican, Fr Jacques Loew, in 1941, the aim of this mission was to reconnect the Catholic Church and the working classes. Those who joined shed their priestly garb and worked in factories, campaigning for better pay and conditions for the working poor. The unions welcomed their presence, but the Vatican was reserved and, at different points, intervened to halt the movement. However, thankfully it has survived to this day.

It was during those years in France that I met the famous Abbé Pierre, whose motto 'Love the poor' was not rooted in any romantic or benevolent philosophy of almsgiving or charity; rather, it was a teaching that called for solidarity with those who suffered the injustice of poverty in order to act for its transformation. He was an intellectually humble man, who took the prophetic message of the Gospel seriously and lived life accordingly. He was an inspiration.

Following this golden period, I had the good fortune to be appointed as a lecturer to St Patrick's College, Drumcondra, Dublin (St Pat's), the training college for primary teachers. Again, serendipity, if not providence, provided. A few years earlier, I had been assigned for my final teaching practice to an all-boys' school run by the Vincentian order at St Paul's, Raheny. When I visited the Leaving Cert class for an observation day prior to commencing, I encountered a roomful of young men, all of whom towered over me. Any mention of religion clearly bored them, so I suggested that I would teach a month-long philosophy course on existentialism instead, which excited and appealed. My supervisor was a saintly priest, Fr Seamus O'Neill, then a member of the Department of Religious Studies in St Pat's. I can only surmise that Seamus recommended me for the appointment.

My career in St Pat's over the past thirty-five years has never been dull. The opening years prior to my departure to undertake my doctorate in Boston College in 1981, passed happily and without incident. It was during this time that my mother, truthfully my best friend, suddenly developed pancreatic cancer and died within eight weeks. Watching her bravely transition from being a beautiful, fun-filled, strong woman to a shadowed, emaciated presence left its mark. Her consolation, constantly repeated, was that now she would be reunited with her beloved Arthur. I hope she is.

2

KATHERINE

'Your silence will not protect you.'

Audre Lorde

This will be a soft telling.

I was born five months after the United States Government electrocuted the Rosenbergs for espionage. It was 1953. A cold wind was in the air though it was only eight years after the ending of the Second World War. The fear of communism masked the desire for new markets and the growth, not of imperialism because Americans had shed the royal exterior as they sought 'the land of the free', but of American capitalism throughout the globe. Much of that fear wasn't yet infecting a quiet town in the most north-western state of America – Spokane, Washington – where I was born. Not much was happening in the 'Inland Empire' as it was called then. While McCarthyism was rampant on the East Coast, those living in Washington state were far away from the centre of political power. Though it was a little different with my parents. My mom, Kathie, was a New York City girl, and she had met my father, Bob, there when he was studying for an MBA (Master's in Business Administration) at Columbia University. He was there *gratis* courtesy of the GI Bill, one of the few ways young men were thanked for fighting in the Second World War. So, though my parents had moved west by the time I appeared, they still had a keen eye for anything happening eastward.

My dad had always said that he wanted to marry a woman who was his intellectual equal, an undoubtedly progressive view for his time. Graduating in 1942 from Mount St Vincent's College in New York, my mom was one of a small percentage of women Americans who deferred marriage long enough to get an education and start out on a career. She worked as the personal assistant of Paul Titus, one of the big boys at Hearst Advertising Services. She had dreams of continuing in advertising. She was very popular with the men and still has a rather large collection of gorgeous linen hankies given to her by various admirers during that time.

In September of 1950, Bob and Kathie married in New York, and soon headed towards Spokane where my father took up a teaching job with the Jesuits in Gonzaga University. He had received his bachelor's of philosophy there, and they both must have decided that it would be a great place to raise a family. First came my brother Bob Jr, and then myself, the oldest daughter. Before they were finished, I had one beautiful sister, Suzanne, and two other brothers, Philip and Mark. My mom had left the glitter and glam of the city that never sleeps. Her dutiful sacrifice of professional fulfilment left its mark, though this struggle never indented her unconditional love for all of us children.

Our home was a happy place, built to their design and its location chosen for a neighbourhood that was filled with kids and spacious residences. But money was tight for us, and there were a couple of years when I had to wear second-hand clothes. No wonder I loved going across the street to my best friend Kay's home where they had a maid, a grand piano, a Mercedes 280 SLK in the drive, a refrigerator in the den (as well as in the kitchen) and a huge bedroom for just one little girl. I adored her. I wanted to be with Kay all the time. I was five years old.

We didn't go to the public school close to home. We were Catholic, and so every morning we took the long car ride to the closest parochial school, Our Lady of Fatima. It was a quiet time in American Catholicism, though in 1958, when I had my first religion classes, a peasant from the north of Italy was elected pope. As I prepared for my First Communion the next year, John XXIII announced the convocation of a new Vatican Council, one that would require the presence of all the bishops of the world, as well as theologians and non-Christian observers, in order to respond with a fresh and open spirit to the agitation for renewal growing at the fringes of the Church.

As a six-year-old, I was, of course, unaware of those stirrings of change so far away. I was, however, in love with God. Every morning, I couldn't wait to get to the church for daily Mass, and I still have a well-worn blue children's prayer book that brought me into a haven of tranquil communication. Where does a kid so young get such an attraction or orientation? I really do not know. I knew that both my parents were people of tremendous faith, thoughtful and active Catholics. This, no doubt, influenced the way in which I interpreted my small world, but my deep devotion so young had origins beyond the ordinary. I literally experienced an affective relationship with transcendence. It was at the centre of my little heart.

My memories of spiritual security are coupled with disturbing remembrances of the 'red scare'. Adult Americans were being told that the communism of the Soviet Union would spread all over the world if the American Government didn't do something about it. What would happen, they wondered, if and when the Russians knew how to manufacture the hydrogen bomb? Towards the end of the fifties, every so often when we were at school an outside siren would split the silence, and the principal would flip the school-bell switch. We as children were told that the Soviets may be attacking, and we had to crouch under our desks until it was 'all clear'. By 1962, based on a series of invented scares about Soviet military build-ups, the United States had overwhelming nuclear superiority.

Close to the time of my eighth birthday, John F Kennedy was elected President of the United States. I remember the euphoria, especially in our Democratic household. His inaugural words still hold such vision:

Let every nation know, whether it wishes us well or ill, that we shall pay any price, bear any burden, meet any hardship, support any friends, oppose any foe to assure the survival and success of liberty. Let the word go forth from this time and place, to friend and foe alike, that the torch has passed to a new generation of Americans – born in this century, tempered by war, disciplined by a hard and bitter peace, proud of our ancient heritage, and unwilling to witness or permit the slow undoing of human rights to which this nation has always been committed.

Could he mean it? His deeds fell far short of the promise. But how could we have known that then? We were the new generation. And though I did not meet one black person until I went to high school some years later, the Black March on Washington in 1963 sent reverberations of 'The Dream' all across the United States. The rebellious soul of oppressed Americans was being eloquently transformed by Dr Martin Luther King into a spiritual call for political freedom. It was one of the first social movements that inspired my life. I would later find that the spiritual urgency for social change is another avenue to the divine.

My late childhood and adolescence, however, were lived far more under the felt influence of apparent change within the Roman Catholic Church than the explosive social rebellions in other areas of American life during the 1960s. An openness to the modern world and a willingness to consider change were being promised by the Church in a faraway land. Little did I know then that I would come to meet some of those who gathered to observe the Vatican proceedings – Gustavo Gutiérrez, Hans Küng, Mary Daly. Each had their own story to tell. Each believed in the promise. All of them suffered because they took the promise seriously in their own lives. But I am ahead of myself now.

In 1964, we left the sleepy town of Spokane because my dad had secured a big job in Seattle, three hundred miles farther west. It took me two years to get over leaving my best friend. I lived for the trips back to Spokane to visit her. They were frequent at first. I really couldn't imagine my life without her. But I simply had no choice, no power to change that as a child. Reality forced the eventual adjustment, though I am certain that meeting another best friend helped to heal my mind and heart. Sally had a beautiful voice and loved every kind of music. Some of my very happiest times were singing with her in school recitals and Easter midnight ceremonies. Other happy though confusing times were nights spent together in her house or mine. My innocent exploration of sexual identity may or may not have impacted on her. To this day, I do not know. This was the beginning of a deep silence within me, at my very core.

I don't think anyone would have noticed that veiled confusion. I loved sport, speech, music and everything to do with school. I stood out. I was a leader. But I didn't talk about everything. Not even to my best friend. Not even to myself.

In the autumn of 1968, some of that confusion dissipated – or perhaps it was just put on hold for a while as my world got bigger. My parents wanted the best for me, and so I was given the opportunity to go to Holy Names Academy, an all-girls Catholic high school fifteen miles from our home. Today it is one of the best college preparatory environments in the state. I was meeting hundeds of girls from other backgrounds and neighbourhoods. Our teachers had high expectations. There were lots of extra-curricular activities. And, by that time, the wind of religious change was blowing fiercely in Catholic schools throughout the United States. There were no recitings of the catechism. Instead, religion teachers experimented with countless ways to make religion relevant to young people's lives. Our freshman retreat was a weekend full of song and religious fervour. I came back to school leading the new liturgical songs before and after classes. Many of us were on a spiritual high. I visited the chapel every day.

Of course, things settled down after a while, as they always do. And I tried to live the 'normal' life of a teenager. Many days I had no difficulty. I loved driving my own car to school. I played sport. I studied hard. Then one day, at the age of fifteen, I met Katie. She was two years ahead of me; she had a soft smile with hazel eyes and long, silky, straight brown hair. She was exceedingly bright, and she, too, was captivated by God.

In the milieu of rules and normal expectations, we both reached across a very wide chasm towards each other.

It wasn't easy to find the time to spend together, at first. Two years apart in school meant that we had different schedules, different groups of friends, different worlds. Over the next two summers, however, we created a world where our friendship deepened, and I remember often feeling that time stood still when we had picnics and lengthy conversations in Volunteer Park, or played chess in her home, or when I listened to her play a twelve-string guitar and sing with a faltering yet sweet second-soprano voice.

What were we to make of how we felt about each other? While it was an utterly pure experience of love, during those first years of our companionship there was always, always something secretive at the essence of our relationship: to ourselves as well as to the outside world. And so, she had boyfriends. I tried them too, once or twice during high school. Neither of us questioned this in the other. Somehow, we managed to hold parallel worlds together: the world of our secret love and the other, regular(ised) world. We continued to do this for the next three years, as she went off to Seattle University and I finished up in high school and then went off to Gonzaga University back in Spokane.

This late adolescent world of self-discovery and silence, coupled with striving for academic excellence and spiritual depth, was only faintly touched by the political turmoil of the Vietnam and Watergate era. Yet, this was my cultural context – awakening each day to the growing movement of people from all walks of life opposing the Vietnam war. In 1970, my oldest brother turned eighteen and only barely missed being drafted into the war; instead, he joined the tens of thousands of young Americans who protested against it on their college campuses throughout the United States. The climax of protest came in the spring of 1970 when President Richard Nixon ordered the invasion of Cambodia; the United States National Guard shot to death four students who were striking at Kent State University in Ohio. While eight of the guardsmen were indicted by a grand jury in 1974, a US district judge dismissed charges against them all on the basis that the prosecution's case was too weak to warrant a trial. The political damage had been done, though, and within that same year Nixon issued the order for US troop withdrawal. The critical 'no' of the American people, the power of public protest, had effected immense social change.

The early seventies were filled, too, with the cumulative effects of the first and second waves of American feminism. The suffragettes of the late nineteenth century and the women's liberation movement of the 1960s broke apart the 'feminine mystique': the image of the woman as mother, as wife, living through her husband, through her children, giving up her own dreams for that. As Betty Friedan concluded: 'The only way for a woman, as for a man, to find herself, to know herself as a person, is by creative work of her own.'

The political activism of black women challenging their poverty within patriarchy, of middle-class white women demanding freedom from sex discrimination in employment, and the Supreme Court decision in 1973 – *Roe vs Wade* – bringing into law that a woman and her doctor had the right to decide about abortion – all of this was my world too. I grew into my young womanhood with a horizon of vastly more opportunities than my mother had. This is not to say that women were free. But I was being exposed to wider possibilities, and I was witnessing the fact that critical analysis and activism could bring about tangible change.

And yet, I muse now what impact it had on my evolving sense of self that as a young adult I lived during an era when every official body classified my sexual orientation as an illness, a crime or a sin. It was not until 1973 that the American Psychiatric Association removed homosexuality from its *Diagnostic and Statistical Manual of Mental Disorders* (the bible of psychology). Up until that time (for my first twenty years), homosexuality was viewed by psychologists as a pathology, a disease to be treated. No wonder, then, that Katie and I invented a parallel world.

It was hard to keep that going at times. Often one world would disappear. The early period of college in Spokane was a time like that. I was excited by the new venture – being away from home, living in a dorm, being responsible for my own new adult life. I had decided that I wanted to study medicine and signed up for science pre-med courses for that first semester, along with one course I chose from a liberal arts curriculum required by all students attending a Jesuit university. I was at *this* Jesuit university because my father had gone there, taught there. Photographs of him still hung on the walls of the administration building. I was baptised in the parish church adjacent to the campus. I didn't apply to any other college; it was my first and only choice.

Destiny opens unexpected doors. Fr Vincent Beuzer SJ was the chairman of the theology department in 1972. He taught me the one non-science class I took in my first semester: the Letters of St Paul. His lectures fascinated me. It was my first hearing of a critical approach to the study of scriptures, and, as I listened to the unfolding of ancient stories interpreted within the context of their own times, the faith of my childhood grew up.

I was still happily engaged in my scientific study, and I perceived this New Testament course as an enjoyable 'requirement'. Six weeks into the term, though, Fr Beuzer called me to his office one day to discuss an essay that I had written on Paul's Letter to the Romans. At the end of our meeting, he turned to me and said: 'Zappone, I think you should consider majoring in theology. Or, at least a double major in theology and medicine.'

If you have ever read the Acts of the Apostles, you may remember that it contains a story about how Paul fell off his horse on the way to Damascus. As told, the story to conveys the suddenness of his conversion to the God of Jesus. One day, Paul was persecuting the followers of Jesus, the next day he heard Jesus's call to preach the Gospel. I didn't even know that I was on a road comparable to Damascus, but my teacher did. Two weeks later, I decided to drop medicine and to take up theology. It was the beginning of an intellectual and spiritual journey that would last twenty years.

It was an inspiring time to be studying theology within a Catholic environment. The impact of the Roman Council was being felt in American Churches and theological centres of study. In 1971, the National Conference of Catholic Bishops held its ground-breaking synod 'Justice in the World'. It was viewed as the beginning of a new way of doing the work of the Church in America. The Church was the *people* of God, not simply the hierarchy. It was open to being transformed, and theologians in every country encouraged a shift in focus from private spirituality and doctrinal matters to community, society and culture. Gonzaga fostered a close-knit community, and hundreds of us would gather regularly for theological reflection outside of the classroom as well as attend Saturday evening Masses sponsored by 'campus ministry' teams. I learned the double bass in order to play and sing at those Masses. There were more lay people than priests or religious studying theology; there were more women than men. It felt like the beginnings of a quiet revolution, one which had the potential to make religion relevant to and powerful in the modern world.

I did not miss home much. I had made lots of new friends. I met Tom the first day I arrived on campus. He lived in the boys' dorm next to mine and moved in at the same time. I recognised him that day because I had noticed him the year before as a senior in high school when our choir joined the Seattle Prep choir to give a concert at Christmas time. He was good-looking, dynamic, smart, artistic. We were known as 'a couple' that first year, and everyone thought I would marry him. We danced, sang, ate, but did not sleep, together. Neither of us wanted to. We didn't even discuss it, and our friendship – confusing at times – paradoxically deepened.

I returned to Gonzaga the following autumn, though I did not last beyond the winter. In the early seventies, it was exceedingly unusual not to complete a degree at the college where one began, unless one was dropping out altogether. That was not my circumstance. I was enthralled with theological learning more than ever. But the parallel world of my love affair with Katie was calling me back to Seattle. Many, many times I was asked, 'Why are you leaving Gonzaga?' But I never spoke the truth; instead, I offered a lengthy rationale about 'Tough times for my folks' (my father had recently lost his job) or 'The theology department at Seattle University looks more to my liking.' How could I speak the truth then? I am reminded of a book written during that time entitled *On Lies, Secrets and Silence* by Adrienne Rich. I am telling the truth now. I hope it is not too late.

Katie had an apartment on Columbia Street, a couple of blocks from the university. I spent some of my time there (when her roommate went home for weekends), and I also moved back home. I continued my theological study at Seattle University; she was completing her theological degree that year. We had eight months together before, once again, the two-year age difference separated us as she went off to New York City to begin a master's degree at Fordham.

My last two years at Seattle University were a mixture of deep loneliness for her, confusion about what that could possibily mean and a rigorous training in theological scholarship under the tutelage of some of the best Jesuits in the country. It was there that I learned to become a systematic thinker with philosophical leanings towards the classics. It's hard to imagine now how attendance at a seminar in St Thomas Aquinas's *Summa Theologica* could generate such excitement within me. But Fr Reichman knew not only how to engage young minds in a reasonable debate about faith, he also provided me with the technical tools to order concepts and write words so that theses could be deftly elucidated towards proven conclusions.

My spirit continued to be caught by the transcendent presence of something divine. My theological endeavours could not be disentangled from the daily experience of being called by God to 'Come, follow me.' At twenty-one, I interpreted that to mean to prepare myself to teach religion to adolescents. Had I been a man, I probably would have joined the Jesuits (the vow of heterosexual celibacy was not an issue). I suppose that exclusion from the possibility of leadership, authority and priestly ministry was one of my first felt experiences of oppression. (I could not feel the oppression of my sexual identity because of the silence within me.) As I continued my training in the 'Fathers of the Church', the 'Trinity', and the 'Theology of Man', it did not occur to me to apply some of the insights of a dawning feminist consciousness coming through my reading of Simone de Beauvoir's *The Second Sex* to the study of Christian theology. Further, the bibliographies of my courses did not contain any of the early feminist theological writings, such as Mary Daly's *The Church and the Second Sex*, published in 1968.

Once again, I had the experience of living in two separate but parallel worlds until they started to converge in late 1975. Some of my women friends had heard of an invitation to gather in Detroit, Michigan, in November of that year to discuss the ordination of women to the Catholic priesthood. A couple of us decided to go – I had never been that far east. It was the first of such gatherings, and the Women's Ordination Conference continued to meet for the next twenty years. While I do not remember much of the content of the conference sessions, I was present in the plenary hall when the organisers invited any woman who felt called to ordination to stand up. One by one, hundreds of women stood that morning to publicly claim their call. All of us were forever changed.

In October of 1976, Pope Paul VI completed a document, *Declaration on the Question of the Admission of Women to the Ministerial Priesthood*. In it, he quoted Thomas Aquinas: 'Sacramental signs represent what they signify.' The Pope added: 'The same natural resemblance is required for persons as for things. When Christ's role in the Eucharist is to be expressed sacramentally, there would not be this "natural resemblance" which must exist between Christ and his minister if the role of Christ were not taken by a man. In such a case it would be difficult to see in the minister the image of Christ. *For Christ himself was and remains a man*' (emphasis mine). As long as Jesus was male, women would not become priests. While the Church was preaching justice on social issues, this did not extend to the realm of women nor to the sexual domain. This has never changed. I really believed then that it could.

I continued to pursue my theological career and feminist interests at the Catholic University of America in Washington, DC, where I completed a master's degree in religious studies in 1978. I chose the location for two reasons: it brought me closer to Katie who was living in New York, and it was one of two pre-eminent programmes in religion and education during the period. It was a tumultuous time in American Catholicism. The American bishops were often found to be at odds with Rome, especially in their efforts to break new ground on birth control, homosexuality, clerical celibacy and women's ordination. There was so much hope on the horizon.

And yet, internally, I was growing more and more depressed as the months went by. In January of 1977, I sent a letter to my parents: 'I know it's been a long time since I have written and part of it has been my busy schedule, but the other part has been that I've been depressed lately and I didn't want to worry you.' I will never forget the extraordinary generosity of my parents' response, especially my mother, to that letter. She had a fear of flying and had never flown before. In the early spring, all of that changed as she boarded a plane, with my father, to come and visit me.

Why was my psyche so fragile? While the pressures of graduate school were fierce, it went beyond that. Something fundamental shattered within me during those eighteen months. I think it was then that I began to realise that I could no longer live in two worlds or between worlds. The healing finally came, gently, through self-discovery and acceptance. I packed my bags in March of 1978 and headed to New York.

Living in New York City in the late seventies was challenging. Day by day I felt my soft Seattle skin harden until I had enough armour to protect my soul from the despair of the poverty and violence that played itself out on the streets of the Bronx. One afternoon, I was walking on Fordham Road and came upon a man laying on the street, bleeding profusely from knife wounds. I just kept on walking. I was too frightened for my own safety to stop. (And so I was left with a scar on my ambition for social change that still lingers today. Scars can be avenues towards deeper insight, though. I have learned that personal empathy – the ability to feel the emotions of another – is a prime and necessary ingredient in any agency for systemic change. The revolutionary path goes askew unless I bring my soul and heart as well as my mind to the work. Analysis without empathy produces solutions for the powerful only.)

What a contrast it was for me, then, to leave the Bronx each morning on the subway to a stop that opened onto another world – 5th Avenue and 84th Street. New Yorkers call it the 'Upper East Side', and it was upper in every way. Immaculate streets, doormanned apartments, elegant ladies and slick gentlemen arriving in white stretch-limousines or yellow taxi cabs to begin another day. I was chairing a department of religion for the upper school in Marymount School of New York. It was here that I made my first clumsy efforts to make religion more relevant to the lives of rich young women whose parents lived or worked in New York and travelled all over the world. The Shah of Iran's daughter and the daughter of the Plaza hotel's manager were some of my charges.

I think I managed to engage their minds, somewhat. But I know that I caught their hearts when we would take the long bus journey from the school to the southern tip of Manhattan. Dorothy Day lived and worked here in the Bowery, in a place called Maryhouse. In the mid-1930s, she and Peter Maurin founded the Catholic Worker movement in order 'to create a society in which it would be easier for people to be good.' They published a newspaper that contained a critical analysis of the social issues of the day, established houses of hospitality for people who were hungry and homeless and held regular round-table discussions for clarification of thought about questions pertaining to the social order. She was an anarchist and a spiritual leader, a simple and brilliant woman who believed that we are all responsible for one another and the common good. Maryhouse provided hospitality to homeless women, and I would bring my students down to help with serving lunch. We were all fearful at first – that we might get mugged, knifed or have our money stolen. But unconditional respect and love pervaded the atmosphere and melted our fear. When Dorothy died, eighteen months later, tens of thousands of New Yorkers lined 5th Avenue to say goodbye as her pine coffin travelled from the Bowery to St Patrick's Cathedral.

During the three years I taught high school, a slow-burning restlessness grew. There were still so many things that I did not know about theology or how its study could be the source of social and spiritual change. But that was not the primary source of my disquiet. One early summer evening, after taking my usual run through the campus of Fordham University, I conceded to myself that my thirteen-year companionship with Katie was over. The details are not relevant to this tale. The separation, though chosen on my part, was searing. What would I do? Where would I go? For several years I had heard about a doctoral programme in Boston College. Entry was highly competitive, but it seemed to be the right course to suit my interests. It was the only place I applied. I was accepted. In late August of 1981, I set off to a town where I knew no one.

3

LOVE STORY
IN BOSTON COLLEGE

Open the book of tales you knew by heart,
begin driving the old roads again,
repeating the old sentences, which have changed
minutely from the wordings you remembered.

Adrienne Rich

The heavy heat of a Boston summer had started to subside during the first week of September 1981. One hundred and seventy acres of Boston College's tree-covered Chestnut Hill campus nodded to the gentle approach of a New England fall as Ann Louise left her graduate housing in Foster Street in Brighton and Katherine sped in an orange Volkswagen Beetle from an attic room in Newton towards McElroy Commons, the location of an orientation session for graduate students in theology and religious education. Both of us were anxious, for very different reasons, yet expectant that we would find new professional opportunity through doctoral study in a strange town. Neither of us imagined anything more than that.

Katherine entered the room relieved that she had finally made it to this day. Leaving New York had felt like an uprooting from solid ground. There were lots of students in the room, and chairs were being moved around to form a semi-circle that would hasten warmth and make way for the professors' introductions. She walked towards the back rows, somewhat shy of the activity and started to sit down. Her shoulder tapped, she turned around as Tom Groome, one of the professors, introduced himself and then pointed towards Ann Louise in the very back row. 'She's our other doctoral student. She's from Ireland.'

Her smile was beautiful; her eyes warm with generosity and optimism. But it was the voice – the refined Irish female voice – that took Katherine totally by surprise. She had never met an Irish-born woman before. Did they all sound like that? Not possible, Katherine thought. Ann Louise's clothes were different too, more formal and less casual than American styles, and Katherine would later learn that the burgundy sleeveless jumper Ann Louise was wearing had been knitted by her beloved mother. During that first encounter, Katherine took in the utter vivacity of this woman from an unfamiliar land.

Ann Louise had arrived somewhat earlier. When accepted into this new interdisciplinary doctoral programme some months earlier, she had learnt the disconcerting news that there would be only one other candidate. The thought of studying with just one other student for the next number of years didn't appeal. So this would be the day when all would be revealed. Suddenly the door opened, and this very attractive woman with black curly hair entered; she had an air of confidence and authority that set her apart. Dressed in her tailored suit and carrying a leather briefcase, she sat a few rows ahead. Her confident demeanour allowed Ann Louise to muse: Well, thank God one of us knows what we are doing here! Ann Louise quickly warmed to this woman, Italian in appearance and German in her sense of purpose. What she didn't know was that she was Irish at heart. She was called Kay at that time.

On the first day of classes in early September, the front page of *The Heights,* Boston College's independent student weekly, carried an article announcing the appointment of Fr Avery Dulles SJ as the Gasson Professor for that year, a Chair established to support the visiting professorship of a prominent Jesuit. Fr Dulles, considered to be 'one of the country's leading theologians and systematic professors', was also the son of President Eisenhower's Secretary of State, John Foster Dulles. (He was elevated to the position of Cardinal in the Catholic Church by Pope John Paul II in 2001.) We were both excited at the opportunity of studying with him, each having read several of his works in our earlier degrees. Ann Louise signed up for the graduate seminar in Christology, and Katherine took his course on Theological Epistemology, designed to 'apply the philosophy of knowledge to theology'.

Nothing exemplified more the Catholic ethos of this university than the presence of such a distinguished theologian. Its ethos was and still is a primary rationale of its existence. Boston College was founded in 1863 by a County Fermanagh-born priest, Fr John McElroy. It was an institution created in response to a period of bigotry and intolerance for the Irish Catholic immigrants of Boston. Catholics were originally denied domicile in the Puritan Protestant Boston until 1789 with the adoption of the state constitution after the American Revolution. As late as the 1830s, Catholics comprised only 2 percent of the US population, but, due to the famine, some two and a half million Irish left their homeland, and in the decade from 1846 to 1856, almost 130,000 of these Catholic people entered Boston. They were desperately poor, had been deprived of education and were therefore destined to become the labouring and domestic classes. The Catholic bishop at the time sought a means to begin to change the future for these Irish, to prepare them to participate in and to lead Boston civic life and take up positions of trust and responsibility in city and state. Through the assistance of Fr McElroy, the Society of Jesus answered the bishop's call to found a low-cost college for day scholars.

By the early 1980s, the Chestnut Hill campus, bordered by Commonwealth Avenue and Beacon Street, was nestled between settled upper-class neighbourhoods, and its Ivy-League character was bolstered by high tuition costs of $6,000 per year (standing at $37,410 per year in 2008). The city of Boston was cresting the wave of the 'Massachusetts Miracle,' a model of economic growth, public–private co-operations and consensus politics. It was still suffering, though, from the bitter controversy over court-ordered bussing during the mid-1970s that was designed to promote racial integration in the city's public-school system. Judge W. Arthur Garrity Jr, a Harvard-educated Irish Catholic, found that the Boston school committee had 'knowingly carried out a systematic program of segregation' and that the entire Boston public-school system was 'unconstitutionally segregated'. Students were bussed to different areas of the city to break the segregation. It was a heart-breaking time for Boston, with ugly racial incidents earning it the label of the most racist city in America.

Boston suffered other inequalities. A 1982 Brookings Institution study on urban life concluded that Boston ranked in the bottom third of all major US cities when measured against things like unemployment, poverty, crime and municipal debt. The inflation rate was 12 percent by 1980, and, in the New England region, unemployment rates climbed to levels not seen since the days of the Great Depression. It was no wonder, then, that Boston was also home to many community organisations formed to prevent destruction of working-class and ethnic-minority neighbourhoods, drawing on grass-roots political power to negotiate with business and city on behalf of the people.

Those were the muted rumblings in the city background as we made our way back and forth between the main campus, where classes were held in handsome limestone and granite buildings styled in English Collegiate Gothic architecture, and 31 Lawrence Avenue, an old Boston three-storey wooden home recast into offices for the Institute of Religious Education and Pastoral Ministry. The institute was a burgeoning academic centre, offering graduate degrees to students from all over the United States and countries farther afield. It held a premier reputation for interdisciplinary doctoral study in religion and education, bolstered by the scholarship, writings and pastoral sensibilities of Drs Mary C Boys, Thomas Groome, Claire Lowery and Padraig O'Hare. As PhD students we also had access to courses and professors in what is called the 'Boston Theological Institute', a consortium of nine theological schools in the greater Boston area. At different times during our two years of coursework we studied at Andover Newton School of Theology in Newton Centre, Episcopal Divinity School, Harvard Divinity School and Weston School of Theology, all in Cambridge, across the Charles river. We were enthralled with the magnitude and diversity of theological education available to us.

As the days passed during that first academic term, we began to spend more and more time with each other outside of classes. As anyone knows who has done graduate study, it is an intense period in one's life. For us, though, the academic intensity was soon coupled with a burgeoning desire for friendship and intimacy. This was completely unexpected and caught us both by magical surprise. Katherine was still distracted by grief and just couldn't imagine that Ann Louise was anything other than straight, though it soon became apparent that Ann Louise was not pining for anyone in Ireland. Katherine felt so timid about disclosing her sexual identity to Ann Louise – the cultural gap had her mystified. Americans in general are upfront about personal details, though revelation of sexual identity is usually more covert, except, of course, if interpersonal dynamics open up a safe setting. But what were Irish Catholics like on these matters?

Ann Louise gradually realised that she was falling in love. To speak of love, or at least of 'falling in love', requires us to speak in metaphors – for only this form of living language can allow us 'to lisp the truth' of this transcendent and ever so immanent experience. Ann Louise often speaks of meeting Katherine as being 'surprised by love'. This was an encounter that awakened in her a potential for mutual love that had not been experienced before. It was so easy for her to identify with and choose this love. Despite coming from a very different background, Ann Louise had no hesitancy in accepting the newness of this form of love and, trusting her deepest intuition, gradually became convinced that Katherine would be her life partner.

Money was extremely tight for Katherine. Though she had a full-tuition scholarship and some contribution towards cost of living, this did not cover all expenses. In the first year, in order to make ends meet, she had to take a part-time bookkeeping job with a young man who was starting a landscaping business. Nevertheless, one evening she invited Ann Louise back to her room (in a family home with cooking privileges in the kitchen) to the most extravagant meal she could envisage and proudly dropped two whole lobsters into a boiling pot on the stove so that Ann Louise could experience the Boston delicacy. 'I couldn't possibly tell her,' muses Ann Louise now, 'that I was horrified to witness the death of these two living beings!' We had a wonderful meal, Katherine considerably poorer and Ann Louise with a sacrificed principle.

When we look back now on that the evening, we both agree that it marked a turning point in our awareness that each yearned for the other. It was eminently challenging, however, to find any kind of private space for the flourishing of our relationship. Ann Louise was renting a room in a graduate housing dorm, and the hallway to her bedroom door was highly visible by all others who lived there. Katherine lived in an attic room, with the owners occupying the other floors and another boarder in a room beside her. Of course, had we been an opposite-sex couple, none of this would have mattered much and we would have a very different story to tell.

Little daunted, the power and passion of mutual love enhanced our problem-solving abilities. By mid-October, we were getting into the car each Friday afternoon and heading towards the North Shore. Ann Louise, while not a woman of too many means, never let money stand in the way of a proper and magnificent longing. So, every weekend we found a lovely motel in Gloucester, a fishing town about sixty miles north of Boston.

We had discovered its extraordinary natural beauty on our first visit to a House of Prayer that was attached to the Jesuit Eastern Point Retreat House. It was located in the servants' quarters above the kitchen of the old estate. Sr Isabel Green, a very holy woman, ran the House of Prayer with utter simplicity and profound wisdom. She became our dear, dear friend, and we believe that she was aware of and affirmed our love relationship, though unspoken between the three of us, to her premature death in 1986. But we are ahead of ourselves and have stepped off the chronological path because sweet memory sometimes does that.

On 10 November 1981 – six weeks after we met – Katherine asked Ann Louise if she would spend the rest of her life with her. It was an eternal euphoric moment. We both stepped out of time to a place where potential hindrances do not exist, where cultural gaps dissolve and bodies become one forever. The next morning we went out on to the beach in front of the Good Harbour motel and took the run of our lives. We would continue to run together, often, on the beaches of the North Shore with the unimaginable joy of two embedded spirits. We decided to enter a period of engagement, though, and wait until the following October to make a formal life commitment to each other. It was the biggest decision of our lives, so we wanted to be as certain as we could that a lifetime of faithful love could be ours.

The weekends on the North Shore continued as often as we could manage them throughout the autumn and coming winter months. We often brought books and notes and tried to maintain the proper concentration of doctoral students. One Saturday morning, we went off to breakfast at a local café. We were intensely involved in a theological conversation that continued from leaving the car to eating the pancakes. When we finally got up to return, Katherine realised that she had locked the keys in the car. 'Not to worry,' Ann Louise said confidently, 'we have another set of keys in the motel room.' The motel was a good few miles away, however, and so we decided to hitchhike back – relatively safe in those times. It wasn't long before a lovely woman, Stephanie, picked us up. She was a real-estate agent, and as we started to tell her the story of our frequent visits to the North Shore, she said: 'My husband has a little house in Gloucester that he wants to sell but we can't put it on the market for several months because of a legal dispute about the size of the back yard. Would you consider renting it, for a very small fee? It would be safer to have the house occupied than not.'

We had found a home to be together without even looking for one. The heavens were opening just for us; that is what it felt like then, and it would not be the last time.

It did not take us long to get the bare living essentials moved into the skinny, maroon-coloured, wood-panelled house on Washington Street. Regardless of weather, we never missed a weekend (one winter afternoon it took us four hours to get there after driving through an unrelenting nor'easter snow blizzard on Route 128). What did our colleagues think at the time? We simply would be making up an answer now because there was little comment. Sure, they all thought it amazing that as doctoral students we had a weekend getaway. And we did begin to gather a small, close circle of friends with whom we shared the nature of our relationship. But we also held large parties in our snug home for those who did and those who did not know; the joy of our partnership just kept spilling over, and we wanted to celebrate every moment of life, often.

We did not, however, ever notice the weekly announcement in *The Heights* about a gay and lesbian support-group meeting in Haley House, a centre for social-justice concerns at Boston College. We probably would not have attended. A layer of silence was slowly erecting itself around our public lives while the circle of friends in the private sphere grew. Fear was never far away, though. One evening, we spent hours agonising over whether we would come out to one of our woman professors; at the time, she was Katherine's doctoral advisor, and a friendship between them had begun to develop. The hiddenness of our relationship – within the context of friendship with others – often impacted negatively on Katherine's sense of integrity. But, we were studying *theology*, and who knows how such revelations might impact judgements made by others about our academic progress and consequent professional opportunities. Perhaps it was even deeper than that: coming out in a professional context necessarily would mean a deeper acceptance of the normality and goodness of this way of being human. The journey towards such self-love as a young lesbian woman was not to be, this time. In the midst of our discussons that evening, Katherine felt her head splitting until she experienced herself almost out of body. Later, we would diagnose it as a severe panic attack brought on by the conversation and by emotion that erupted from somewhere within the deeps. Living the tension between our public and private lives was enough to drive us crazy some days, but there was also a push towards an evolving freedom that ultimately became possible for us because of our 'forever love'.

The themes of freedom and liberation were to dominate our theological and educational formation for the next five years. Our professors of religious education were steeped in liberative philosophies of education as well as critical understandings of sacred texts that uncovered the power of prophetic traditions and portraits of Jesus Christ as Liberator. Sociological studies of Christian origins prompted the crafting of theories of education that promoted the learner's action in society as a key requirement for a life characterised as Christian.

During the sixteen years since the closing of the Second Vatican Council, the disciplines of theology, biblical studies, pastoral ministry and religious education had been released from the unhealthy authoritative grip of Rome. This prompted a flourishing of new methodologies to interpret ancient traditions and Church teachings. Developmental psychology, critical sociology, archaeology and historical criticism were among the scientific and literary disciplines used by theologians and biblical scholars to uncover new religious meaning that would be relevant and inspiring for twentieth-century Christians. Religious education was now being influenced by giants of educational theory such as John Dewey, Maria Montessori and George Coe, all of whom shared the belief that we learn through doing and that the educated person engages with society and participates in building a democracy that represents all the people.

These were the intellectual currents that flowed through us each day as we walked into classrooms and libraries and took part in dinner conversations with professors, colleagues and friends. They created an ecclesial and professional milieu where religion was perceived as a potent force that would enable the discovery of meaning and the establishment of more just societies. As future leaders in the fields of theology and education, we were becoming familiar with the huge sea change within Roman Catholicism and other Christian denominations and its implications for finding new ways to re-create engaged and critically intelligent communities of faith.

We were in *Boston*, though. As Thomas O'Connor, the famous historian of this town has said in his book *Boston Catholics*, 'New theological and philosophical *movements* were being discussed in a city of renowned colleges and universities' (emphasis ours). During our second year of coursework – both at the Institute of a Roman Catholic university and three 'renowned' Protestant divinity schools – we began to study liberation theological movements with those at the forefront of those movements. We came into contact with believers who brought God-talk to the doors of movements for social change. This was to revolutionise our lives, forever.

Carter Heyward is a fiery, inspiring, courageous and creative feminist theologian. She was ordained in the American Episcopal Church in 1974 with the first group of Episcopal women who broke their Church's laws by becoming ordained irregularly (that is, before the Church as a whole had approved women's ordination). In 1975, she joined the Episcopal Divinity School in Cambridge to teach 'systematic theology'. By the time Ann Louise took her courses and Katherine heard her public lectures, Carter had come out as a lesbian feminist priest and was developing theories about God based on women's experience of the divine in sexual relations of mutuality.

A wellspring of freedom erupted within both of us. Here was a theological leader, inspiring rhetorical orator and social activist who shared our sexual identity. If she could do it, so could we. Here was a woman who bravely followed her own insights from experiences grounded in the world of the twentieth century, not of a world two thousand years ago. Our intellectual search to make religion relevant and to utilise it as a source to power social change was being exposed to a path we had never before imagined.

Carter's first major text, *The Redemption of God: A Theology of Mutual Relation,* re-envisaged God as the 'power in right relation', and she lectured about the ways in which our human effort to practise mutuality in friendship and intimate relations is a primary source of divine healing in the world. At times, she would equate God with 'our unalienated erotic power', and she would always couple her search for more adequate God-talk with a constant concern for justice and social change in various forms. She linked the efforts of people who are poor and oppressed with the struggle of people who choose to love those of their own gender. She challenged us 'to god' in the world. Along with other feminists, she was rethinking sexuality and God as 'justice-love'. Her soft Southern drawl was often eclipsed by a cacophony of student voices in heated debate throughout her seminars.

We were completely caught up in the possibilities that Carter laid before us. We did not even bother to think about the practical consequence of such radical thought. Why would we do that then? She fed our own fiery spirits, and we were young, we had our whole lives before us. She was talking about a way to draw on the extraordinary energy of our partnership-love so that the world could be a better place, for everyone.

Feminist theology was erupting within Roman Catholic circles as well. The brilliance and bravery of feminist theologian Mary Daly continued to reverberate throughout Boston College (and other theological centres around the world) even though Mary was on sabbatical from Boston's theology department for most of our stay. After the publication of her first book, which uncovered and tracked a deep prejudice and hatred of women throughout centuries of Christian texts, her contract had not been renewed. Student and faculty protest was immediate and widespread. Eventually, after marches and petitions and the establishment of a review committee, Daly was reinstated with tenure in September 1969. By 1973, she had published another text, *Beyond God the Father: Toward a Philosophy of Women's Liberation*, wherein she laid out the classic argument that 'If God is male, then the male is God in society.' She was one of the first to dismantle the maleness of God by outlining its impact on the subordinate position of women in society. She pointed out in one argument after another how the history of Christian theology gave divine sanction to patriarchal social order.

All of this made such sense to us. Daly's early works demonstrated meticulous systematic and rational arguments. Weren't these the prized characteristics of what we were being taught as the best of theology? Yet, we of course were deeply aware of how her approach challenged the very heart of male power and authority in the Church and in society. If she did not get away with it, would it be safe to follow her path? To be honest, questions of safety in this regard did not linger long for us. The truthfulness of her critique and our experience of it in our own lives as women in the Catholic Church emboldened our courage to embrace some of her fundamental insights and to believe that we could encourage others to do the same.

Our first meeting with her took place in the early autumn of 1983 when she returned from her sabbatical. We had only a few days left in Boston before heading off to Ireland, but we wanted to meet this famous woman. So we went to the first day of her graduate class, 'Feminist Critique of Selected Philosophical and Theological Texts'. We felt that we were in the presence of a 'Copernican' thinker, one who was turning much of what we had learned in earlier theological education on its head. It was truly awesome. We were very disturbed, however, by her demeanour. She would look out the window and ask, 'Can't you feel the poison in the air surrounding this university?' She was visibly shaken by teaching in the college again, as if she was shouldering all by herself the essence of centuries of patriarchal effects on woman. This would be the first of many encounters with Mary over the years. Ann Louise would establish a soul-connection with her, though not agreeing with all of

Mary's analyses and future philosophical project. But Ann Louise was able to discover the generosity and softness of her soul underneath the myriad layers of her persona for the world. This would teach us both much about the personal consequences of radical life options.

Issues of homosexuality and sexual ethics came to the forefront of Catholic debate and teaching during our time of theological study. With the origins of the gay liberation movement in the Stonewall riots of June 1969, many lesbian and gay people found their public voice to resist the construction of homosexuality as a pathological condition and to reject heterosexuality as normative (that is, the only way to be normal). Gay theology began to emerge in the 1970s as gay Christians started to reflect theologically on the gay liberation movement. The Vatican had released a document, *Persona Humana,* in 1975 which stated: 'Although the particular inclination of the homosexual person is not a sin, it is a more or less strong tendency ordered toward an intrinsic moral evil; and thus the inclination itself must be seen as an objective disorder.' John McNeil, an American Jesuit theologian, published *The Church and the Homosexual* in 1976. The book is a scholarly liberal critique of official Roman Catholic teaching on homosexuality. McNeil was ordered to refrain from any further public statement on homosexuality and to halt his ministry to gays and lesbians. For nine years he obeyed but finally broke the Vatican-imposed ban when the Congregation for the Doctrine of the Faith put out a 'Letter to the Bishops of the Catholic Church on the Pastoral Care of Homosexual Persons' that reiterated its 1975 teaching, and McNeil was expelled from the Jesuits in 1987 at the age of sixty-two.

A number of other Catholic theologians challenged the Church's teaching. In 1977, a report from the Committee on the Study of Human Sexuality of the Catholic Theological Society of America argued for support of committed homosexual relationships because they fall within the report's criteria for genital expression characterised as 'creative growth towards integration'. The year prior to this publication, US bishops in a pastoral letter on moral values adopted a strong stance in favour of civil rights for homosexuals. In 1981, the Archdiocese of

Baltimore issued a statement saying that the homosexual orientation is 'in no way held to be a sinful condition'. On the other side of the continent, the Washington State Catholic Conference (three bishops of Washington state) published 'Predjudice Against Homosexuals and the Ministry of the Church'. The bishops suggested that Catholic teaching on homosexuality needed rethinking and development; they pointed out that the Church's theological tradition on homosexuality was not infallibly taught.

We lived through these times; we took part in the ethical debates as they were played out at Boston College as well as in Harvard and the Episcopal Divinity Schools. We experienced the freedom of ethical pursuit within Protestant circles and the strength of critical, respectful dissent within the Catholic arena. In the early 1980s, as we moved between several centres of theological education, it appeared as if momentum was growing towards a robust, systematic and rational foundation for a shift in Roman Catholic teaching. Leading theologians and prophetic United States bishops and archbishops challenged the Catholic Church's imagination to stretch towards sexual justice.

Perhaps you could say that we were living within such an exciting and challenging intellectual and faith-filled climate that we genuinely believed the Church would have a place for us some day. But we were still too afraid to place ourselves at the forefront of such change for sexual justice. We channelled our critical and creative energies instead into the promotion of feminist, Latin American and Black liberation theologies.

Rosemary Radford Ruether, a leading Catholic feminist thinker, was a ground-breaking theological scholar-guide in this regard. Her numerous published works place Christian sacred traditions in critical dialogue with feminist and other liberation movements throughout the world. Her *Sexism and God-Talk: Toward a Feminist Theology* (1983) put into published form lectures we received where she critiqued the male-favoured bias of Christian traditions, recovered long-ignored sources and practices of women's leadership and co-equal participation in religion and reconstructed concepts of God, Jesus Christ, redemption and other primary theological themes by including women's experience as revelatory of the divine. We experienced nothing short of intellectual conversion as she laid out how patriarchy and sexism are rooted in dualistic thinking. She traced the history of philosophical and theological scholarship that put forward sharp dichotomies between spirit and matter, soul and body, human and non-human and how maleness was identified with spirit and rationality, and thus superior, and femaleness was relegated to an inferior status because it was identified with matter, body and nature. 'God' could never be anything other than 'male' in this kind of world-view, and women could never be priests or authoritative decision-makers in Christian organisations. Ruether's works, however, promised hope for the future of Catholicism as long as women and men were willing to practise new ways of being Church together, to enter novel ways of living Jesus's vision of a 'discipleship of equals'.

As these freeing insights seeped deep into our bodies and minds, we felt reinvigorated and confirmed in our choice of theology and education as a profession. We were also discovering fresh ways to utilise revelatory texts and traditions in the work of social change. During the last summer of our coursework, we had the opportunity to be inspired and changed yet again. His name is Gustavo Gutiérrez, acknowledged as the father of Latin American liberation theology. Fifteen years prior to our meeting, he spoke for the first time about a 'theology of liberation' at a conference in Chimbote, Peru. Though he had been part of the theological renewal in the light of Vatican II, Gustavo realised that this was still not adequate for guiding and inspiring an attack on the structural poverty in South America. What did the Scriptures and Church teaching have to say to his poor people?

Gustavo invented a new approach to theology by inverting that question. He asked: 'What do the poor people have to say about God as they struggle for freedom?' *A Theology of Liberation* (1973) and *The Power of the Poor in History* (1983) challenge theologians, ministers and educators to reread scriptures and reinterpret talk about God and salvation from the viewpoint of a solidarity with the poor. Every morning Gustavo would come to class, having had an early-morning swim to maintain what little strength his legs had as a result of childhood polio. He would climb to the podium with a limp, a small man in physical stature, a Goliath as he began to lecture.

This is what he said: 'Liberation theology begins with a personal commitment to the ending of poverty. Then you analyse the causes of oppression and systemic poverty, *with those* who experience the impact of it. Theory and talk is not enough. Action to bring about social change has got to come next, and *then* theologian and people reflect on the word of God in light of that whole process.' We were transfixed. What a brilliant way to bring religion and social change together. We both felt his words, and his way touched the deepest parts of our souls. We knew then that we would have to find a way, some day, to follow this call.

Using this method, Gutiérrez discovered the social challenge of the Hebrew and Christian Scriptures: that God is a God *of the poor, for the poor*, and that 'salvation' is a historical process. It is not simply a matter of individuals saving their souls. Those who experience poverty must be empowered to become agents of their own transformation. The divine is revealed in the people's struggle to be free. We wanted to find God there too.

Around the time of that course, Gutiérrez came under suspicion by the Vatican, and in 1984 the Congregation for the Doctrine of Faith (with Cardinal Joseph Ratzinger, now Pope Benedict XVI, as the primary author) issued a 'Critical Instruction on Certain Aspects of Liberation Theology'. The primary purpose of this Instruction was 'to draw the attention of pastors, theologians, and all the faithful to the deviations, and risks of deviation, damaging to the faith and to Christian living, that are brought about by certain forms of liberation theology.' It was also the year that the Vatican conducted a visitation of the Seattle archdiocese, whose leader, Raymond Hunthausen, had also become suspect. The purpose of the visit was to assess the merits of complaints made about the archbishop, including, though not limited to, his welcoming of

Dignity, a lesbian and gay Catholic group, to the cathedral one day.

Were these growing pains? Or were they the fire of entrenchment, burning away any radical challenge to change?

We were in love, condemned by some and welcomed by others. Our desire to be together, fuelled by unimaginable joy and a youthful vision of utopia, carried us along as we continued to take stock of the consequences of a life commitment in one country or another. Our skinny Gloucester house was not available after the summer of 1982, and we certainly did not want to renew contracts for separate lodgings. What would we do? One day we went to visit Isabel to seek her counsel and to take a walk along the rocky beach of Eastern Point. As we described to her our dilemma, she said: 'A monk who stays with me from time to time has been renting a home in Rockport [four miles north of Gloucester] but he is moving on now. It might be available.'

Later that afternoon, we took our first drive to Penzance Road, which is just a little back from the seafront outside the town of Rockport. As we drove up to the wooden house on stilts (the Chinese couple who had built it only needed one floor but they wanted to see the sea), we felt for the second time that we were being blessed from on high. The house had panoramic views of the Atlantic from every side of its rectangular shape. Three bedrooms (two could be our studies), a wood-burning stove and an in-built wok in the kitchen added to the character of this potential new home. But we were now *farther* away from Boston; we would be letting go of our separate rooms and we still did have to attend courses at least three days a week. We asked the question again, what would we do?

Our dear and brilliant friend, Mary Condren, had the answer. Mary is an Irish woman who had also come to Boston College to pursue graduate studies. She had been a leader in the Student Christian Movement and had edited their journal, raising the visibility of feminism and other theological liberation movements long before she came to America. She had finished her master's degree but had decided to pursue a doctorate at Harvard. So Mary was in the process of looking for housing in Cambridge while we were considering the Rockport option. 'Would you consider,' she posed, 'taking rooms with me so you would have a place to stay during the week? It would help with my rent!' And that is what we did. The top floor of 29 Garden Street had just come onto the Harvard housing market. We called it 'The Penthouse' and would stay there three days a week while we took our classes and then we would get into the car on Thursday evening to head to Rockport on Route 128 north.

The fall of 1982, twenty-six years ago at the time of this writing, signalled the closing of our engagement. In early September, we contacted our friend Revd Flora Keshgegian, an Episcopalian priest who was studying in Boston College. We told her about our desire to make a commitment of 'life-partnership' and that we wanted to declare our vows within the context of a ritual. Our spirituality was integral to our individual identities and to our partnership. We knew of no other same-sex couples who were doing this then, but we believed it was the right and most meaningful way to proceed. It was a daring move for those times, yet it fitted with the creativity and experimentation towards spiritual freedom within mainstream traditions. Flora agreed, and we hold vivid memories of preparing with her the Eucharistic ritual and the exchange of vows. As any good Catholic or Anglican knows, people marry each other, the priest does not perform this sacrament. In fact, it didn't really matter to us whether the act of union would be considered a sacrament or not. Indeed, we did not view it as 'marriage' because that was a legal act which was forbidden.

We did feel, however, that we were moving into forbidden territory in some way, and this gave us great delight! It was our first small, though not insignificant, public step towards pushing the boundaries of sexual justice. While that was important to us then, all we really wanted to do was what couples all over the world do if they are in love and want to spend the rest of their lives together. Our friend Paula Wheeldon had a jeweller friend whom she suggested we go to for our rings. Paula said: 'I'll tell her what you are doing. She'll be fine with it.' So, as part of the preparations, we took the 'T' into De Caprio jewellers of Boston. We entered the store with a slight hesitancy and asked for Paula's friend. We were graciously welcomed. It's amazing how a simple act can mean so much. There we stood, at the glass counter, choosing settings and stones (ruby for Katherine – it's Ann Louise's birthstone; topaz for Ann Louise – it's Katherine's birthstone) and giving instructions that the engraving for each ring should read:

'God is Love – KAL'.

On 16 October 1982, we gathered together twelve close friends in our Rockport home to share a Eucharist together, to witness our life-partnership vows and to pronounce our union. For everything there is a season and a time for every matter under Heaven. For us, this was our time to plant, to build up, to dance, to laugh, to embrace, to gather stones together, to love.

It was not the time to tell our families.

4

STRANGERS IN THE
HOMELAND

Returning to Ireland in October 1983, having just completed our doctoral comprehensive examinations in Boston College, and with the knowledge that a new academic year in St Pat's would commence the following week, caught us up in a vortex of activity that left little room for anxiety about how our relationship would be perceived in Ireland.

Reflecting back, Ann Louise would say that her delight in Katherine's presence and the project of creating a home together in Griffith Court, where she had lived before folding up her tent and heading to Boston some years earlier, diverted attention away from the radical relational choices that we were making. We were in love and excited at this new stage in our relationship. Here was Katherine, willing to leave her beloved USA and live in suburban Dublin, in a sparsely furnished home that didn't even possess a washing machine! There was horror on Katherine's face when it was first revealed that Ann Louise used to wash her clothes in the bath. Obviously, the vestiges of a vow of poverty remained. Furthermore, there wasn't one mirror in the whole house – maybe this was related to the vow of chastity! Anyway, all that was to change, and change rapidly. We came into the twentieth century with a bang, borrowing the money to acquire all the necessary modern conveniences within a week. We restored the garden together as we listened to U2 play in nearby Croke Park, and we bought our first dog,

Habermas, called after the German philosopher Jürgen Habermas, who wrote turgid prose and had formed part of our doctoral examinations. Our Habermas gave much greater joy and delight than the other.

On her return to Ireland, Ann Louise sensed a gradual dawning of her difference in terms of her relationship. She had left Ireland as an insider, open, happy-go-lucky, nothing to hide. She had lived her life out loud, but now had to observe the wisdom of silence. For the first time in her life, she experienced herself as an outsider, a stranger to the status quo and the accepted norms of relationship. While people say that one's relationship is nobody's business and is part of one's private life, she came to experience that this is true only as long as you conform to the publicly prescribed norms for relationship as set out by Church and State. Returning home as an outsider, never happier, but cautious and fearful, was a very new and conflicting *modus vivendi*.

Founded in 1875, 'to provide training for Roman Catholic lay teachers independent of the State,' by 1974 St Pat's was a recognised college of the National University of Ireland (NUI) and funded by the State. But the managerial system didn't keep pace with such developments, and the college continued to be managed by the Catholic Archbishop of Dublin, with the stated ethos being to promote all things Catholic. Of course, Ann Louise could have 'come out' gaily and lost her job, as was the fate of Eileen Flynn in New Ross some time earlier (Eileen was a teacher in a secondary school managed by the Catholic Church who became pregnant out of wedlock, and the Church, consistent with the contradictions of its pro-life position, sacked her – she had to leave, along with the unborn she carried.) However, at this time, Ann Louise had a job and Katherine had none, we had a mortgage and needed to make monthly repayments, so we decided together that we would keep quiet about our relationship and choose very carefully those we would trust as we formed a circle of friends, some old, some new.

In mid-October, Katherine received a phone call; a gentleman who spoke with a soft Mayo cadence was at the other end of the line. It was the first time Katherine had heard an Irish accent that sounded different from those in Dublin. He introduced himself as Seán Freyne, Head of the School of Hebrew, Biblical and Theological Studies in Trinity College, Dublin. He said he had heard through one of his students that Katherine was now living in Dublin; she, in turn, had heard via Katherine's doctoral adviser, who was her uncle. (Such was Katherine's introduction to the way business is often done in Ireland!) Prof. Freyne wanted to put on a course in liberation theology for the Michaelmas term beginning immediately, but he had no one to teach it. 'Would you be interested?' he asked. When she went to meet Professor Freyne for the first time to have lunch in the Common Room at TCD, Katherine felt as if she was stepping into a period of cultural history different to anything to which she had ever been accustomed. The formality of the high-ceiling rooms, chandeliers, open fires and antique furniture complimented the sophisticated, club-like ambience where members (academics of the college) came for coffee at eleven or sherry after dinner. This sense of beautiful foreignness would lessen over the years but never diminish altogether. Katherine accepted his offer and thus began her nine-year association with Trinity.

It quickly became evident to us that the Ireland we had returned to was in crisis and that the bottom had fallen out of the economy. Although Ann Louise had lived away from the country for some time, both in France and in the United States, she didn't anticipate that the economic gains of the 1960s would have dissipated to the extent they had and that the country would be in such a malaise. She could recall 1963, just twenty years earlier, prior to entering religious life, the discussions around the table in her home where business friends of her parents, in buoyant mood, proclaimed that Ireland had finally broken with the depression of the 1950s. At that time, the country was sustaining an annual growth rate of 4 percent, and young people leaving school in the middle classes were filled with optimism as they had every hope of employment and a secure future in Ireland.

Clearly, governments had mismanaged the economy, for if you encounter a country in chaos, what else could you blame but the failure of leadership in the interval? It also became clear that some of the earlier optimism was grounded in policies that were unsustainable. As a public-sector worker, Ann Louise was among the lucky ones with a secure and pensionable position, but then 64 percent of the jobs that were created during the 1960s and 1970s were in the public sector. There were few jobs in the private sector and a clear failure to build indigenous industries. Large farmers, large property-owners and landowners were fine, but there was growing evidence of a working and non-working class of people who were suffering hardship as never before. Unemployment in the early 1980s had risen to 15 percent and there was a sense of powerlessness – that nothing could be done to redress it. As we (re-)entered Ireland in 1983, even those holding a Leaving Certificate and indeed graduates of the universities couldn't find employment and were emigrating in droves.

Studying at Boston College had influenced many changes, not least a radical change of mind. The return to St Pat's therefore challenged Ann Louise to a substantive review of both the content of what she would now teach and the pedagogies or methodologies of how she would teach. While the general course headings remained the same – for example, Moral Theology, Pedagogies for Teaching Religious Education – Ann Louise creatively manoeuvred the course content to teach areas that were now of far greater import and interest. Topics such as liberation, feminist and black theologies and the ethical issues emerging from these reflections were now included.

One of her most formative experiences in Boston was the opportunity to work as a graduate assistant with Paulo Freire. Paulo, a small, unassuming man, came from north-west Brazil each summer, with his wife Elsa, to teach the graduate students. Probably the most famous educator of the late twentieth century, with a worldwide reputation, this man was unusual because he actually lived what he taught, putting his theory into practice – something he would have named as *praxis*. Furthermore, he spoke the truth about the injustices in his own country where the vast majority lived in abject poverty while a tiny minority of landowners lived in decadent opulence. Although a lawyer by training, he had left that profession, convinced that education was the key to the transformation of poverty. He developed an adult literacy programme in 1963/4 that was immediately successful as it listened to the participants and taught people according to their interests and needs. He never arrived to teach with a prescribed curriculum; rather, he and the participants creatively constructed the content for each course, or 'co-intended the curriculum'. As the consciousness of local workers was raised, they no longer acquiesced to their oppression but agitated for change. This threatened the minority rich landowners, who quickly used their influence and insisted that the government expel the leader of this radical education movement. As a result of a military coup in 1964, Paulo Freire, this humble revolutionary, was imprisoned and later forced into exile.

To sit next to this man and to introduce him in a lecture hall of some five hundred students, packed into tiered rows, was an extraordinary privilege. But it was daunting too. Paulo sat in total silence, looking up at the assembled masses. Eventually, he spoke quietly: 'I will take the first question.' These students were used to straight lectures – in fact, value for money was measured by the number of pages they filled at each lecture, and they had paid 'big bucks' to be here. Uncomfortable shuffling followed, and no one spoke. For an awful moment, Ann Louise thought that she would be managing a riot. The soft voice was heard again, this time reminding the students gently of his theory of education. He didn't believe in 'banking education' – pouring facts into other people's minds. Rather, he believed in education as an exercise in freedom, a dialogue that happened in a mutual relationship of respect. The goal of education was to reach communion between human beings, and this could happen only in shared speech and mutual listening. Of course, all his books, from his famous *Pedagogy of the Oppressed*, stated this clearly, but no one in this audience of master's students anticipated that he would dream of putting such a theory into practice! After what seemed like a lifetime of silence, the first question was asked, and the course began.

Having worked with this man over a number of summers, Ann Louise could no longer think of teaching or the art of education in the same way. Indeed, it is amazing in this twenty-first century how the majority of teaching practice reflects a nineteenth-century hierarchical world order where the very structure of lecture halls promotes the false belief that the teacher's role is to pack the minds of those in passive attendance with endless detail that could be acquired on the Internet in formats that might prove more stimulating. The persistence in educating in this manner promotes 'a culture of silence' and does little to develop thinking citizens who are critically conscious and creatively capable of promoting positive change in our society, especially for those who have least. Freire died in 1997, leaving us with this request: 'You don't have to follow me. You have to reinvent me.'

This indeed was a challenge which Ann Louise took seriously when she returned to St Pat's and reviewed her own teaching methodologies from the past. From then on, when she gave students course outlines, they were informed that these were merely draft proposals and, following a Freirean approach of co-intending the curriculum, they were requested to add topics and make amendments. Where possible, a dialogical approach to teaching and learning was used. Truthfully, this worked better in small seminar groups than in large lecture halls, but students were always encouraged to interrupt, to question and to critique. For some, this was all a bit alarming, and they were more comfortable to receive other people's ideas than to articulate their own, while others engaged the dialogue with verve.

Our studies in Boston also drove us towards interest in and integration into different social-action groups forming in Dublin in the early 1980s. While at Boston College, Ann Louise had become immersed in the study of the 'just war' theories and formed part of discussion groups on the Church's position on nuclear war led by world experts in this area such as Bryan Hehir SJ and John McDargh. This was a period when 175 wars were being fought in the world and 125 of them had some religious ingredient. Humanity was spending $900 billion on guns, with the USA leading the pack, spending $1 billion a day while its annual deficit rose. The question remains: why are governments permitted to spend such huge resources on nuclear weaponry and none on preventing nuclear war from happening?

The objective of our study was to understand the link between the Christian faith and the international politico-military order. It was of particular interest to examine the just-war theory and find out if this traditional doctrine could speak a prophetic word in a nuclear age. Although the just-war theory is not exclusively a Christian preserve, doctrinally and historically it has been linked with the Catholic moral tradition going back to the fifth century and St Augustine. St Thomas Aquinas, in the twelfth century, asked the question in a telling manner: 'Is fighting in war always a sin?' As students in Boston College, our debates into the night concluded that the answer to the question in a nuclear age is a resounding 'Yes'. It was straightforward logic. There were clear rules for war, some of the principles involved the immunity of non-combatants from direct attack and proportionality. In other words the values sought by the use of particular military means must outweigh the harm caused by these means. On the basis of these principles alone, no nuclear war could ever be justified. At this point in history, we know from the devastation wreaked by the dropping of the atomic bomb on Hiroshima that the nature of nuclear war is to violate both of these principles. When we talk about nuclear war, we are talking about a warfare that is qualitatively different from classical warfare. Pope John Paul II was correct when he stated, 'War should belong to the tragic past, to history, it should find no place on humanity's agenda for the future' – a point already made in the Vatican II document *Gaudium et Spes,* which rejected acts of war 'directed to the indiscriminate destruction of whole cities or vast areas with their inhabitants.' However, when it came to condemning nuclear war and calling all Christians to a position of nuclear pacifism, the Church reneged on its own teaching and gave in to the lobby of the mighty arms industry, all except a few courageous bishops, such as Archbishop Raymond Hunthausen in Seattle. He invited all citizens in Washington state to deduct 60 cent from every tax dollar they paid, as that was what went into the arms race, which he believed was unethical.

Returning to Ireland, we became part of the Irish Women for Disarmament movement, and a group of us travelled to Greenham Common to remember the fortieth anniversary of Hiroshima. The preparation for this trip was a learning in itself. While the group shared a commitment to pacifism, we had clearly divergent ideas on non-violent protest strategies. There was a strongly held opinion by some that there should be no leadership positions of any kind and that all decisions would be reached by consensus. By the time we got to Greenham Common we were exhausted with negotiations between ourselves – and arrest by the US military who guarded the nuclear base would have offered light relief! It was a clear lesson in the powerlessness of structurelessness!

Living in Greenham Common dissipated the belief that peace isn't of interest to people. Here were hundreds of women living in tents in the freezing cold, signalling their commitment to building a world without weapons. At night we danced around the fence and sang by fires, by day we wove webs of coloured threads, symbols of life, into the imposing barbed-wire fence that protected the base. The faces of the young American servicemen from inside the compound gazed back at us in wonder. As we left the base, the words of the philosopher Herbert Marcuse came to mind: 'The success of the system is to make unthinkable the possibility of alternatives.' Greenham Common imaged in lived solidarity an alternative to war. None of us was arrested on that occasion, but that was all to change the following June.

In the early summer of 1984, it was revealed that President Ronald Reagan was to visit Dublin, so the group mobilised again and planned to demonstrate in the Phoenix Park, protesting on the nuclear issue but most especially at the brutality of US policies in Central and Latin America. Unfortunately, we had booked our tickets to leave Ireland on 1 June to work in Boston College in graduate summer programmes and to continue writing our dissertations. The Gardaí, who overreacted to this peaceful protest, arrested the members of our group, who were present on 3 June. Many of our friends spent three days in the Bridewell prison, incarcerated under no known law. All this happened as President Reagan drank beer in Ballyporeen, in rural Ireland, his newly discovered 'home place'. This was an extraordinary response by officials of the Irish State to a group of women non-violently protesting the violence of a regime that had been implicated in over 50,000 deaths in San Salvador alone between the years of 1979 and 1984.

Since our return to Dublin, all our efforts to find a parish that reflected the perspectives of a Church in the modern world proved fruitless. As well as our training in theology, we both had always nourished our spiritual lives and longed for a Christian community willing to engage with the exciting developments coming from black, liberation and feminist theologies. It seemed clear to us that even the liberal agenda for renewal set by Vatican II was proving too much for a fearful and restricted Irish Church. Gradually, the People's Theology group was formed, a diverse group of Christians who came together weekly to express and celebrate our spiritualities and to support each other in the various actions with which we felt challenged to engage. Most of us were on the fringes of the Church because the Church was rejecting or limiting us or because we were rejecting the limitations of the Church. We broke bread together and didn't agonise if this entailed transubstantiation or not!

While were we not 'out' publicly about our relationship, it was clear to those in the People's Theology group that we were a couple living a committed relationship. The solidarity of this group allowed space to reflect openly on issues related to our identity that were engaging public debate at that time. We watched, appalled, as the Norris case for decriminalising homosexuality, taken by David Norris, unfolded in 1984 and discussed the judgement by the Supreme Court as a majority of judges continued to rule that homosexuality and criminality were equated. In other words, the legislation criminalising same-sex sexual activity between men was constitutional. Reading the text of the judgement, we were shocked although not surprised at the explicit influence that the Catholic Church had on this negative Supreme Court judgement. In his review of the moral status and possible consequences of male homosexuality, Chief Justice O'Higgins gave precedence to the fact that 'Homosexuality has always been condemned in Christian teaching as being morally wrong.' As writer Leo Flynn, commenting on the case correctly said, 'The framework deployed by the Court is incommensurable and contradictory.'

Lesbian sexuality was conspicuous by its absence in this judgement, because, of course, lesbianism was not even recognised in law and had never been criminalised in the state. However, this did not mean that lesbians were not being discriminated against on the same basis as gay males. In fact, some of our lesbian friends were choosing to live in poverty rather than take jobs as teachers in a school system controlled by the Church that would force them to deny their identity in order to get a well-paid job. While we truly admired their integrity, we didn't follow their example. Clearly, the Norris judgement confirmed our outsider status in both Church and State. It was doubly important for us to form part of solidarity groups where our difference was accepted and the intolerance of Church and State towards our identity was vehemently rejected. Later we discussed the Catholic bishops' pastoral, *Love and Sex* (1985), where it was stated that: 'It's not Christian to despise homosexuals and exclude them from society.' The language of double negatives was neither consoling nor pastoral.

Returning to Ireland with a strengthened feminist consciousness, we soon became aware that the early 1980s had been 'difficult and demoralising years' in the country for the feminist movement. While feminism in Ireland has had a long and complex history, the absence of women from positions of power in successive governments persisted, despite growing protest from women's groups. Although all women have had an equal right to vote in Ireland since 1923 (they had a limited right since 1918, restricted by age and ownership of property), and despite the fact that women continued to be the majority gender in Ireland, there remained strongly held traditional views regarding women's responsibility within the private world of family, and an unquestioned socialisation of women to the belief that child-rearing and housework were exclusively their domain. In fact, at that time, only 30 percent of all women and 17 percent of married women were considered as 'workers'. Furthermore, the myth put forward by most political parties that the voters prefer men was bolstered by the fact that in the Dáil which had commenced in 1982 there were only fourteen women elected (8.4 percent) out of the 166 seats. Gemma Hussey, Minister for Education, was the only female at the cabinet table, and she lamented in her diary of that period, that she'd be judged 'Not only as a Minister but as a woman too'!

As feminist women, trained as educators and theologians, it seemed obvious to us that we should strive to raise consciousness and work towards social change by sharing the new insights from feminist theology. Fr Jimmy McPolin SJ, President of Milltown Institute of Theology and Philosophy, had heard of Katherine's work in Trinity. He invited her to come and teach feminist theology, not in the degree programme (that would have been too risky at the time) but in their newly established adult-education series. While Jimmy had some inkling that people might be interested in the topic, we all underestimated the thirst for this type of theological education. For the opening evening, the institute had prepared a small lecture room. But people started to arrive in droves, and it soon became apparent that even their largest lecture theatre would not accommodate the numbers, mainly women, queuing for insight that would offer spiritual nourishment and allow them make sense of their lives. The first series of ten lectures was extended into a further series, and the numbers continued to grow. Not only was the content of these lectures transformative, but Katherine's capacity to communicate vivaciously in a manner that embraced the broad diversity of her audience was equally new.

One day, at our home in Griffith Court, there was a knock on the door. Katherine opened it, and there stood Betty Hegarty, beautifully dressed and filled with liveliness, humour as well as a seriousness of intent. She had heard about the lectures in Milltown (on the Southside of the city), but that was a long way to travel from Howth, on the Northside, where she lived. 'Would you come to the Northside if I gathered a crowd?' she asked Katherine. The Sutton Dingy Club was chosen as the location, and it proved particularly popular, with Betty proselytising all her friends and neighbours on the Hill of Howth to come and hear the 'good news'. Word was out, newspaper articles were written about this popular new phenomenon called 'feminist theology'. *The Irish Times* ran an article on the Milltown lectures, noting that the series 'is proving as popular with the ladies as any aerobic keep-fit, or *cordon bleu* cookery class. Week by week the number of men attending is also on the increase. And that's not counting the Jesuit Fathers who keep a watchful eye on the proceedings.' There was a prophecy hidden in those words. Soon after, Katherine gave a lecture on a book entitled *Our Right to Choose*, a scholarly theological argument that abortion is not always an unethical choice. Katherine was called to the President's office, and the series came to a close. Negative responses to the course were not confined to Church quarters. One well-known feminist wrote to Katherine telling her that she wanted to 'knee-cap' her for 'giving religion a good name!' Ann Louise had to offer Katherine an interpretation and context for the violent image.

During this period, Fr Pat Wallace invited Ann Louise to speak to the Dublin diocesan annual meeting. He assured her that this mixed assembly of monsignors, canons and parish priests all wanted to learn about these new developments. Pat, always a dreamer who wanted the best for the Church he loved, completely misread the situation. Midway through her presentation, one of the more burly canons, dressed in full cassock with red buttons, jumped to his feet and began roaring, insisting that this 'heresy' be halted instantly. As Ann Louise gazed at him, she had the image of all his little red buttons popping off in response to his explosive outburst. Needless to say, the remainder of the lecture was not delivered.

While we experienced the Church's teaching on homosexuality as an infringement of our human rights, we also found the exclusion of women from positions of power, decision-making and leadership in the Church oppressive. What other organisation could justify, in the name of God, the exclusion of half the human population from full participation in its institution? Yet the Catholic Church persisted then and now in doing exactly that. People often ask us why we ultimately left the Church, and this is a core reason. As women, we concluded, to remain would be to participate in our own oppression, and nothing, in our opinion, could justify such a stance. During the time we had studied with Rosemary Radford Ruether she put out a worldwide appeal to all women in the Catholic Church not to give one more cent of their money to support their local Church until women were given full equality in the Church. Sadly, this and other creative attempts to transform the sinful sexism of the Church from within have failed, failed utterly.

5

FINDING OUR
HOMEPLACE

It was only after moving to Ireland that Katherine learned that her maternal great-grandmother, Catherine Brady McGivney, had been born in Virginia, County Cavan, in 1854 and that eighteen years later she took a boat across the long and arduous sea to an island named Ellis. It was only after moving to Ireland that she learned as well that her grandmother, Mamie McGivney Neumann, travelled twice across that same sea in the early twentieth century to return to the home of her mother and to visit relations in Cavan and Oldcastle, County Meath, including a favourite uncle who happened to be a priest. Katherine grew up during the melting-pot era in America; it was not a period when the stories were passed on or people searched for their 'roots'. She was and felt utterly American.

Only once had she travelled outside the USA before arriving on Irish soil in the early 1980s. During the first two years in Dublin, she used to say to Ann Louise that she was going to write a new dictionary because every day she heard a word or a phrase used in a way she had never heard before and whose meaning she didn't know – simple words or phrases, like 'boot' for the American 'trunk' of a car, or 'I'll call', meaning that the person would end up on your doorstep rather than telephone you! How was it, then, that she felt such a forceful sense of being at home in Ireland – in spite of the annual trip to the Aliens section of the Garda Station in Harcourt Street where her passport was stamped 'permission to reside'? It was the language, again. She would also hear phrases that she hadn't heard since her grandmother had spoken them to her years before, her soft, American accent undoutedly affected by her own mother's Irish one. Irish people would often say that Katherine had a soft American accent too. Culture was travelling through the blood.

Katherine thought a lot about these things as it slowly dawned on her that we had to choose which country to live in, 'for good', so to speak. Large-scale emigration had resumed in Ireland – there was a net outflow of some 75,000 persons over the 1981 to 1986 period. Irish people with educational qualifications, but unable to find work in Ireland, went to live elsewhere. There was a huge irony in Katherine's consideration of immigrating as an American while so many Irish were emigrating to her original homeland. This was never lost on the Irish – especially the shopkeepers. 'Why did you come to Ireland?' they'd ask, then with even greater wonder, 'Why are you staying?' What could she tell them? The truth? Some of the truth had to do with a growing feeling of being Irish in her soul. Some of the truth had to do with becoming part of a culture that carried a huge embrace of freedom from oppression. These pieces of the truth made it easier to choose the land of her great-grandmother for the sake of 'forever love' with Ann Louise. She knew that Ann Louise adored her homeland and that it would deeply unsettle her to move away from Ireland. But Katherine's lifelong commitment to Ann Louise – so easily embraced – would eventually melt any genuine desire she held to make a home together in the USA.

We were still spending a lot of time in America, though, during this period. While we had completed our doctoral comprehensive exams in September 1983, we had one more formidable task ahead to finish the degree, namely, to write and defend a dissertation. Unlike European doctorates that were dissertation only, the norm for an American PhD included three phases: coursework, exams and dissertation. We worked on our dissertations as best we could during the academic year, and Katherine became the proud owner of the first-model Apple Macintosh, holding 412 kilobytes of memory in the hard drive to assist with the task. Her parents had sent her the money to purchase it because she had very little income from teaching – the original personal computers cost five times as much as they do now. It was immensely challenging, however, to combine research and writing with Ann Louise's full-time job and Katherine's part-time courses that added up to full-time work. Living a continent away from the Boston College library and our advisor (this was the era of BE, (before email!) compounded the toughness of this task.

The solution? We wondered if our dear American friends, Joe and Doris Mahoney, could help us out. We had met them in May 1983 through a newspaper advertisement. At that time, we were coming to the end of our tenure in the Rockport home because the owners had raised the rent for the summer. If we wanted to stay, it would cost us per week in the summertime what it had cost us per month as a winter rental. Ann Louise sat down one evening and composed an ad for the *Gloucester Times*: 'Two doctoral students currently enjoying winter rental in Rockport urgently seek accommodation for summer June 1–September 30. Home in Ireland available for house swapping.'

It was that last line that was the winner. On the evening of the first day that the ad ran, the telephone rang and Katherine answered. A man asked, 'Where is the home in Ireland located?' Katherine replied, 'On the Northside of Dublin.' There was a pause. 'Is Dublin OK for you?' continued Katherine. 'Oh, I don't want to stay there,' came the reply. 'I have my own house in Portmagee, County Kerry. I was just interested to know where yours was.' Joe Mahoney then told Katherine that he would be willing to rent one side of their US home to us. They were about to move out of this side into another section for the summer, and it was available at the beginning of June. The Mahoneys were located about ten miles closer to Boston, in a tiny place called Prides Crossing. 'Would you like to take a look?'

We drove to the Prides Crossing train station the next day to meet him. There he stood, an Irish cap on his head, next to an ancient, banged-up Mercedes. 'Follow me,' he invited, with a laughing glint in his eye. He drove across the street and into the entrance of an old Massachusetts estate, flying past two magnificent granite columns. We followed him and started the long climb to the top, passing hundreds of acres that had been divided into a number of tracts for separate homes over time. Where would this lead? Joe finally reached the top bend in the hill and drove around to the left. There it was, aptly called The Old Fort. A twenty-one bedroomed mansion stood in front of us – a bit faded, but a mansion nonetheless. 'Our side' had the original kitchen (with two huge catering ovens), a separate room for playing pool, two studies, two bedrooms (one with a heart-shaped bed), a living room, dining room and an outdoor porch attached. There was a path down to a private beach on the Atlantic – and Joe wondered if a couple of hundred dollars a month in rent would be OK?

It was a talismanic summer as we alternated between studying for exams and learning how to windsurf on the beach. Doris and Joe were both the age of Katherine's parents and minded us like daughters. Surely they might consider renting it to us again for the next couple of summers so that we could have concentrated time in Boston to complete our dissertations? That is exactly what happened.

Spending one quarter of each of the next couple of years in America helped to ease Katherine's transition to the social and economic reality of Ireland. With such high unemployment rates, and political moves to cut public expenditure, there was little hope of her securing full-time employment within a university context in the near future. Ours was a dreamy optimism, though. What mattered most was to be together, and our vibrant love helped us to feel that anything was possible. Both of us had good health. Ann Louise was a racquetball champion, and Katherine was a runner. Ann Louise loved every kind of music, and Katherine played guitar, often into the night, when we gathered our friends in the small sitting room of Griffith Court in front of the coal fire. Our petite, narrow back garden bore tulips, daffodils, sweet pea and several other flower varieties that had been transplanted from Ann Louise's mother's garden. The strangeness of being in Ireland (for both of us) started to subside.

Teaching liberation theology in Trinity College – one of the most elite academic settings in Ireland – was a complex adventure for Katherine in those early years. This theology insisted that the Christian is one who stands in solidarity with the poor. The theologian ought to do likewise, not out of some obligation to give alms or charity, but because the sacred texts reveal that the God of Jesus stands on the side of the poor. What did it mean, though, to take this stance? For the Latin Americans, it meant three things: be with those who experience poverty, reflect on the workings of society together and act towards radical social change for the eradication of this oppressive social condition. Most people are poor not out of free choice but because social circumstances limit their chances in life. It was critical, then, to understand the origins and elements of social circumstance in order to change them. This was central to liberation theology's interpretation of Jesus's command to 'love your neighbour as yourself'. Love is emancipatory action in history. To do justice is to know God. Likewise, to know God is to do justice. This was Katherine's strong belief and commitment.

Katherine simply could not teach this 'content' in theory only, if she was to maintain spiritual integrity. Further, a central tenet of her educational philosophy is that we 'learn by doing' and we come to know the truth of something by reflecting on our action. Aristotle talked about it as '*praxis*' in his treatises on how humans know. As part of her courses, then, she invited her students to step outside their everyday lives and to come with her to people and places where they had never been before. She had previously met some of Ireland's leaders who were bringing together ethical and social concerns within their own life's work. Fr Fergal O'Connor, Dominican and former Professor of University College Dublin's Politics Department, met her one morning in his home, St Xavier's Dominican Priory on Dominick

Street. He was an outstanding example of lived dialogue between theory and practical social engagement, founding a hostel for homeless girls in Dublin in addition to giving his legendary lectures at university. Victor Bewley, Quaker and Managing Director of Bewley's Cafés, invited her to have coffee in his Grafton Street office to talk about his work with the Travellers. This research sparked other ideas for Katherine and built her confidence to teach in an unorthodox way – at least, it felt very unorthodox in the Trinity setting.

Some of her students agreed to accompany Katherine on regular visits to one of the first refuges established for women who were experiencing domestic violence. It was located on the Howth Road, though it took them hours to find it the first day because of the 'no sign' policy intended to protect the women from their abusers. Katherine had memories of her New York days in the Bowery, although this was a considerably smaller setting, and much of the time was spent in companionship and practical support to the women and their children. They had little training ahead of time. Katherine just kept asking her students to listen and try to understand how the world looked from the women's and children's point of view.

Other students agreed to visit the district courts with her. From week to week they observed the class differences between those who were before the judge and those who were part of the legal and judicial system. Katherine prompted her students to ask was this accidental or could it be a consequence of social policies and life circumstances? Most of these students had never considered these issues before, and their initial resistance ebbed over time. Indeed, Katherine still meets them from time to time, and they thank her for teaching them how to ask critical questions and for helping them to see the privilege of their lives.

At the beginning of her third year of teaching, Katherine was contacted by a Mercy sister, Joanna (Kathleen) O'Connor, who directed the Brown Street Family Centre in Weaver Square, part of Dublin's inner city. She wanted to know if Katherine would set up a women's group with her in the centre. Though she hadn't ever done anything like that before, Katherine saw it as a fortuitous opportunity. No students came for this venture, but it was the most formative situation for her own learning, and she began to understand the impact of Irish economic and social policy from those who had received little of its benefit. Chris McCarthy, a resident of the flats and community leader, became one of her prime teachers.

Current critical review of these times confirms some of the social and cultural dynamics that Katherine and Ann Louise started to uncover in the various settings, particularly in Katherine's work with the women of the Brown Street Centre. Each week she asked the question, in one form or another: 'Why are things the way they are?' As the trust deepened across utterly different life experiences and opportunities, it became apparent that these women's lack of educational qualifications and their upward immobility as a social class were the primary causes of the poverty they experienced. Virtually all of them had entered post-primary schooling, but most left early without completing the Leaving Certificate qualification.

Brown Street was one example of the many projects and organisations at local and national level that created improved conditions and opportunities for those who were getting left behind. The first issue of *Poverty Today*, the newsletter of the Combat Poverty Agency (set up by statute in 1986) captures this well with a picture of Irish people protesting and holding placards that read '1.3 million on Social Welfare' and 'Are Social Welfare Payments Adequate?' In 1988, the agency received grant applications from 219 projects throughout the country who were working with minorities – women, family groups and the unemployed. In 1985, Sr Stanislaus Kennedy founded Focus Point, an agency to provide services to and advocate on behalf of people who were homeless, especially women and young people. The Community Worker's Co-operative, a national network of those active at community level working for social change, was established in 1981. The Irish National Organisation for the Unemployed came into existence in 1987 to lobby for the interests of the underclass. Women's Aid (set up in 1974) finished its first custom-built refuge for women experiencing domestic violence in Rathmines, Dublin, in 1986. Over the decades, each of these national organisations, and several of the local ones, developed into highly influential agencies for social change.

This was the milieu that we discovered as we left our academies each day. The Irish spirit of rebellion for justice was palpable in our burgeoning circles of friends and colleagues. Katherine felt more and more enticed by this culture of political activism and love of liberation. Maybe this was the right place to seed our own dream?

We had talked about it often since our earliest days in Boston College. There we met a number of people who inspired us by their anger at the lack of justice in the richest nation in the world and their creative work to change that. Ann Louise studied with Professor Letty Russell, one of the first women in the 1950s to be ordained in the United Presbyterian Church. Letty had served for many years in the East Harlem Protestant parish and had worked with mostly black and Hispanic people, enabling them to become leaders in community activism and local development. As part of her teaching at Boston College, Letty encouraged students to get involved with justice projects in Boston's inner city. Ann Louise found her way to Rosie's Place, a shelter for homeless women, founded by Kip Tiernan at a time when some women were trying to pass themselves off as men to get a meal in the men-only Boston shelters of the early 1970s. The shelter had recently been reconstructed due to a fire and was now a beautiful, light-filled, open place. Each week, a different parish in the greater Boston area took responsibility to bring delicious food and offer hospitality to the 120 women and children who called each evening for their meal. Ann Louise was deeply moved by the dignity and respect that marked all relationships here. At the end of each evening there was space for only twelve families to be offered accommodation for the night. She watched her friend, Sue Costa, speak to each of the women and their children with concern and attention, trying to ensure that they would have somewhere to go rather than spend a further night on the street. Ann

Louise learned how groups of people working together in a setting of mutual respect could reshape social circumstance so that their lives could have a chance for the better.

We were unaware, however, that during the summer prior to our own arrival in Boston, a small group of people had purchased together a seventeenth-century house in West Gloucester, Massachusetts. They were to have a considerable influence on how we shaped our dream. One afternoon in the spring of 1982 we noticed a poster in Boston College stating that Rosemary Haughton, the author and theologian, was going to give a public lecture on her latest book, *The Catholic Thing*. We both knew Rosemary's writings and were intrigued to hear how she would interpret the relevance of the Catholic tradition for the social issues of the time. We attended the lecture and were deeply impressed by her simplicity, brilliance and soft anger. Towards the end of her talk, she mentioned Wellspring, a house that she and others had purchased to become their home as well as a place to pursue a common commitment to social justice by offering hospitality to those who needed it.

At this stage, we were living in our Gloucester house, and the next weekend after we finished breakfast at Charlie's, a restaurant beloved of locals, we decided to see if we could find Wellspring. Three policemen were eating at a table near us, and we asked them if they had heard of the house and if they knew where it was. 'Just your luck,' one of them said, because he had read an article about the house in the *Gloucester Times* the week before. He gave us directions, and we jumped into our car with considerable enthusiasm for the adventure. About fifteen minutes later we pulled up the drive of this former Stagecoach Inn. Our knock on the door was answered by Nancy Schwoyer, and she invited us in to share a pot of tea she had just made for herself and Rosemary. They told us about how Paul (an assistant superintendent of schools) and Mary Jane (a schoolteacher) Veronese had sold their family home for the down payment on the property. They talked of other members of the group, all prepared to leave their previous employment and homes in order to develop together what soon became one of the first family shelters for homeless people in the state.

Wellspring Inc. has become a national leader in the fields of family shelter programmes, education programmes for people on low income and the development of affordable housing. Their public-policy work has been influential in law-making and public expenditure to end homelessness. The vision of its earliest years contained the possibility for all of this. What impressed us most, however, was how the friendship shared between Rosemary and Nancy, and between all members of the community, provided a relational power effective enough to develop new social and economic systems for the towns and cities of the state of Massachusetts. Subsequently, we sat often at their table, having meals with their guests who had been homeless. We gathered by their fireside to reflect with guests, members of the community and public-policy experts on lessons learned from their work within a setting of mutual respect, care and shared resources. We witnessed conflict – its resolution, its hardship. We felt the potency of faithful hope.

These experiences remained in our minds and hearts as we came to Dublin. While we had no desire to relinquish our academic professions, we had abundant puissance to envision a lifestyle that embodied a venture in social change. Our life partnership was and still is the nucleus of this capacity. The youth of our love then also fostered a remarkably free imagination; potential barriers were viewed as opportunities, and we took great delight in solving unanticipated problems together. There is an American feminist songwriter, Cris Williamson, from this period who wrote 'Waterfall', containing a first chorus line which goes like this:

Filling up and spilling over, it's an endless waterfall,
Filling up and spilling over, over all.

We thought it aptly described the source of our desire for each other and for our shared desire for the common good. We sang it often.

We were trained as educators as well as theologians. We knew that education could be a weighty tool for personal and social transformation. We quickly became aware of the growing gap between those we met in university and those who had little chance of getting in. We had witnessed the double burden that women experiencing poverty carried in Irish society – as women, they had less access than men to third-level education or higher-paying jobs and had sole responsibility for childcare and home duties. Their gender compounded their experience of economic oppression. While we continued to work and to complete our dissertations, we also started the search for a property that could be both our home and the setting for an educational undertaking that might indent into these gaps and burdens. Griffith Court was too small, though it had been a happy home – a place to dream and to gather friends. We had few material assets. We decided simply to share what we had. Ann Louise had a sum of money from her part of a family inheritance, the pubs her father had owned on Dawson and Wexford Streets. That could help with a down payment, and we believed that the sale proceeds of Ann Louise's house, combined with our joint income, could finance the rest.

In June 1985, our two-year search for a fertile site came to an end. It was described as an 'old hunting lodge' situated in the Dublin mountains in the rural village of Brittas. It was five minutes up the road from housing estates in West Tallaght, a new suburb of Dublin characterised by poverty and isolation. The house itself was quite small and had a dilapidated appearance. It was a wooden house with a cedar frame and shingles, slightly American in its appearance (most Irish homes were made of concrete blocks at the time). It had a good bit of land, though, almost an acre and a third, with a small paddock adjacent to the house and a garden that was lined with trees planted a hundred years previously. At the back of the house, a former owner had built a four-car garage to protect his antique car collection. The current owners had turned it into a stable. We saw the potential for something else.

Three months later, we purchased The Shanty – named by the English Major Gamble who had built it in 1889. Later, we sat drinking coffee in Bewley's of Grafton Street and wrote a letter to friends and family telling them of the impending move:

> For some time now we have dreamed of founding an educational centre. At the beginning of the summer we came upon The Shanty, an old cedar home in Brittas, County Dublin. At the back of the house is a four-car garage that we hope to convert into this centre.
>
> Our long-term goal is to form a small community of people who are committed to the work of the centre. We hope that both the communal and educational setting will promote freedom from sexism, classism and any other kind of social inequality.
>
> We understand this to be a spiritual as well as educational venture. We want to have a table that is open to all – for food, drink, compassion, merriment, visioning, storytelling and decision-making. This is our dream.

We had found our homeplace.

6

THE BATTLE WITH
THE BISHOPS

Graduation at Boston College each year is a huge affair, thousands of students who have paid fortunes to acquire their degrees, line up to be conferred in the enormous football stadium, as the proud parents sit soaking up the glory of it all. The doctoral students always lead that procession. In 1986, four thousand students graduated, and a hundred doctorates were conferred, but we were not among the recipients.

Influenced by Virginia Woolf's analysis of patriarchal processions in *The Three Guineas,* we felt that as feminist women we would have little integrity if we marched publicly in this hierarchal ritual. Woolf, in her social satire, calls on women, 'the Society of Outsiders', to stand apart in solidarity and thus critique 'the great patriarchal machine'. This parading of personal distinction in order of merit could hypnotise the mind, she maintained, but 'it is our aim not to submit ourselves to such hypnotism.' Using irony to full effect, her work sought to destabilise systems of perception and value that are essentially male. She was particularly allergic to institutional pomp and circumstance. As a pacifist, she drew clear analogies between processions of war, patriotic processions, religious processions and academic processions, where women remained a token presence with no real share in central power or decision-making processes. In her opinion, by attending such an institution we were already guilty of 'adultery of the brain' – but by choosing to abjure this official pageantry and to absent ourselves, we would, perhaps, procure some absolution if not redemption?

So, as colleagues and friends graduated in Boston College, located in the grandeur of Chestnut Hill, our attention was focused in West Tallaght, in south-west Dublin, an area blighted with some of the worst effects of poverty and social deprivation that the Irish State had ever known. While Dublin has always been a socially divided city, the emergence of these urban pockets of unrequited poverty, far removed from the core of the city, was new. In fact, it was the deliberate policy of emptying the inner city of the under-educated and the unemployable, along with their families, into new housing ghettos where residents shared common challenges, that created the environment of desolation we encountered during that summer of 1986. It was true that by the mid-1980s the buildings in the inner city were dilapidated and in decline and the city population was decreasing, with unemployment at over 35 percent and reaching 80 percent in some local-authority housing areas. However, the enactment of a policy to move residents to the far-flung suburbs of Dublin, breaking up the networks of support that families living in poverty relied upon, was ill conceived.

For some, there was an initial euphoria that they had finally got a house from the Corporation or the County Council, for, of course, they were aware that there were 3,500 names on the council waiting list in the 1980s. The other cause for delight was that they had got a house, not a flat, and so had escaped the sentence of being relocated to Ballymun, north of the city, to one of the 2,866 flats that had been built almost overnight like lego blocks, it seemed, in pre-cast units that reached for the sky, upwards for sixteen stories. Within weeks of this development, rumours abounded that the lifts didn't work, and rats and children mingled on the concrete stairwells.

However, as some 28,000 gradually settled into the four areas – Jobstown, Fettacairn, Brookfield and Killenardin – known as West Tallaght, the issues of 'multiple social deprivation' became evident. While the Dublin mountains could be seen in the distance, the local areas looked like abandoned building sites with nothing but endless, monotonous rows of small, grey concrete houses. There was inadequate infrastructure; there were no amenities and infrequent buses to serve this unemployed population – all adding to a sense of isolation and feeling of disempowerment. The odd shop in a converted house, which sold the basic staple foods at exorbitant prices to these captive consumers, contributed to the poverty of this young community. Later, when a few purpose-built shops arrived in Jobstown, they were barricaded like Fort Knox, and people had to face the indignity of doing their shopping through wire grids.

No description could capture the sense of desolation that marked this place in the mid-1980s. It was the stories of the women, in particular, who lived in West Tallaght that gave a glimpse from the 'bottom up' of the consequences of the careless 'top down' decisions of planners and government who created, at a distance, this inhumane environment.

One very pregnant woman, living alone, shared with us her terror that she would go into labour in the middle of the night. She had no phone, no money for a taxi and didn't know any of her new neighbours, none of whom had a car anyway. As she was about twelve miles from the nearest maternity hospital, her concerns were more than justified. Another woman, who lived on a street that had been built over a year before, described how the shared desperation was bonding the women there. Making a stew one morning, she discovered that she had no onion. She set off to 'borrow' one, and felt welcome, though disappointed in her quest, as she called at every door – until, finally, at the last house, 'the only one with a man in it', she came upon the desired onion.

Walking these streets, hearing the narratives of the lived experience of poverty, convinced us as never before that an aesthetically pleasing place and space is fundamental to human flourishing. We learned, first hand, of the power of place to hinder a sense of human well-being. One hears discussions about West Tallaght where there is insinuation and innuendo – that the people living there are to blame for the 'disadvantage' of this place. A more accurate reflection is that this segregated place and space breeds difficulties for those who were never consulted about it and were given no active role in deciding to live in this isolated social vacuum on the periphery of Dublin.

While the solidarity of working-class communities had been broken up by this evacuation to suburban wastelands in order to reinvigorate inner-city economic growth, it didn't take long for the resilience of people in these new areas to find expression in community development groups that agitated for some amenities to meet their social needs. It became clear to us that one of the greatest supporters of these fledgling efforts to build a community in Jobstown was the local parish priest Fr Liam Murtagh and his team of priests and nuns. Here was a group of people who had not only read the Irish bishops' episcopal letter, *The Work of Justice,* but they were living its radical pronouncements on justice and society. This document talks about God as a liberator of the oppressed and asserts that 'the poor, the victimised, the persecuted, are the privileged ones in the Kingdom of God.' In a later paragraph titled 'Justice before Alms', it moves away from any patronising notion of charity as it states: 'Justice involves returning to another something which is rightly their own. We have to give back what is not ours before we can give away what is ours.'

The tradition of the social encyclicals was being revived here and placed in an Irish context. The subtext offered a welcome, albeit rare, critique by the official Church of the State's social policies, which were wreaking devastation in the poorest communities. The Jobstown parish team, by their many activities among the people, were translating this and the Latin American theme of living an 'option for the poor' into a culturally appropriate *praxis* as they lived dedicated lives of respectful partnership in this community that thirsted for recognition and human rights. As few attended Mass, Fr Murtagh, dressed in his old anorak, would walk over to the football pitch each Sunday morning and chat to the men he encountered there. Sr Ruth (Anne) Hartnett walked the roads, building connections with the women, some of whom were living in fear behind closed doors. It became clear to us that when the time came to bring our idea for an educational project from seed to flower, we would need an endorsement and an introduction from this group of people who were so revered and respected in this community. We were equally convinced that we needed a team of people to share the vision and plan the project with us before we could advance.

In the autumn of 1986, Katherine received a phone call from Mary Sweeney, inviting her to give a lecture at a course being run by local women in the Dominican Priory in Central Tallaght. These women, who had previously completed an outreach programme from UCD in Women's Studies, had now decided to plan their own course with the intention of developing some action for women. Katherine accepted the invitation and furthermore asked if she could join the group. As relationships became established, she shared our vision for the development of an education project for women in West Tallaght and invited those who were interested to join us for a weekend of study and reflection in our home. The theme of Feminist Spirituality was agreed.

On that autumn Saturday, we waited apprehensively in our beloved Shanty. The wood-panelled living room was ready, the fire was lit under the copper canopy, scones baked and handouts prepared. The gates were open to the tree-lined property, and the rough-haired collie dogs (we now had two), Habermas and Julian, were in attendance. To our delight, fifteen women turned up for what was to be a unique weekend.

We started by sharing our own knowledge of emerging theories in liberation theologies, and these women placed their experience of being Irish women in search of change, challenge and new meaning in dialogue with these new insights. The weekend was a mixture of deep thinking, critical and creative dialogue and moments of quiet and spiritual reflection. Each day after lunch we took a walk in the woods behind our home. We began as we hoped to continue, with an educational approach that embraced all dimensions of being human in the world.

We shared our dream. We believed, then as now, that education is the key to the transformation of poverty. Most of these women knew about the plight of the 28,000 people now living in West Tallaght, where unemployment was running at 70 percent and rising. Our vision was to build an education project that would focus especially on offering opportunity to women who carried the main burden of managing poverty, especially within the family. We were clear that the enactment of this idea was impossible on our own. We needed a group of women to join us in this adventure. At the end of the weekend, eleven from the group signed up. We simply called ourselves 'the management team', and so the project was born. We agreed that we would meet every second Wednesday evening and that meetings would alternate between planning the project together and continuing our study of liberation theologies, feminist theory and liberation theories of education. What we could not have foreseen during that first autumn encounter was that twenty-one years later most of these women remain involved in the work of The Shanty Educational Project, now called An Cosán, and form part of our community of friends.

Following months of planning and research into local women's interests and needs, we were ready to offer our first course. It was decided that Ann Louise and Katherine would request our first formal meeting with the parish team. It was refreshing and renewing to meet a group of Christians who were utterly committed to working for the welfare of those they served. Furthermore, they were not territorial and simply wanted to support any initiative for the betterment of the lives of the people in West Tallaght. As there was no single building in the community in which to hold the courses, we stated that we would open our home and provide transport for the women who wished to attend. We also suggested that the warmth of a home context could be a positive educational environment, especially for women who may have had a negative experience of schooling. However, we did need space for a crèche in the community. Without hesitation, they offered us rooms in the parish centre in which to develop our first childcare programme. We were all acutely aware that return to education or work was impossible for women without the provision of childcare. The Irish academic Mary Daly, in her excellent book *Women and Poverty* (1989), states that there is very little information about poverty among Irish women in the mid-1980s, yet we do know that by 1988 there were only nine known workplace crèches in the country.

It was suggested that Ann Louise should go to different houses with Sr Ruth to be introduced to individual women whom the parish team identified as leaders. Their advice, that we should offer our first course to women leaders in the community, was a pearl of great wisdom. A meeting room in the presbytery was recommended for the introductory mornings, before transporting people to our home six miles up the road. Again, this was insightful advice, and we facilitated the first two weeks in the Jobstown presbytery, while Rose Cullen and Catherine Long co-ordinated the crèche facilities. This allowed the women to get to know us and to become accustomed with the idea of leaving their community to head into a rural setting and participate together in the first course. Looking back, we, as a management team, never cease to be amazed at the courage and pioneering spirit of that group of women. They didn't know each other, they certainly didn't know us, and yet their thirst for education and a better life allowed them to step beyond fear and take a chance.

The participants had requested a course that would rebuild their confidence and communication skills, which, they stated, had been depleted by their struggle with poverty and isolation. They also asked for training in negotiation and advocacy, as so much of their time was spent battling the bureaucracy encountered in extracting their social-welfare entitlements (there were thirty-five categories under which claims could be made) and dealing with County Council/Corporation officials in relation to rental and housing problems. While embroiled in their own individual struggles, their vision also included a desire to build their community and make Jobstown a different place.

Betty Hegarty, a trained personal-development instructor and respected educator, was employed to deliver the opening course in dialogue with the group's expressed interests and needs. Ann Louise, who was able to reorganise her lecture timetable in St Pat's, became Betty's assistant. Joan Foran and Sheila Norton organised transport from Tallaght to The Shanty, and so the first course began.

Before the group would arrive we always had the fire lit, the house warm, some home baking ready. While we thought of this as a tiny gesture of respect, many in the group reflected later that on mornings when the bleakness of poverty was militating against their attendance, the anticipated warmth of a home context and fresh scones coaxed them on and allowed them to stay the course. At the end of the year, nobody had dropped out of the programme.

The learning from this course and those that followed was mutual. As the participants shared the experience of their lives, our own classism and privilege was profoundly challenged. It was during this period that we learnt the lived detail of the injustice of poverty in the lives of Irish women. While few would contest that the roots of poverty are located in the general social and economic position of women, the effects of poverty are multiple and varied. From these opening sessions it became clear that women's lack of opportunity to earn an independent income was the greatest contributing factor to their poverty.

It is true that women's dependence on husbands or the State for an income as they attended to households and reared children was not confined to areas of social deprivation such as West Tallaght. The Irish Constitution of 1937 had enshrined, if not romanticised, this notion in Article 41 on the family. The text, which remains unchanged to this day, deserves mention:

2.1 In particular, the State recognises that by her life within the home, woman gives to the State a support without which the common good cannot be achieved.

2.2 The State shall, therefore, endeavour to ensure that mothers shall not be obliged by economic necessity to engage in labour to the neglect of their duties in the home.

There is no doubt that this constitutional endorsement of women's role in the home has socialised many women, in the middle classes in Ireland, to feel a sense of guilt if they choose to work outside the home. However, no such choice was open to women living in West Tallaght in the mid-1980s, as there were no jobs available. Their experience of guilt was of a very different nature: they grieved that they never had adequate resources to provide for their family. In that opening course we learned of the drudgery of work in homes marked by poverty. Women described working up to fifty to sixty hours a week for no pay, living on an inadequate allowance, trying desperately to make ends meet, while waiting each month for the children's allowance to buy basic items of clothing for the children. The fact was that men got the social-welfare money and women were lucky to get a share of it.

The idealism that may have inspired the constitutional article above had no applicability to this context of penury. Women in West Tallaght were obliged to work in the home, they had no choice, their childcare needs were neglected by the Irish state, and they received no independent income. It was not evident what aspect of the 'common good' was achieved by this situation. Rather, women narrated with innumerable examples that they experienced the financial dependence and control of their lives as deeply stressful and quite unjust.

One woman told stories of waiting for her husband outside the dole office and pleading that he would hand over a decent amount of 'his' social-welfare payment to her so that she could manage the house for the coming week before he went off drinking with his buddies. One of the early role-plays in the course was building the negotiation skills that she would use to get agreement from 'himself', the husband, to allow her to get 'split payment'. Such a system, which depended on his permission, would mean that the woman could get the dole (social welfare) amount split at source, setting aside an agreed amount for herself and the children. In a state that claimed to revere the traditional family, when social welfare *was* divided, the married woman got £30 and either £10 or £14 for each child, depending on age, while women parenting on their own got £49, with the same allowances for their children. Obviously, both amounts were entirely inadequate, but the point is, as many lone parents shared openly, in their opinion they were better off on their own!

Even when a man handed over the majority of the money, as some did, there was never enough. One of the stories often told was of the 'roving ten pound note'. The dole was paid out on different days for different households, which meant that there was always a house with a bit more cash than the rest. The understanding was that if you ran out before 'pay day' you could borrow the 'float'.

When women shopped they did so with absolute attentiveness, getting whatever bargains were going. It all took a lot of time, but managing poverty constantly used up a huge amount of one's time. One woman who had four children mentioned that she always counted the apples on sale in a bag – they might weigh the same, but the one with twelve rather than eleven apples would allow her to put an apple into each child's lunch box for three days.

We too had to confront our presuppositions about life lived under the shadow of poverty. Ann Louise recalls the day when she approached a woman taking a break in the purpose-built 'smokers' house' behind The Shanty. She gently suggested that perhaps the women might think of giving up cigarettes but quickly learned that her suggestion was both inappropriate and intrusive. 'Listen, love,' she was told, 'I have six children and I'm on my own. We have one rule in the house: when I light up a fag at the table the children sit down and give me a few minutes' peace. So I can tell you now I am not about to give up the smokes!' Correctly chided, Ann Louise learned to keep her health warnings to herself!

Managing a meagre budget was always difficult, but being surprised by unexpected calls for money made this task well-nigh impossible. Impromptu requests from schools for money for this or that caused real tension in households. Having a child for First Communion or Confirmation was a huge anxiety. Dressing children for these events frequently pushed women to resort to moneylenders, then be forced to pay back their borrowings with exorbitant interest over many years. On hearing these stories, our management team, working with the participants, took various local actions to change customs that clearly, advertently or inadvertently, added unnecessary pressure to women's lives.

Some of these actions were successful; others failed to indent deeply rooted customs and vested interests. For example, the campaign to get a credit union in the local community succeeded, and many women in the early courses led this initiative and volunteered to staff it. In all assertiveness training courses we included a unit on financial management that provided a comparative analysis of the lending rates at credit unions and those of moneylenders. However, the call to move sacramental preparation from being located in primary schools to parishes was strongly resisted, though a number of parents living in poverty did feel that, if they had the choice, they'd prefer to have a parish-based preparation with local catechists and a quiet celebration of First Holy Communion and later Confirmation when their child was ready as part of Sunday Mass. This would take away much of the unnecessary hype, loss of school time and undue financial pressure.

The opening courses reconfirmed our commitment to advance a project for radical social change in West Tallaght. Informed by the experience of women who had left school early with no qualifications and who were now caught in a poverty trap, it was clear that accessible, affordable education and training, along with the provision of free childcare, was key if their desire for a different life was to be realised. It was now time for us as a management team to take the learnings from these foundational courses and allow them to inform the development of a transformative model of women's community education. But first it is important to hear the voices of some of those first participants as published in our newsletter from that period, *The Shanty Times.*

We were a group of women who met as strangers and ended out as friends. We came from different backgrounds, yet we all shared the same sort of problems. A bond grew between us. It gave you a feeling of belonging, of security, of friendship and most of all a feeling of trust in each other. You could be yourself and not just feel that you were a mother or someone's wife. *Ann Doyle* (1987)

In response to the fact that Jobstown, with over a thousand children in the primary schools, still had no secondary school, another participant wrote:

We as parents are faced with another crisis in Jobstown. Not only do we not have a community college/secondary school, but we are now faced with massive cutbacks in our schools. Although I know the country is in a bad way financially, it would seem to me that while some cutbacks are needed, it is us, the ordinary people, who must pay the price, all the time. We must be on our toes in the future for our children as they will need all of our help if they are to have any hope for the future. *Ann Cuddihy* (1987)

It was during the years of planning and starting The Shanty that the 'Battle with the Bishops' began. In early June 1984, prior to leaving for Prides Crossing to continue research on the PhD theses, Ann Louise had applied for the position of Head of the Department of Religious Studies. As St Pat's was a college of UCD, the interview panel comprised a number of academics from the university, along with Fr John Doyle, President of St Pat's, who chaired the board. Ann Louise had no idea how many people were interviewed for the job, but she did know that another member of our department, a Vincentian priest, Fr Joe McCann, had also applied. A week after the interview, she met Fr Doyle in the corridor, and he quietly congratulated her – she had got the job! As a 'formality' he needed to inform the Archbishop of Dublin, Dr Dermot Ryan, so he requested that she didn't make the result public.

We set off for Boston in celebratory mood. We loved our life in Prides Crossing, and this was the summer that Doris and Joe expressed a wish that we would plant an organic vegetable garden, as they had always dreamed of growing their own produce. So we bought *The Cabbage*

Patch Garden Book, and, following the instructions to the letter, we planted a large area with every known vegetable. Each morning we would rise at 6.00am and weed before the sun came up; each evening we'd water at sundown. It was an idyllic time. By September we had enough organic produce to feed all the households in the surrounding county!

At the beginning of July, Ann Louise got a phone call to say that Fr John Doyle was coming to Boston and would like to meet her. She found it strange, as he had never mentioned any such visit at their last meeting. However, she was very fond of him and looked forward to showing him Boston. On the day he was to arrive, she got a further phone call to say that he had had a heart attack at the airport and wouldn't be travelling. Within twenty-four hours she was informed that now Fr Seamus O'Neill CM, the former head of the department was coming to see her. At this point, it was clear that something was wrong. Ann Louise will always recall driving the thirty miles to Boston for that meeting. She had a deep premonition that something momentous was about to happen; in fact, at one point she had to pull off the highway and just calm herself before going on. Upon arrival at the agreed restaurant she immediately asked Seamus if something was the matter, but he assured her that all was well and so she had a great lunch and a good chat with the man who had always been so supportive and who, she believed, had recommended her for the job in St Pat's many years previously.

When the dessert arrived, his mood suddenly changed, and he informed Ann Louise that he was there to deliver very difficult news: the Archbishop of Dublin, Dr Dermot Ryan, had vetoed her appointment and in her place wished to appoint the second candidate, Fr Joe McCann, as Head of Department. While agreeing that this must be difficult, Seamus begged her to accept the Archbishop's decision. Ann Louise assured him that she would never accept such an injustice and that, furthermore, the university had appointed her to this position, the university was funded by the State, and that upon return she would take up her position as Head of the Department. They parted shortly after.

She presumes he flew home that evening but never asked.

As Ann Louise drove back to the Old Fort at Prides Crossing, many thoughts vied for attention, but what she experienced as the betrayal by Dermot Ryan was to the forefront of her mind. They had known each other for years. He lived at the back of her family home when he taught at UCD; in fact, their gardens were adjoining. He had taught her as a student, and they always got on very well. When she was awarded the scholarship for Paris, he sent for her, and they chatted for hours in the long library in the Archbishop's Palace on Drumcondra Road. This was the first of many meetings. He was always extremely interested in the latest theological ideas from Europe, and he asked that she would call by each term during her studies. Most meetings remained at the level of academic conversation but on one occasion he invited her down to his study and sought her advice on a new colour scheme he was considering. When she decided to undertake doctoral studies in Boston College she informed him, but he was resistant to that idea and told her that really she should think about marrying and having children, rather than further studies, as time was not now on her side! While they agreed to differ on that point, they parted amicably.

Back at Prides Crossing, Katherine was shattered by the news.

Rather than returning to Ireland immediately, we decided that, despite the distractions, Ann Louise would try to continue with her dissertation research and at the same time get as much information and assistance as possible by phoning colleagues and friends. Naturally, her first call was to the Archbishop himself to hear his reasons for his decision. However, he refused to take her calls, and eventually one of the priests in the palace came on the phone and told her that the Archbishop would not, 'now or ever', speak to her about his decision. On hearing this, Ann Louise's dear sister, June, drove to his home in Dublin 4 and requested a meeting. Horrified by this uninvited caller, the housekeeper slammed the door in her face. Calls to the local branch of the Union of University Teachers were received differently; representatives Pauric Travers and Celia Keenan were more than empathetic.

The clash of contradictions surrounding this sequence of events was exacerbated by the fact that at that time Ann Louise was engaged in an intensive study of the work of the philosopher Jürgen Habermas. What she was experiencing was the antipathy of his theory of 'communicative competence'. He believes in the possibility of transparent and non-manipulative exchanges between human beings. Trust between people is built up by the ordinary practices of open communication. He critiques the suppression of dialogue by the exercise of power, and he calls for 'communication free from domination'. The failure to engage in intersubjective communication blocks the necessary knowledge that could lead to liberation and the resolution of conflict. Left in a limbo of silence, Ann Louise experienced what Habermas correctly speaks of as 'structural violence' – inequality created by injustice rooted in distorted communication. In the eighteen months that followed, all that she ever received from the Archbishop was legal letters, despite her persistent request for dialogue. How Church leaders informed by a gospel that claims 'God is Love' and that 'we should love one another' can dismiss the fundamental right to speak in the face of injustice is incomprehensible.

While many colleagues were kind in their commiserations, the fact that St Pat's was a college managed by the Archbishop of Dublin meant that the weight of the law rested on his side. Shortly thereafter, Ann Louise received a letter from the Archbishop's firm of lawyers, Arthur O'Hagan, restating his position. As an extraordinary quirk of fate, one of the founding partners of this firm was Ann Louise's uncle, Freddie Gilligan, and Arthur O'Hagan had been a close friend of her dad's.

While she filed the letter, she told the new President of the college, Fr Sam Clyne, that as she had been appointed to the job she was going to become 'acting' Head of the Department. It calls for little imagination to appreciate that the opening meetings of the department were tension-filled, with Ann Louise 'acting' and the Archbishop's man for the job in attendance.

Archbishop Ryan never broke his silence. Within a few months he was appointed to Rome, then, following a brief illness, he died. He had the unusual honour of being made a cardinal posthumously. His successor, Archbishop Kevin McNamara, a small, taciturn, dour man, was equally unwilling to speak to Ann Louise but continued the legal correspondence via O'Hagan's. The matter was still unresolved when he also died. Friends commented wryly that while Ann Louise was not winning the battle with the bishops, they seemed to be dying in their efforts. The next man appointed, Archbishop Desmond Connell, had also taught her. True to tradition, he too refused communication.

It goes without saying that this sequence of events took their toll. Without Katherine's devoted love, a wonderful home life and a sense of humour, it would have been impossible for Ann Louise to sustain the ongoing tension of this situation. Then, out of the blue, some eighteen months later, she got a letter stating that she would be appointed, *but only for four years*. Usually at that time an appointment to a head of department position was for life. This, it seems, was a clever legal compromise, as it was clear she would not give up the fight. It was the conclusion of the initial phase of this saga, a regrettable example of what Habermas calls 'systematic distorted communication' and a dismal failure of communicative ethics.

7

BUILDING A MUSE

It became evident very quickly that our home, small to begin with, was entirely inadequate to meet the ever-growing demand for courses. Word had spread rapidly among women in the local community that there were opportunities to return to education with childcare provided and with no prohibitive fees, and there was avid interest in this possibility. While we heard some middle-class critiques about 'taking women out of their communities to this house on the hill above Tallaght', the participants themselves were clear – they loved getting on the minibus and taking the six-mile trip up the road into a calm environment. Some women, especially those parenting on their own, often arrived frazzled, perhaps having spent the previous evening plea-bargaining with bored youths who sat in menacing numbers on the little wall in front of their sitting-room windows threatening to throw the bricks they held through the glass. There was mixed opinion as to whether it was better to keep the curtains open and stare them down or close the drapes and hope for the best. Others lay awake listening to 'joyriders' screech past in stolen cars, praying that when the inevitable moment came for the vehicle to be burned out, it wouldn't be in front of their house. Calls to the police proved pointless as 'they had abandoned the area'; even bus drivers refused to come into this vicinity at night.

So many women remarked that as they walked up the path to our home, lined on both sides with herbaceous borders of seasonal blooms, a sense of peace descended, and this relativised the trauma of the previous evening. This energy of stillness and tranquillity around The Shanty is something we inherited, and it continues to envelop the property to this day.

The search for suitable premises to locate the expanding project back in the local area, which was always our long-term objective, bore as little fruit at this time as it did when we had last tried some years previously. Apart from an effort by the local parish team to conduct a door-to-door weekly collection inviting each household to contribute a pound a week to fund the building of a community centre as a recreation space for youth, there remained no building to house any educational and training activities. As mentioned previously, when we bought The Shanty we saw the potential of converting the four-car garage there into an education space, but that idea now seemed a daunting task as we both had busy 'day jobs' and gave any spare time we had to the project in its current incarnation. However, the management team, by now expert at problem-solving, came up with a suggestion: they would ask the men in their lives to undertake the garage conversion. Within weeks, in February 1989, The Shanty Building Committee was formed. Fergus Roche led the volunteer building team; his wife, Maura, was chairperson of the management team at the time. Marie Moran's husband John was a professional builder and generously directed all the technical aspects of the building. It was clear early on that a large group of skilled volunteers was also needed if the tight deadlines set for an autumn opening were to be met. Fergus owned a hairdressing business, as did four of his brothers. Their approach to gathering the volunteers was novel: as men were in 'mid-shave' in the barber's chair they'd be reminded, 'By the way, you owe me one', and so the services of electricians, plumbers, bricklayers and painters were acquired, and on Saturdays and Sundays they'd arrive in droves. We'd cook, feed and encourage as we watched the walls go up from our kitchen window nine feet away.

From the beginning, every step of development in The Shanty Educational Project called for a new level of fund-raising. Initially we funded the courses by requesting that all fees accruing from our weekend work, especially courses to religious communities on the topics of liberation, feminist and black theology, be contributed directly to the project. However, these sums quickly proved entirely inadequate to meet the growing costs of providing excellence in education. The management team assumed responsibility for running various fund-raising events around the Tallaght area. We often laugh as we recall together some of these adventures, like that day in the heart of winter when we stood for hours in the carpark of the Cuckoo's Nest, a pub in central Tallaght, holding a car-boot sale. While business was brisk, and we all sold everything from our attics and elsewhere, we almost died of the cold, and in the end made very little money, although we had great fun! We think back on those days, and we marvel at the generosity of the management team, giving time, even at weekends, to make this project work – among many others was Mary Sweeney, a widowed woman with six children who always brought a positive attitude and wisdom aplenty to the task at hand.

A more successful event was the fashion show held in Jobstown, organised and planned by a group of local women partnered by Julie Kiernan and Cora Marshall from our management team; this event brought in a profit of £500. The profit resulted from the huge support by local women, as they each paid £2 into the event, a substantial contribution for those living on a social-welfare budget. Not enough has been written about bottom-up fund-raising, where people living with the injustice of poverty give so that, in this case, the 'education poverty' in their communities could be transformed. As Seamus Heaney correctly states: 'The future lies with what's affirmed from under.' Sr Ruth Harnett, writing about this event in *The Shanty Times* (1988) stated:

> One of the great features of The Shanty is that these women are now part of a wider community of women associated with The Shanty and they had recently been involved in a fund-raising fashion show for the project. It was marvellous to see them on the night – their ability, poise and confidence was remarkable. It was obvious that they had really begun to believe in their own ability and resources in a way that would have been unthinkable a year ago.

A major factor in all of this has been the atmosphere of trust, love and genuine friendship created by Ann Louise and Katherine for the women who come to their home. The ongoing contact and opportunity for growth created by association with The Shanty community is such a support for the women and it opens up new avenues all the time.

Fund-raising for building materials was a different task, and as the building commenced it was democratically decided that Ann Louise and Katherine should go to the suppliers to secure the necessary items, from concrete to tiles, from building blocks to toilets! Initially, we undertook this task hesitantly, as neither of us had ever before asked anyone for anything. However, a seasoned fund-raiser, offering us no sympathy, simply snapped: 'Always remember you're not asking for yourselves.' This was a salient lesson, and we got on with the task. Our confidence grew with every success, to the point that we were visibly taken aback when we didn't get everything we asked for. The phrase, 'Only the best will do', had become a cant for all involved in the building enterprise, and it influenced our approach. On one occasion we were bartering with a supplier for a large quantity of bricks, as it had been decided to surround a beautiful, purpose-built, copper canopy over the fireplace with an interior brick wall. Having listened to our fund-raising pitch, the manager of the firm kicked for touch asking us first to walk around and choose the brick we'd like before he'd negotiate. Pointing out the one we wanted, he burst out laughing: 'Well,' he said, 'all I can say is that you've good taste – that's the most expensive brick we sell; and Bono was here yesterday and chose that one for his new home.' Completely disarmed, he gave us the lot free.

By the end of these endeavours we had everything but the roof. We even had a larger minibus to transport the growing numbers of women back and forth. Family and government brought us to the finish line. Ann Louise's sister, June, and a team from Tallaght West, spent months selling raffle tickets in every shopping centre available for a car she had extracted from a car dealer and raised a huge amount of money. Katherine's dad, Bob, devised and carried out an ingenious plan to get everyone to buy a tile for the roof. Finally, Minister Michael Woods, a close friend of Ann Louise's mentor Fr Pat Wallace, under the scheme of grants to voluntary bodies in the social-services area, contributed some monies made available to him from the National Lottery.

One of the lessons from engaging in the task of fund-raising was the innate goodness of people. Once the issues of social and economic injustice in our country were understood, it was our experience that people were spontaneously generous. However, another realisation was that due to the segregation of the social classes and the ghettoisation of those who live in poverty, the culpable ignorance of the privileged in this society was appalling.

The building took seven months to complete, an unrivalled record, for, not only was The Shanty Educational Project left with a fully furnished, beautiful space at The Muse in order to grow and expand our work, but there was no snag-list, nor any post-building problems to be sorted. Our belief that an aesthetically pleasing educational space is integral to the emotional well-being and needs of learners was confirmed by the enthusiasm that greeted the opening of The Muse by the new participants in October 1989. To capture in words the spirit that went into creating this living space is difficult, suffice to say that hundreds of people contributed in large and small ways. Throughout the period of the build everyone had seemed inebriated with a common sense of empowerment that their engagement with the work was, indeed, making a difference. Many commented that they were really glad to find a way to give something back to society and to share their resources.

With the opening of The Muse, the first phase of our burgeoning 'career' in fund-raising ended, only to be rapidly reignited as soon as we started planning for the next development phase. But with the building complete, we were relieved and deeply happy that this stage of the dream had been realised due to a large group of people from many diverse backgrounds joining together in solidarity to break the cycle of poverty.

Funding the growing number of courses remained an ongoing struggle. There was neither recognition of, nor funding for, adult community education. This designation was to differentiate it from 'adult education', where the middle classes attended and paid for evening courses in their hobby of choice in their local Vocational Education Committee (VEC). While a philosophy of lifelong learning is to be promoted in every situation, our work had a very different agenda. It is interesting to note that during this period the Government invested 0.4 percent of its overall education budget in adult education, but the category that we named as 'adult community education' didn't have a budget line and therefore didn't exist in their terms. An AONTAS (Irish National Adult Learning Organisation) report in 1988 stated: 'As course fees increase for adult education courses throughout the country the poor and generally disadvantaged members of our society are being excluded from adult education.'

It became clear that we needed a development committee, a group committed to the ongoing development of our work, with a special focus on fund-raising. A volunteer group of seventeen women, all of whom came from middle-class backgrounds, quickly formed. They all knew of and believed in the work of The Shanty. Betty Hegarty, who had worked for years as a tutor in the project, became the first chairperson of this group. Most of these women also took up a volunteer engagement with the daily workings of The Shanty – for example, Nuala Wallace, Managing Director of a large cash and carry business, gave a morning a week, taking charge of hospitality and sharing the recipes for her delicious home baking. Maureen McGuinness drove the minibus on another day. As they formed friendships with women in Tallaght West, they described how their own lives and perspectives were being changed. These cross-class relationships enabled mutually supportive encounters. Maureen, whose husband was a director in Dunnes Stores, arranged that the women and children would be the models for the promotion of Dunnes' autumn collection. The advantage to the participants was that they got to keep the clothes. Once a month over a meal in The Shanty, the development committee would meet, and, amidst howls of laughter, we'd plot and plan a way forward. Many of these women admitted that they had never been part of an all-woman group, and they simply loved it. Meriel Kilroy, another member of the group, offered that she and her husband Howard, a leader in the corporate sector, would to do a jazz lunch in their home to kick-start this new phase of fund-raising; it was a fun-filled, family event, with as many in attendance from West Tallaght as from Dublin 4.

The growth spurt in our own educational endeavours with working-class women called us to step back and articulate a theory that reflected the practice of what we called 'women's community education'. Listening to the women's stories of prior negative experiences of education at school, one could only deduce that their return to learning required an environment and a pedagogy that would be markedly different from that earlier experience. As Albert Einstein correctly reminds us: 'We cannot solve our problems with the same thinking we used when we created them.' In our writing from this period we highlighted a set of principles that should inform the theory and practice of a feminist pedagogy.

This pedagogy resulted from critically reflecting on our work in different Shanty courses, observing what enhanced and what hindered women's learning, but above all the results drawn from engagement with our imaginations. Ann Louise has written frequently on the importance of engaging the imagination – first to try to imagine something new, then to create it. Hearing the story of Nuala Wood, for example, allows one to realise just how new and imaginative women's community education needs to be, if, together, we are to recreate a belief that education has a positive contribution to make.

Nuala is about the same age as Ann Louise. They started school on the same day in September 1950 – Nuala in a primary school in Drimnagh, Ann Louise, as already mentioned, in Loreto, Foxrock. Nuala lived in a corporation house in Drimnagh and was the third daughter in a large family. Growing up, her father repeatedly told her that she was 'nothing but trouble' and her mother, with equal frequency, told her of her father's disappointment when she was born because she wasn't a boy. In her published story, Nuala describes vivid memories of her primary-school years. Early on, she sensed that the poverty of her home influenced teachers' negative attitudes towards her. This was never confirmed until she reached sixth class. During the summer prior to this final year at school it dawned on her that her only way out of poverty was to get a scholarship to secondary school and so continue her education. So, on the opening morning of the school year, she got in early and made her way to the top of the line as her class queued in the yard before entering the school. Upon reaching the classroom, she sat in a desk in the front row. This was part of her plan – to do well she wanted to be close to the teacher, the blackboard and away from distractions. Suddenly the door opened, and the nun entered. She fixed her glare on Nuala and shouted: 'What are you doing in that desk? Don't you know children from the corporation houses sit in their proper place at the back of the room? These desks are for the girls in the bought houses!' To this day, Nuala weeps as she recalls that long, humiliating walk to the back of the room. That was the day her education ended, and it laid the foundation for a life of hardship. Along with the other 'corporation girls', she spent the final year at school running errands, selling raffle tickets and making holy pictures for the nuns to hang in the prams of new-born babies! The one skill she remembers learning was to darn the heel of a sock so that in the future she could mend her husband's socks, a skill she has never used to this day.

She left school on her fourteenth birthday, the permitted legal age at the time, with a minimum grasp of basic English, and began working the following day in a tailoring firm 'picking threads'. She was quickly promoted to machinist and worked from 8.00am to 5.00pm earning £2 9s 3d per week, £2 of which she willingly handed over to her mother.

At forty, following two unhappy marriages, she got a house in Jobstown, having decided she'd be better off on her own. Her one desire was to rear her children to become 'four first-class citizens', and if this entailed resolving her deep anger at the education system and returning to learning she was willing to give it a try. Sr Francis, a nun living in the local community, persuaded her and her neighbours, Jodi, Brigid and Margaret, to come along. She wrote:

> Coming to The Shanty has helped me. I had always felt that I missed out a lot, feeling handicapped by this in many ways. I made sure that my children got a good education and as they learnt it bounced back on me. But as they grew up I found myself feeling left behind. I used to get depressed and wouldn't go out or be bothered with friends. But coming here over the past few years has shown me my own importance as my own person. My classes mean everything to me. They have made me much more confident. I realise that I have rights, that I too am entitled to have a good life. I'm positive in my thinking now, am more at ease in my own mind and I'm sure I'm easier to live with. (1990)

It would be convenient to dismiss Nuala's story of educational classism as an exception rather than the rule, but our experience of twenty-two years of listening to the tales from school of working-class women who lived in similar circumstances allows us to conclude that unfortunately they were the rule for that generation. Nuala's story and other similar accounts left us in no doubt that the pedagogy employed in our various courses had to take account of these experiences.

Reflecting on the teaching at The Shanty, Ann Louise developed, in dialogue with the participants, and published what we called a feminist imaginative pedagogy, a five-step process, outlined below, and trained tutors to use it, where applicable, in their courses. This methodology was strongly affirmed by authors Brid Connolly and Anne Bridget Ryan in their book *Women and Education in Ireland,* (1998).

1 An Opening Circle

Each session, usually three hours with a break in the middle for a half-hour of tea, scones and a chat, commenced with an Opening Circle. We will elaborate on this practice later; however, it grew from our conviction of the need to integrate spirituality into our educational work. In their evaluations of our courses, women stated that they deeply valued these times of quiet and named them as essential for their learning.

2 Naming of Presuppositions

No knowledge is ever neutral or interest-free. It has been our experience that negative feelings and thoughts that we bring to a topic can block our receptiveness to new learning. On the other hand, the opportunity to pause and reflect on prior understandings of a given issue can bring to consciousness previous, positive understandings of the issue under consideration. The study of Travellers in our Social Studies Diploma (one of a number of courses we've run with university status) is a good example.

Many participants knew Traveller women and, indeed, had stood with us protesting for Travellers' rights on the Tallaght by-pass. Others were filled with negative bias, as they had accepted without question much of the stereotyping and maligning of this ethnic minority. Other topics, such as female prostitution, abortion and homosexuality, often unveil opinions peppered with prejudice and bias which must surface and be dealt with gently within the group before any real learning can take place.

3 Articulating Women's Experience

This pedagogy is grounded in giving voice to women's experience and giving authority to the power of women's knowledge. The exploration of female experience is a highly imaginative act. It opens up a space where we can break the silence about our feelings of oppression induced so often by male imagery of who we are or ought to be. Through creative exercises – combining storytelling, music and art – false imagery, which objectifies us, can be critically examined, exposed and rejected. Irony and humour are key in cracking open encrusted false consciousness, allowing women to tell the truth about their own lives. We always recall the intervention of Carmel Habington (a wonderful member of our management team) when she heard that popular song 'You Are the Wind Beneath My Wings': 'I have no desire to be the wind under anyone's wings,' she commented, 'I want to fly myself.' From our work, we realise that there is no doubt that the female imagination is the site for the birth of women's subjectivity. A further illustration of this stage in the pedagogical process is the reflections on the theme of motherhood as expressed by women in the creative-writing class. Bernie Cahill, a participant from Jobstown, compiled a list of the ideas different women shared on this theme:

> 'Motherhood is not idyllic – it is a struggle from beginning to end. Especially for low-income families who often do not have sufficient funds for the bare necessities of life.'
>
> 'Worry and anxiety of the impending birth with its consequent bills, in addition to rent and other basic commitments, began to put a strain on our marriage. In desperation, my husband took to drink and this additional problem precipitated the breakdown of our relationship.'
>
> 'Guilt lies heavy when one cannot afford things needed by a family. "I want" – how often do we hear these words and feel powerless to respond positively to them?'
>
> 'The mother feels inadequate to cope with the struggle and becomes resentful, and this resentment often festers like an open wound when the mother feels she cannot speak to anyone about it because of shame.'
>
> Bernie concludes: 'Poverty can cause pain, and the torment can tear one apart. No one understands the worry of a mother for her children, from the cradle to the grave, and this causes emotional and physical problems, and yet no mother can afford the luxury of being ill.'

As women broke the silence about their experience of motherhood, one by one, they shattered the mythology that romanticises this role. (Bernie herself died of breast cancer shortly after penning this piece.)

4 Critical and Imaginative Social Analysis

The movement from reflecting on one's own experience of oppression to engaging in an analysis of its causes encourages a shift away from any residual feelings of guilt or victimhood. Here we encourage thinking that sees the foundations of oppression as clearly located within the systems, the structures and the institutions of society. It had been our experience that teaching the skill of critical thinking is extremely difficult, especially when we live in a society where the victim is blamed and the protester is dismissed as a crank and easily silenced. Women such as Nuala Wood often come to The Shanty willing to blame their own lack of intelligence, some even describe themselves as 'stupid', instead of questioning the system of education that never gave them a chance to succeed. Some of the finest moments in those early years occurred during the basic English courses taught by Toni Ryan, an empathetic educator and literacy expert. As women mastered literacy skills, they wrote to their local politicians, naming the educational handicap they had lived with and demanding a change in the education system so that the acute personal and social disadvantages they had lived with would not be repeated in the lives of their children. This awareness that society is socially constructed and therefore can change is a real moment of liberation in any educational journey and includes the education of the social imagination.

5 Theoretical Reflection

Although no one will argue the need to link theory and practice in a feminist pedagogy, little is written about the challenge of providing a sound theoretical base as the foundation for reflection and social action. In the early years of constructing a method of education in dialogue with the needs of women, many of whom had left school at fourteen, there were many resistances and challenges. Some women could see no need to reflect on different theoretical perspectives, they were in a rush to gain the skills that up to now had been denied them. Others spoke about what they perceived as a gap in their conceptual ability. While highly intelligent, they had never been trained or given time to think strategically. Wrestling with ideas, taking time to ponder and think about different ways of understanding the world, these were luxuries not afforded in lives lived managing poverty. It is our belief that literacy in the fullest sense entails understanding the prevailing patriarchal ideology (accepted set of ideas that presumes male dominance) and to do so we must understand the nature of ideology, so that we can begin to articulate an alternative set of radically new ideas. The need to read, to think and to write cannot be overstated, but the space and time to do so causes continuous hassle. One woman in the Women's Studies Diploma course shared with us the information that her haven in her home was the toilet – she'd hide the books in there and for those minutes was left undisturbed, especially by her husband who was extremely jealous of these 'new-fangled ideas' she was acquiring in The Shanty.

We found that the theoretical dimension of any theme can be presented imaginatively, creatively using video or audio tapes, pre-read articles and books or simply teaching in a dialogical style using the flip chart as a vehicle to illustrate with diagram, art or cartoons the ideas under consideration. There is no idea too complicated that cannot be communicated by a good teacher. Sr Bernadette Flannigan, who taught a number of women 'the higher realms of mathematics' when they expressed a desire to do Leaving Certificate maths, proved that point.

6 Engaging Praxis

No one who has ever attended a course at The Shanty is in any doubt about the link between theory and practice. Furthermore, while the imagination is central to the different movements of a feminist pedagogy, nowhere is this more true than at this stage – envisioning the future. To envisage the future creatively is to stand in the present and see reality other than it is. Because the creative imagination is the place of seeing what should be, then a feminist pedagogy educates for a new order – a world beyond patriarchy, beyond the rule of the fathers. This stage allows us to hold the 'is' and the 'ought' together in a new way that rekindles the belief that dreams can come true: this is how it is, this is perhaps how it ought to be. Such pedagogy can provide a space to heal the hopelessness and despair that can take over the lives of women who live with too much hardship and too little privilege. Such hope-filled imaging and social action is seldom accomplished alone.

At several courses, having reflected on the women participants' own experiences of motherhood, the group ultimately studied recent feminist theories that offered new insights. For example, their study of the French philosopher Julia Kristeva allowed greater clarity that motherhood is but one role that a woman chooses in her life. Kristeva reminds us that 'We need a new discourse on motherhood, one that liberates the logic of the maternal body and that in so doing is creative of new and more mobile subjective and cultural identities'; becoming woman is a more exciting prospect than simply reducing oneself to being a 'mother for others'. Another feminist philosopher, Luce Irigaray, states that in the end the failure of the mother to be a self enrages the daughter: 'I received from you only your obliviousness of yourself.' As illustrated in the work of both philosophers, motherhood is one, albeit a very important, role in any woman's life; furthermore, the freedom and choice to become a mother rests with the individual woman.

The chosen praxis by the group reflection on women's role in society was to form a local group called 'Jobstown Women's Own'. Ann Kielty writes about this development:

> Wednesday 22 February 1989 saw the launch of Jobstown Women's Own, a group which was set up to bring women together in positive way to enjoy each others' company and to provide a space in women's lives which they could call exclusively their own. Ann Louise and Katherine were the two invited guests to this launch of the first women's group in Tallaght West. A national newspaper published an article about the group.

> 'Isolation is a major problem facing the women of Tallaght. Now a new women's group has been set up in Jobstown to combat this and bring women together. Five women set up the group, all of them have completed a number of courses at The Shanty Educational Project. Mrs Kielty commented: "We wanted to put something into the community, and do something for the women of the area after we did the courses as there isn't anything in the area for them at the moment."' (*Evening Herald*, 6 March 1989)

(It should be mentioned that all submissions to Government for the ongoing development of this locally led group failed, and so Jobstown Women's Own folded shortly after its formation. Even more poignant was the sudden death of Ann Cuddihy, Secretary to the group and an untiring community leader and social activist, who had taken courses at The Shanty since the beginning. One of the women commented at the time, 'Sometimes it's all just too much to try to keep going; her heart gave up in the end.')

With The Muse up and running, over seventy women attending eight different courses and even two groups of men now settled into their own programmes, we both felt exhausted and agreed that we needed more leisure. Although we have always walked about three miles each day with our dogs in the woods behind our home, we needed a new hobby. A new riding stables had opened close by so we decided to take up horse riding. The owner and instructor never quite grasped that we were new to this sport and within weeks we were on 'hacks', galloping like lunatics, clearly out of control, through the aforementioned woods. Though fearless and risk-takers by nature, this stretched us to the limit, but we trusted and loved the horses we rode. Katherine would climb up onto Bianca, a huge, sixteen-hand former racehorse, while Ann Louise rode Bess, a darling animal who would jump anything we encountered *en route*. We'd return home each Saturday exhilarated, refreshed – and so relieved that we had survived another day!

There was growing concern at our management-team meetings about the quality of childcare we were offering as part of the project. While we always offered 'sessional care' for participants' children, which now was run in the new community centre by trained childcare staff, the time had come to establish an early education and childcare facility for the children themselves. At this time, 25 percent of Ireland's entire child population lived in poverty, and the percentage was much higher in West Tallaght. In *The Shanty Times* of winter 1991, we wrote an editorial that reflected on the recently published 'Convention on the Rights of the Child' published by the United Nations (UN). It had taken ten years to produce the final document, which was adopted by the UN in November 1989. However, to become law, it required twenty of the then 166 nations to sign up to the fifty-four articles that dealt with the basic civil, economic, social, cultural and religious rights of children. The good news at the time of our editorial was that eighty countries had already signed. Much to our chagrin, Ireland was not among them. Our own analysis proved accurate: in order to sign up to the Convention, our government would have to tackle the growing levels of child poverty and the rapid deterioration of child welfare in our land.

Our editorial concluded: 'To tackle the injustice of child poverty, we have a dream. Our dream is rooted in a belief that good childcare and pre-school education are rights for all children and are a pro-family measure. The Government has no programmes in West Tallaght to meet this end. Our dream is to construct a "Rainbow House". We will acquire two houses in the West Tallaght area and create them as a children's space: a space of beauty, colour, joy, play and fun. Although this dream is in its infancy, we strongly believe that educational care for children is care for the future.' Before we published this newsletter, we went to St Thomas's senior primary school in Jobstown and told the children about our idea. Following a discussion about their ideas, the children were invited to draw their images of what the Rainbow House would look like – Brian O'Reilly's drawing was published in that edition of our newsletter. Many of the other drawings were saved and now hang on the walls of An Cosán, which illustrates that dreams come true and images become reality. In fact, what happened in this instance illustrates that there are moments in life when reality surpasses our dreams and images of what could be achieved.

All our courses had now moved to The Muse, and, with a broad range on offer, the question always remained: are we reaching the women who are most isolated in Tallaght West and least inclined to return to education? Reflecting on Nuala's story and the stories of many women like her in West Tallaght – women who had worked in their youth as machinists in factories – we decided to put on another set of courses in creative traditional handcrafts, starting with the art of quilting. Here we joined with an established group of quilters in the nearby rural town of Blessington. We knew these women, who were members of the Irish Countrywomen's Association (ICA), as they ran the country market at weekends in Blessington, which we attended with religious fervour, and there they often displayed beautiful quilts that their group had made. These courses were an immediate success, allowing women to return to education via a route in which their own skills and background could be affirmed. Apart from learning the ancient and complex craft of quilting, many of the participants quickly saw the economic opportunities that came with acquiring this skill. As Katherine's fortieth birthday was approaching, Ann Louise commissioned a king-sized quilt for our bed, in Katherine's favourite colour, blue. On the day itself, the women who had created this magnificent piece of art, along with their tutor Ann Coe, carried it up to our dormer bedroom and 'dressed the bed'. Consonant with the tradition of quilting, each woman had embroidered her name on the back of the quilt. Reflecting back, this is one of many occasions when, though we didn't speak publicly about our relationship we did not hide it. When Katherine arrived, she was simply overcome – not only had she received an heirloom that would always be with us, but it had been created by a group of women who one year previously had been living their lives in isolation behind closed doors. This 'micro-enterprise' continued under the stewardship of one of our management team, Julie Kiernan. The women made wedding gifts and presents for their own families and sold personalised quilts as christening gifts.

The second handcraft training programme also began as a course in The Muse. It then developed into a large community enterprise that over a ten-year period sold on the national and international markets and was represented at all the craft fairs during those years. But the full details of that development come later. It began when we heard that the artist Mary O'Rourke had a workshop as part of her family farm up in Glenasmole, a few miles away. We set off to see her work and explore the opportunity of developing further local women's interests in ancient

Irish crafts. Mary's studio itself was a work of art. Inside the large stone cottage, fleeces from her Jacob's sheep – a type renowned for excellent wool – were piled high in one area. The smell of oil from the wool filled the air. Carded and spun wool hung in skeins from the rafters in a magnificent array of colours, all from natural dyes. One woman worker stood rhythmically feeding wool through a carding machine and receiving the flat combed product from the other side. This she passed to another worker, who sat at a spinning wheel quietly spinning the carded wool in the traditional manner. It was like stepping back in time, although, observing the finished products that Mary was creating, it was clear that she was developing items for the top end of the current craft industry. She agreed to run a weekend course – and was surprised by the huge turnout.

Driving the bus around the estates in West Tallaght, and sometimes assisting women negotiating on the doorsteps with reluctant husbands and partners for this day out, gave further insight into the challenge for women with no income to get any time for themselves. Once we arrived in Mary's studio, the tension fell away, and we all became absorbed in learning the various skills. We sat enveloped in wool at every stage of its transformation from fleece to felt. There was no sense of unease or estrangement among the women, although they never had been in such an environment. Mary, as well as being a gifted artist, has a huge heart and embraced us women in all our differences. The sounds of country life filled the studio that nestled in the Dublin hills about eight miles from the raw suburb we had left behind some hours earlier. Towards the end of the day, each one of us had made a small gift to bring home. As this opening weekend came to a close, the women pleaded with Mary to allow them to come back. She agreed, and so on one Sunday per month for the following year we began a triangular relationship between Glenaraneen, Glenasmole and West Tallaght, all locations equidistant from each other. Ann Louise willingly became the bus driver for these outings. She loved the setting, the day of chat with the women and the opportunity to learn this craft. We got some spinning wheels delivered to the women's homes in West Tallaght so that 'homework' could be accomplished, and we also purchased one for our own home. Coincidently, we had four Jacob's sheep in our paddock (all called after mystics), so, as we were producing our own raw material, the prospects were endless!

These simple beginnings in the winter of 1991 formed the foundation for our community enterprise. We were always aware that although income is but one factor among many that influence the opportunities that people enjoy, in order to reverse women's poverty, women's economic dependence must be addressed. Along with providing educational opportunities for women and children, we needed to find a way to enable women to get back to work. This would be the central theme that we addressed at the celebration of our fifth anniversary, when we welcomed an exceptional woman.

There are few in this country, certainly in our age range, that won't recall vividly the day that Mary Robinson became Ireland's first woman president. In May 1990, we attended a fund-raiser for her in the home of a mutual friend, and over the following eight months supported her campaign in any way we could, like every other feminist in the land. When word broke on that dull December day that she had won, unrestrained joy was unleashed. We rang our friends and quickly gathered our feminist spirituality group. We drank champagne, danced and sang. Some hours later we listened to her victory speech, when she said: 'I don't know whether to dance or sing, so I have done both.' We understood. She correctly praised 'Mná na hÉireann' that evening, 'who, instead of rocking the cradle, rocked the system'. Quoting the poet Eavan Boland, she said: 'As a woman, I want women who have felt themselves outside history, to be written back into history.' This was, indeed, a moment of success, and the women of Ireland, certainly our circle of friends, sensed a common achievement on that evening.

Some months later, our mutual friend, Barbara Fitzgerald, godmother to Mary Robinson's daughter Tessa and a member of our development team, requested the President to visit The Muse to celebrate the fifth anniversary of The Shanty Educational Project. On 4 December 1991, one year after her inauguration, she honoured us with her presence. As the Special Branch scoured the property and hid in the bushes for the duration of her visit, we all crammed into The Muse and savoured every moment of this special celebration. Women from the community welcomed her and spoke of the enormous sense of pride and appreciation they felt that she had come to share in the festivities. The Chairperson of the management team, Marie Moran, reflected in her speech: 'Since I joined The Shanty my life has been enriched and I know that we will continue to fill this place with love and hope and turn even more of our dreams into reality.' Clearly informed about the work of the previous five years, the President in her response was rich in her praise: 'We have – in women, in their organisational abilities, in their creative approach – a major resource.' She honoured our work as a model of locally based women's community education and asked that we continue the dialogue with the structures of the established order which could clearly learn from such a creative response to endemic poverty.

8

SOUL-FILLED FEMINISM

We developed The Shanty Educational Project because we were passionate about women's lives and because it was one of the most radical feminist ventures we could imagine. As social activists, though, we believed that nourishment of the human spirit needed to be at the core of our work from the very beginning. It was the most natural thing in the world for us to bring our own quest for a wholeness of body, mind and spirit to the work of changing the status quo. It was part of who we were, part of our upbringing, part of our own way of being together. This is why celebration, ritual, times for stillness and a table filled with home baking were integral to a raising of consciousness that patriarchal culture inhibits the full human development of everyone, but especially women and those who live with the injustice of poverty.

What surprised us from the very beginning was the extraordinary thirst for this way of working. As we indicated earlier, our management committee was keen to study feminist theology and to learn about the ways in which women's experience provides a well-spring to debunk the maleness of God and an impetus to search for new interpretations of women's stories in sacred texts. We remember one evening, as we considered the story of the Samaritan woman in John's Gospel, when Mary Sweeney, having listened to some of the new thinking, offered her own interpretation of the story. She suggested that the nameless Samaritan woman must have had extraordinary authority, and the trust of her own people, in order to convince Samaritans to hear the good news of a *Jewish* man. Mary mused further that Jesus was probably aware of her authority – and his need for someone of her stature – and that was probably what prompted that famous conversation at the well.

We were in awe of Mary's insights, a Tallaght woman who had left school early in order to help her family make ends meet. Her interpretation was similar to that of the renowned German feminist biblical scholar, Elisabeth Schüssler Fiorenza in her book *In Memory of Her*. Fiorenza's work identifies several women leaders in the early Jesus movement and argues that male biblical interpretation erased memories of women's authority and their equality with the male disciples. So here we were, a group of women raised in the Catholic tradition, becoming aware together of the ways in which our religion negated women's stories in the Bible. But we were also seeing together a picture of a strong biblical woman, with lots of courage and confidence to speak in a public forum. You could feel the liberation in our sitting room that evening. If the Samaritan woman could do it, so too could we take our courage in our hands and speak publicly against the injustice of women's poverty in Ireland.

As mentioned before, our meetings always started with an 'Opening Circle', an activity we had devised to honour the presence of each person who had come, to engage our hearts and souls as well as our minds and to create a space for quiet reflection on what we wanted to do together. We often began with a poem, followed by moments of stillness, and then invited each person to reflect on the meaning of the poem for their own lives. It created a prayer-like atmosphere. It was an opportunity for self-reflection within a group who held a common purpose, and we felt strengthened by the feeling of care it created between us. It was so powerful in its simplicity and its impact on us as a group that we brought this practice into the coursework with participants and into meetings with the fund-raising committee and board. It was not Catholic or even religious in tone. It was, and continues to be, time set aside to let our souls be touched by the care we have for each other and by our common search for what it means to be human within a community.

Over time, committee members and course participants often wrote their own poetry to be brought to the circle. Our Shanty newsletters throughout the years are filled with examples of this spiritual creativity, revealing how students were learning to become the women they wanted to be: women finding the personal power to change themselves, their families and to build a proud Tallaght community. Margaret Murray, originally from Drogheda yet finding her way in the early eighties to a council house in Tallaght as a single mother with children, was inspired to write the following poem when her three-year-old daughter tried to blow out a very special candle which Margaret had received at the end of a Shanty 'think-in' attended by members of our various committees. Margaret said, 'As I was writing the poem I thought I was writing it to my daughter, but as I wrote the last line I discovered to my surprise I was writing the poem to the little girl within myself.'

Don't Blow My Candle Out

Little girl, don't blow my candle out,
Let its warm glow light up your lovely face,
I want to see your laughing eyes of freedom
Outshine my bright candle.
Little girl, don't blow my candle out,
Let its strong flame draw out your innocence
So I can remember mine
And let your spirit's shadow dance freely on the wall
In tune with my candle's flicker,
Little girl, don't blow my candle out,
It's all I have to light up my path
So I can find my way back to you
Little girl, wait for me there
Don't blow my candle out.

We continued to feed our bodies and souls through the celebration of rituals and meals together at every significant point in the life of the project. We knew *we* needed this – there were so many times we felt absolutely drained by the fifteen-hour schedule we kept, juggling the development of the project with a commitment to our academic careers in university settings. We didn't always make a successful transition between these two worlds, and from time to time members of our management committee got angry with us for using 'big, middle-class words'. There were other difficult times when some of the community-development workers in Tallaght resented the growth in demand for Shanty courses, or when we simply got worn down by what felt like endless fund-raising. This was the hard slog of radical change. We needed celebration when we got things right, and those who worked with us wanted it too. As one of our friends often states, 'We work hard and we play hard.' Where appropriate, we incorporated a ritual as part of the celebration. There was a huge thirst for ritual – symbolic words, actions and song – that helped us express the meaning of what we had achieved together and how we had cared for each other in spite of weariness or conflict.

A ritual in our four-car garage, before it became The Muse, was a magical example of this. As twilight dawned in mid-February 1989, a day of hard work at The Shanty drew to a close. We had invited our management and building committees and their partners and children to do a huge clear-out of the garage so that we could begin to transform it into The Muse.

We had fifteen people working there, while Ann Louise and a group of women prepared a beef and Guinness stew for fifty! When others joined us at 6.00pm we gathered in a circle in the emptied garage space. There was still a tree stump in the middle of the space (left over from earlier times), and we used it to hold candles, incense and Shanty crocuses coming to bloom. Katherine began the ritual saying, 'You bless The Shanty by your presence here, and we thank you for all you have done to bring us to this point.' Then Fergus Roche, Chairman of our building committee, threw the first bit of plaster on the back wall to symbolise the beginning of the 'skudding' process. Rose Cullen, management member, read from her reflection on one of the past courses:

> Our first Shanty leadership course has been a great success. At first, most of us had a problem with seeing ourselves as 'leaders'. The word gave us images of power over people rather than images of empowering others. However, after a few weeks we all came to realise our hidden leadership abilities which we are constantly using whether it be with our family or working with others in Tallaght. Some of us have started women's groups, others work as leaders in Brown Street Family Centre ... Nurtured by a secure environment I feel I have learned to be a better communicator, gained confidence in my leadership abilities and made some great new friends.

Fr Liam Murtagh, Jobstown parish priest, offered a blessing for health during the building conversion and a prayer that our work would continue to flourish. Ann Louise closed the ritual by saying, 'May the memory of this day and all past and future activities of The Shanty sustain each one of us during the twilight of our lives.' It was time to eat!

Once The Muse was up and running, with courses from Monday to Thursday, we reserved Friday as a day for spirituality. We called it 'Isabel's Day at The Shanty', a quiet day sponsored for groups of five to fifteen, where women came to enjoy the beauty and peace of Glenaraneen. We named the day after our friend Sr Isabel Green, the wonderful holy woman who ran the House of Prayer in Gloucester, Massachusetts. We wanted to remember her after her untimely death from cancer, part of our effort to retrieve women's stories in spiritual traditions. The day resembles her formula for soul-time within a communal setting: a cup of tea and welcome, quiet time, walks in the Dublin mountains and a hot meal, lovingly prepared. So many times we have been told by women as they leave that this was the first time in their lives they ever experienced anything like this, just for them. As the years have progressed, women and men involved in community development and education from all over the country have found their way to our table. We often meet people in our day jobs who say: 'The Shanty? I've been to your home on a Friday!' Twenty-two years on, every week our gate opens to people we have never met but who thirst for stillness and personal renewal. What a contrast to the sign as one enters Clonliffe College, a Dublin Roman Catholic seminary, that one is entering 'private property'.

Placing spirituality at the heart of our work was a risky venture in the early years, even though it, more than anything else, sustained our drive for social justice. While we shaped this ethos together with those who were part of our work, others looking in on us often misunderstood what was happening. On the one hand, the Catholic Church still had such a grip on people's imagination that it was hard for some to acknowledge that spiritual growth could rightfully happen outside the confines of religion. One day, we met judges for the first AIB Better Ireland awards, and they told us that a prominent state agency had not recommended our application for the award because we were operating some kind of 'cult'! (We won, anyway, after Joe Mulholland, Director General of RTÉ, and Farrell Corcoran, Head of Communications in Dublin City University, saw with their own eyes what we were doing.) On the other hand, as we said before, there were some activist feminists who were disgusted with us because we were 'giving religion a good name'; this didn't stop us, but we often felt isolated from those who might otherwise have been comrades if we weren't into the spiritual thing.

This isolation diminished over time as we brought our soul-filled feminist fervour into the public domain, largely through our work as feminist theologians and teachers. While much of feminist political activism in the seventies and early eighties had been focused on battling the Catholic Church's regulation of women's sexuality, we found that there were thousands of women throughout the country who, while aware of the male dominance in religion, were keenly interested in their own spiritual growth. As they heard us on public radio or read about us in the newspapers, we were invited to give public lectures and to teach women's groups throughout the country. Katherine took up much of this work, becoming the 'wandering preacher/teacher' as she travelled to Mayo, Belfast, Donegal, Galway, Limerick, Cork, Connemara, south-west Kerry and many, many other rural locations.

In these rural settings, women would gather in a meeting room of a local hotel; in cities Katherine often spoke in university lecture halls. In each place she sparked an enormous interest as women considered the possibility of Churches freed from patriarchy, or spirituality as something that promoted women's self-realisation, rather than subordination and self-sacrifice. Feminist consciousness-raising was now happening for some *through* the process of theological learning. For others, especially those who had worked within the political context, their feminist horizon extended towards transformation of the Churches. For still others who had left religion long before, they discovered personal nourishment in the common ground of women exploring their spirituality together. One woman captured much of the sentiment throughout the country: 'How angry we feel about the Church, how it treats all women, including religious sisters. The Church doesn't provide any vision for the future. We are all at different stages in the development of our awareness, but we have all agreed that there is no going back. We need to find some way to express our own feminist spirituality.'

As a way to answer this desire, we co-founded, with others, *Womanspirit: the Irish Journal of Feminist Spirituality.* In its first guise as a newsletter entitled, 'Women in the Churches' (May 1986), Marianne McGiffin and her colleagues invited us to work with them to transform it into a publication in feminist spirituality; Marianne was a former theological student of Katherine's at Trinity College and continued her interest in feminist theology by starting this publication. Eleven women, from the Catholic and Church of Ireland traditions, met regularly in the first two years to plan and publish the magazine. We gathered in each other's homes to sketch the contents of each issue and to agree on who would approach whom to get articles or reports on various women's events. We contributed our own financial resources, even when subscriptions started to come in. There was no academic or institutional support for this type of venture. Those earliest meetings were filled with extraordinary enthusiasm, generosity *and* conflict. We mirrored, in many ways, the diversity of women gathering throughout the country. Did we want to reform religion from within or take the radical road out? What was the connection, if any, between spirituality and political action? Were we reformists or radicals?

By the fifth issue in the spring of 1988, we printed a policy that attempted to respect the dynamic pluralism of women's views:

> *Womanspirit* is a country-wide resource to facilitate groups and individuals interested in Feminist Spirituality in its most inclusive and holistic sense.
>
> This means that while it is Christian in its origin and primary orientation, *Womanspirit* wishes to promote and nurture a creative and mutually enriching dialogue between women of all traditions and spiritual journeys. … it places a high value on the personal … it develops a critique of the factors which oppress women in the various areas of their lives and it supports the transformation of individuals and social/religious structures.

Katherine and Marianne, co-editors armed with this inclusive policy, felt a missionary zeal to support the growth of what was fast becoming a new spiritual movement characterised by extraordinary diversity. *Womanspirit* was a vehicle for women to express the personal in a public forum. Anne O'Reilly Kelly, a colleague of Ann Louise's in the religious-studies department at St Patrick's College, wrote about her personal journey: 'I am the surging power and the gentlest echo, the rush of energy and the exhaustion of birth, the soaring spirit and the earthy rootedness … While my story has always been a womanstory, now I write consciously as a Christian feminist – a woman seeking to express the experience of being Christian in the language and symbols most appropriate to women's experience' (Vol. 1, No. 3, 1987). Ronit Lentin, now director of ethnic studies in Trinity College, narrated her Jewish feminist journey: 'Every day as I get closer into line with my women [of the Jewish tradition], I negate that vengeful, aggressive male deity. Every day I get closer to Shekhina, that ever-present female divinity, to whom I don't have to pray because she knows that I am journeying to her centre. Because she knows I am on my way' (Vol. 2, No. 1, 1987). Joni Crone, radical lesbian activist, talked about herself as a 'spinster' and feminist spirituality as 'the web which connects my body, my emotions, my thoughts, my actions with the bodies, emotions, thoughts and actions of other women, so that together we move against the tide of patriarchal misogyny moving against us for centuries' (Vol. 2, No. 2, 1988).

Womanspirit carried regular interviews with Irish women, often penned by Bernadette Quinn (a founder member of the Irish Women's Liberation Movement), to encourage women's leadership in the spiritual and political arena. They were well-known women working in the political or theological field – Mary Harney, Joan FitzGerald, Nuala Fennell and Mary Condren – and not-so-well-known women working for change at local level like Chrissie Ward, activist in the Travellers' rights movement, and Annette Halpin, founder of Tallaght Women's Contact Centre. The magazine also reported on seven Christian feminist conferences throughout a period of four years. It published a list of forty-five women's groups meeting throughout the country, publicised feminist theology and spirituality courses happening from Belfast to Caherciveen and offered a forum for ethical debate. We intentionally sought out the views of activists as well as scholars, middle-class and working-class women. At the time when Ivana Bacik, then President of TCD Students' Union, was taken to court by the Society for the Protection of Unborn Children for publishing information on abortion, *Womanspirit* published the views of theologian Linda Hogan and Shanty community worker Sheila Norton side by side in the winter 1989 issue. From very different perspectives, both women argued for the right of women to choose. In Linda's words: 'As competent moral agents, capable of assessing all the relevant factors, women ought to have procreative choice.' From Sheila: 'Women have a right to choose. It's their life. God forbid that the attitude of my parents' generation should ever again prevail. Please give people the facts, so that at least they can be clear in their thinking. Ignorance is a terrible thing' (Vol. 3, No. 4).

We can't really do justice here to the richness of this journal nor the efforts of those who worked with us voluntarily to sustain its publication over seven years. Best to leave that to a future graduate student in gender and women's studies. It was hugely important in our lives, though. Looking back, it represents the vitality and growth of what we were once part of – a collective effort to radicalise religion and, in the wider terrain, to infuse Irish political feminism with the power of soul. This fitted well with our work at The Shanty, and we shared learnings across these two arenas. We also brought the energy of this politico-spiritual movement into our university work, and while the fit was strong for several years, it slowly unravelled and was eventually severed. Were we too forthright, too honest, too radical to stay forever in theological departments of established institutions? In an earlier chapter we wrote about Ann Louise's battle with the bishops. Here now is Katherine's story.

She was the first one to teach Latin American liberation theology in Trinity College, and we have already described her unorthodox pedagogical approach to that subject. She brought new life into an ancient college, founded in 1592, originally viewed as the university for the Protestant ascendancy. Even the name of her department – the School of Hebrew, Biblical and Theological Studies – reflected bygone times. With the relatively new leadership of Professor Seán Freyne, head of the Theology School, there were strong efforts to bring theology into the modern world. He had invited Katherine in, and, as each term progressed, she developed another new course so that students could discover the relevance of religion for twentieth-century Ireland. She taught feminist bibilical and theological studies (again, the first one to teach this subject in Trinity) and eventually developed a full year's curriculum entitled 'Christianity and a Just Society' that included Latin American, feminist and South African liberation theologies. A former student, reflecting on those times, wrote:

At thirty-four years of age, I was in the final year of reading Biblical Studies and Theology to degree level … a competent student … tutored by honourable men … with the promise of good grades … untouched. Then, in that fourth year of study, she came to teach feminist and liberation theology. Another wordy American, I thought. Pen and paper poised, I sat, ready to imbibe theory and far-off Latin American practice. A safe distance. A chance aside began her musing about a friend's child who was disabled … and then, she CRIED … long tears trickled out of her eyes, trapped momentarily in her glasses, yet slipping through … This theologian who was only supposed to teach … Swamped, sweltered by embarrassment and discomfort at the lack of familiar order in that concrete-blocked room with no window – no vista of escape – I stayed, rooted by this crying theologian. And I saw the disabled boy in my heart's eye, and greeted myself, still wary, barely born. Opened to the pain of life within me, I too knew the sorrow of the unliberated. Liberation theology had begun. I had heard the heart-voice of a woman and recognised my own.

As a way to engage students further in the study of theology, Katherine developed a course called 'Religion and Literature for First Years', and they studied together Margaret Atwood's *The Handmaid's Tale*, Alice Walker's *The Color Purple*, and Elie Wiesel's *Night*. For most students, it was the very first time they had ever considered that 'God' could be dead, black or female. Students were stunned, engaged; no one was unchanged. Her classes were rarely straight lectures; she did not believe in the banking model of education. She treated her students as active learners, often taking notes from them as they debated the questions she set for the session. At the time of the completion of the single European market, she co-taught a course with her colleague, Werner G Jeanrond, entitled 'Religion and European Integration'. The previous year she had been invited by the Professor of Education to develop a course in religious education for those studying to teach at second level. The Women's Studies Centre also signed her up to teach feminist ethics and spirituality.

Katherine played a central role in breaking down the strict divisions between fundamental, systematic and biblical theology and constantly challenged students to link deep thinking about classical texts with radical reflection on the state of the world in which they were living. Her interdisciplinary approach reflected methods being used in other European and American universities in order to recreate what was called 'practical theology'. The great American theologian David Tracy argued that practical theology should be focused on human and world transformation. Johann Baptist Metz, the well-known German theologian, added that this type of theology calls for social criticism of the Church itself and its function within society. In May of 1990, the Church of Ireland chaplain at Trinity invited Katherine to preach on Trinity Monday, a day which marked the beginning of 'Trinity Week' to celebrate the close of another academic year. Katherine was the first woman to preach in Trinity's chapel, and she used this opportunity to concretise the challenge of practical theology by asking the university community to consider how they could create a future for Irish society that is wisdom-filled. In her concluding remarks, she said: 'Our challenge involves not only the pursuit of wisdom within these walls [the original campus is enclosed with stone-faced walls], our challenge includes listening to the wisdom that is sculpted within the *lives* of those who suffer, those outside our walls. How will we create economic theories for the benefit of all without the wisdom of those who experience poverty? How will we talk credibly – and authentically – about God without knowing the wisdom of those who have suffered at the hands of the Churches?' And then Katherine ended her sermon by naming the God who is Wisdom as 'She'. Those with heads bowed jolted up! At the garden party afterwards, hosted by the Provost, Tom Mitchell, many remarked to Katherine that she spoke courageous words, and they hoped that it wouldn't come against her.

Katherine adored her early years in Trinity. She loved her students; she loved challenging their hearts and minds and being challenged by them. She often had to pinch herself as she walked through the cobblestoned campus to remind herself that she really did have the privilege of teaching here. She felt completely alive during heady debates. Students touched her heart deeply as they shared their spiritual struggles, intellectual disbeliefs or personal joy or tragedy. Seán Freyne – a man alive with God, Bible and theology – became a close friend, and early on he invited us to meet his wife Gail and their beautiful little daughters, Bridget and Sarah. They became our 'second family'; because both of the girls' godmothers lived in the USA, Katherine became Bridget's 'Irish' godmother, Ann Louise Sarah's.

There were three men besides Seán with full-time posts in the department and some part-time faculty, but no other part-time lecturer taught as many hours as Katherine. Each year she would teach a bit more, eventually carrying close to a full-time load. She kept hoping that some day a full-time post in practical theology would be created, especially after her work in building up that field. By the end of her eighth year in the department, though, there was no post in sight, and she felt exhausted and disempowered. She had worked tirelessly to design and teach courses, to advise on undergraduate and graduate theses. She gave public lectures, attended numerous committee meetings and published scholarly articles. But she continued to be exploited by the university system that paid part-time lecturers for the hours they taught and little else. It was a pittance. She felt degraded, too, because she had no equal standing with the men in the department, despite her commitment and contribution. Seán had managed to get a small additional fee for her advisory work, but by 1990 she was making a meagre £3,000 for the year's work.

When Katherine returned to Trinity in autumn 1991, she hoped that she would be invited to take up a one-year, full-time post that had been vacated by a young Irish biblical scholar. While the post was not designated for her expertise, the department already had three full-time biblical scholars and only one full-time theologian. Instead, Seán hired a young man who had not finished his PhD (Katherine had hers for five years) to teach a minimum course-load and get full salary. She asked to meet Seán and was told that the University Dean, 'in his wisdom', felt that if Trinity gave her the money (instead of this young man) it might hurt her chances of getting a permanent full-time post, *if* it ever came up. That was the last straw. Katherine told Seán that she would leave at the close of that academic year unless there was the possibility of applying for a full-time position. 'I have functioned as the token woman long enough,' she said. Seán got angry and asked if she wanted to 'disassociate' herself from TCD immediately. 'There are others who could teach your courses,' he said.

At the time of their conversation, there was a slight chance that a full-time position would come up if one of the full-time faculty members resigned his post. Katherine, reluctantly, decided to stay on one more year. Six weeks later, she published her book, *The Hope for Wholeness: A Spirituality for Feminists*. Seán hosted the launch in the atrium of Trinity College, and the well-known feminist Monica Barnes TD agreed to launch it. It was an extraordinary evening with music by Nóirín Ní Riain and Margaret Daly. The place was packed. It was the high point of Katherine's theological career. She and Seán had made amends, and both were hopeful that the future might change for the better. Several months later, though, two things happened that should have been a warning to Katherine. Two department members wrote a letter to Seán asking him to resign his headship after he had agreed to sponsor a lecture by Frances Kissling, director of Catholics for a Free Choice, an American Catholic organisation that promoted women's reproductive rights. At the time, we interpreted it as a move to disempower Seán, especially because of his commitment to women and feminism, and as an indirect manifestation of their fear that Katherine might get a post. Soon after that, Katherine heard from students that a colleague told them that she would be leaving her part-time post the following year. When Katherine confronted him on this, he said that it had 'just slipped out' in his effort to protect her from students pestering her about supervising their dissertations.

In May 1992, a position finally surfaced with the resignation of one of the department members. A post in practical theology was advertised, and Katherine applied, with the support of Seán. From that moment on, two of Katherine's colleagues – and also members of the selection committee – never said a word to her about the post. In fact, one of them told her that he must protect *himself* and have no conversations with any potential candidates.

Katherine took the summer of 1992 to prepare herself for the interview. In September, she met the committee and was thrilled with her morning presentation and afternoon conversation. Ann Louise had been waiting in the Trinity chapel for her throughout the day. They met up as soon as Katherine was finished, Ann Louise greeted by the words 'I think I've got it!' When they returned home, they waited in hopeful anticipation for a phone call from Seán. It never came.

Instead, the Trinity Human Resources Administrator phoned her to tell her that she did not get the job. She apologised for the 'brutal message' that she had to deliver. Ann Louise was looking on and could see Katherine's face register shock. When Katherine put the phone down, Ann Louise just shouted, 'No! No! No!' and then held Katherine close, both of them in tears. An hour later, Seán was at our back door, devastated. He said, 'Not one member voted for you.' Katherine told him to stop; she did not want to hear any more. Later that night, in a half-kept diary, she wrote, 'They put a bullet through my soul.'

Over the next number of months, Katherine received hundreds of letters and telephone calls from colleagues, students and friends. One of her former first-year students wrote: 'I want to tell you how sorry, indeed upset, I was to learn on my return to Trinity this term that you were no longer in the department. *I am annoyed now that as a class we were dissuaded from sending in a petition on your behalf last year when it became known that you were to apply for a permanent position.* I personally was fascinated, humbled and inspired by your course.' Fr Enda McDonagh, Professor of Moral Theology in Maynooth University, wrote: 'I must say that I had assumed you would get it and was very surprised and disappointed when you didn't. There is so much good that you do, personally and socially, pastorally and theologically.' Grace Jantzen, Professor of Theology in King's College, London, wrote: 'What happened is scandalous.' Sarah Coakley, Professor of Theology at Pembroke College, Oxford, penned: 'I am still in shock for you.' Several students sent letters saying they were 'humiliated by Trinity's treatment' of her and 'devastated' that Katherine would not return because 'many of us began to believe that we as individuals have the ability to make a difference in our world.'

Katherine had decided that she would not, could not, go back to Trinity to teach the agreed courses in the Women's Studies Centre. She wrote a letter to the co-ordinator to explain her withdrawal and received a sympathetic letter in return. In November of that term, however, the centre invited Ann Louise to open an exhibition by a woman artist in the Trinity museum. Ann Louise felt, in her integrity, that she could not offer her words without first protesting the fact that Katherine had not been appointed to the position in theology. In the opening pages of her address, Ann Louise annotated the history of Katherine's engagement with Trinity over the previous nine years and the failure and injustice of the university to appoint her. Two weeks later, Katherine received a letter signed by all of the students in the M Phil programme at the centre, expressing their regret at her withdrawal. To Katherine's horror, however, they attached the copy of a letter they had sent to all the members of the Women's Studies faculty. In it, the students objected to the manner in which the centre informed them about Katherine's withdrawal – a short announcement sandwiched in between two others, without any additional information. 'We were offered no explanation for Katherine's exit and no opportunity to ask any questions about it' they stated. 'And then we hear later about the full circumstances at the opening of an art exhibition. We would like to make it clear that Katherine Zappone's course, "Feminism, Ethics and Spirituality" was one which attracted many of us to the Women's Studies programme. Her absence is a source of considerable regret to us.'

It was a terrible time for Katherine. She felt so humiliated that it took her almost two years to walk down Grafton Street again without fearing that former students would see her. Katherine was a public figure and had met thousands of people in her lecturing travels throughout the country – at her last public lecture in Trinity's largest theatre there were people sitting in the aisles because all the seats had been taken, and the organisers were concerned about a potential fire hazard that the over-fill might cause. Though her students had loved and supported her, Katherine felt a deep sense of shame which engulfed her and shut off any desire to meet them again.

It was not the first nor the last time that our love for each other would sustain us through the dark times. With Ann Louise's support, Katherine decided to enter an MBA (Master's in Business Administration) programme in UCD. As there was little opportunity for any other full-time post in theology coming up for some time (and other theology departments throughout the country were controlled by the Church), Katherine felt that it was critical to re-train. She had a natural instinct for business – her father was a great influence on her in this regard – and she believed that she could learn many new things that might support our work in the Tallaght communities. Ann Louise left the words of Adrienne Rich for her, as Katherine set off for the first day of classes:

> When you have buried us   told your story
> ours does not end   we stream
> into the unfinished   the unbegun
> the possible

9

1992—1996

THE RISING TIDE?

The Michael Smurfit School of Business, located on a twenty-acre campus in the village of Blackrock, County Dublin, manifests the origins and potency of Ireland's Tiger economy. UCD had purchased the land and buildings in 1991 to house its graduate school of business. Following an acrimonious debate in the Dáil in 1988, the Irish Cabinet made a profoundly questionable decision to close the doors of Carysfort, the College of Education that had operated from this site since 1877. Carysfort, a recognised college of the NUI and run by the Sisters of Mercy, trained up to three hundred Irish primary-school teachers per year. Cutting off investment in this form of education, just as the Irish economy started to take off, lacked vision and common sense. Economic growth leads to changes in demographics, and today Ireland is still trying to play 'catch-up' to ensure that there are enough qualified primary teachers for the enormous increase in population. When Katherine arrived in Carysfort back in 1992, the red-brick administration building was being transformed into a state-of-the-art, technologically smart, oak-panelled and granite-walled ambience, modelling itself on the Ivy League American business schools. Ireland's average GDP growth rate was preparing to double itself for the entire following decade.

Katherine enrolled in the 'part-time' MBA programme so that she could dedicate some of her time to enterprise development at The

Shanty project. This meant that she was in classes every afternoon from 4.00pm until 9.30pm. She carried a load of seven courses for each of two terms, ranging from organisational psychology and information technology (being somewhat familiar with these) to marketing, micro-economics, accounting, business strategy and international finance (having never studied these before). The year held terrible grief, with the loss of the job in Trinity. Every day as she drove the Dublin mountain backroads from The Shanty to the Blackrock campus, tears streamed down her face. The journey took about forty-five minutes; by the time she arrived she still had to struggle to gather herself for another evening of study. She also suffered hearing loss, which compounded the effort to learn new things. She discovered, though, that by taking copious notes she could force her brain to sustain its attention even as it worked doubly hard to translate the sounds to words through hearing aids. Ann Louise recalls Katherine coming home on 16 October exhausted and depleted. She'd had enough; she felt out of her depth in this foreign world and didn't want to go on. Ann Louise listened and held her gently, stating not only should she continue but she'd get first place in the end. (This prophecy proved to be true.) Over the course of the next number of months, Katherine gradually became enthralled with this new world, and the lads – her fellow students (twenty-three men and two women!) – were wonderful comrades as they worked together through lectures, essays, case studies and exams. They were all going somewhere: an MBA meant promotion, a higher salary or a better job.

Entrepreneurs in West Tallaght did not have such a smooth path. As the Irish tide began to rise, people living in peripheral housing estates met one barrier after another when they tried to access government-sponsored training programmes or grants. Newly developed socio-economic policies and programmes, funded largely by European Union structural funds, often lacked efficiency and heart. For her MBA thesis, Katherine interviewed a number of fledgling local entrepreneurs in West Tallaght. Their stories shocked her. Terry McManus's experience typifies what many of them went through. Terry left school at sixteen years of age; there was no career guidance at his school, and he was not encouraged to do the Leaving Certificate. He was apprenticed as a painter/decorator, went out on his own with another painter, and they spent five years making a little less than £2 an hour. They decided it wasn't worth it, closed up shop, and Terry spent the next two years unsuccessfully looking for work. Eventually he was approached by members of a local enterprise centre to see if he was interested in setting up his own business. Terry said, 'I decided I had nothing to lose so I'd give it a try.'

For the next four years he went back and forth between FÁS, the enterprise centre and the local bank trying to get started in business. The centre sent him to FÁS with a business idea for 'reusable appliances', an idea that had worked in Denmark. Terry managed to get a £5,000 enterprise development grant from FÁS and also requested training for himself and others interested in the business. Several months passed before anything was set up. Eventually they received training, and FÁS suggested that two of them go to Denmark to 'see how it was done.' Then FÁS gave them a business consultant to work with, who insisted that they needed a business plan for their idea. With the finished plan, the consultant presented them with a bill for £1,000. They were also asked to pay £2,000 for the trip to Denmark. The rest of the money was spent on equipment and payment to FÁS for their training. The £5,000 grant money was gone, and they hadn't yet set up in business! When they finally did, the venture lasted less than a year. That was the last time Terry looked for state support. Today he is successfully self-employed – and studying for qualifications as a psychotherapist through our organisation.

Terry's motivation, resilience and perseverance impressed Katherine. Many other men and women demonstrated a similar desire to 'get ahead', for themselves, their families and their communities. Not unlike Katherine's fellow students in UCD, they were willing to take risks, to study and to hope for a better future. How could their entrepreneurial spirit be harnessed, though, in a way that could bring about the future they desired? Katherine thought: Ask them. Respect their views. Work with them to access tailored supports, ensure that financial investment is sufficient. Believe in their intellectual and leadership abilities. Link training and enterprise/job opportunities. Work with them to change government policies and programmes to incorporate *their views, their perspectives*. She and Ann Louise believed that the Shanty education ethos held the potential to fashion a new focus on enterprise and job creation. Others believed that too.

It had become clear to all of us that education must be coupled with enterprise if the cycle of poverty is to be broken. We established the Shanty Enterprise Committee and were fortunate enough to have Jean Byrne, a successful small-business owner and marketing expert, to chair it. She and her colleague Brenda Quinn spent several months researching enterprise supports in Tallaght while members of the Shanty management committee asked course participants about their employment interests. With great expectations, women from different social backgrounds worked together once again to explore innovative possibilities. Within six months we developed a tourist-targeted plan for five small businesses, to be located together along the main motorway from Tallaght to Blessington. There were to be tea rooms, a retail shop for wholefood baked goods, a food-production enterprise, a garden centre, a golf driving range and a specialised, high-quality craft-production unit. We used every business and political contact we had and went to great efforts to source state support but with no success. Undaunted, Jean initiated conversations with Get Tallaght Working (a co-operative voluntarily established to develop enterprise for Tallaght) and the Tallaght NOW offices (an EU-sponsored programme to promote women's enterprise through training and start-up grants). Get Tallaght Working indicated that they had space available in the Tallaght Enterprise Centre for a kitchen and restaurant. For the next four months we pulled together a team of food/restaurant consultants, contracted a marketing feasibility study and got informal agreement from NOW to provide training monies. Just as we were ready to finalise the lease agreement with Get Tallaght Working, it transpired that the IDA (Industrial Development Authority, the state agency that owned the enterprise centre) did not have planning permission for retail outlets at the centre! The venture died then and there. Lack of communication and inefficiencies between agencies blocked our path and wasted our time.

But, as many an entrepreneur knows, success is not a straightforward road. We regrouped to begin again. This time we looked to our own. On weekends, Mary O'Rourke's Glenasmole studio was still bursting at the seams with women who wanted to learn the ancient crafts of spinning, dyeing and felting. In an earlier chapter, we described Ann Louise's love of being with women as they came alive after a hard week of rearing children on social welfare by following Mary's example of spinning at a wheel or colouring the wool with natural dyes. Together they created beauty. Everyone was energised at the end of the day. Why not transform the spinning workshops into a business venture?

We invited Mary to join the enterprise committee along with Aideen Loftus, whom we had hired to work as an administrator to the growing project. Jean had several business contacts in the crafts world, and Mary was well known as a textile artist through her work within the Crafts Council of Ireland. Margaret Murray, a member of the Shanty management team, spun fleece to wool like no other, and we asked her to become part of the team too. Learning the best-kept business secrets at the Smurfit School, Katherine came to meetings with theory ready to be applied! Dara Hogan, Ann Louise's cousin by law, also joined the team and brought with him significant wisdom through his management and accountancy experience. Our enthusiasm could not be beaten, and we set off with different tasks: designing hand-felted products, test-marketing them, researching grant possibilities, developing a training programme, putting together a business plan and remaking an artist's studio into a handcraft production plant.

There was one big snag, however. While the women desperately wanted jobs, and a better life for themselves and their children, fear of losing their social-welfare benefits proved too great a risk. They had every reason to be afraid. The rules were convoluted, appeared to be different for everyone, and if anyone asked for clarification they felt that the social-welfare officer might try to take something away from them. This had happened to some of their friends. The biggest terror for everybody in this environment was the fear of 'losing their book' – the cheque-like book they would take to the post office each week to be cashed into welfare benefits. We asked Deirdre Tinney, a friend of Jean's, to help us. We decided to hire someone to do research on entitlements and cut-off points so that the women's positions would not be jeopardised. What we found was that the 'lone parents' of the group could earn up to £6 per week per child without having their social welfare benefits reduced. Lily Ward, a lone parent with one child, received £79 in social-welfare payments per week, and out of that she had to pay her rent, electricity, food and any other bills that might come up. If she earned more than £6 per week, she'd lose some of the £79 unless she could prove that she paid someone for childcare, and then that expense could be claimed back. Or, if the wife of a long-term unemployed man earned over £60 per week, his social-welfare benefits would be cut almost in half! And what man would wish to suffer such indignity? Marie's husband would lose £55 per week if she were to earn £61 per week. Such were the disincentives, especially for women, to take up employment. As some of the women used to say: 'It would do your head in! You take one step forward, they bring you one step back.'

We believed, then and now, in the power of imaging the positive and in the potency of solidarity across classes. In spite of the Irish State's disincentives, Margaret and Katherine together persuaded a group of twelve women to begin a training programme in making hand-felted products in autumn 1993. Women came three mornings a week to Mary's studio to card, felt, machine and finish the products Mary had designed. There were 'Molly dolls', 'Jacob slippers', tweed patchwork caps and vests, wall hangings – we tried and tested lots of ideas. The enterprise was christened Weaving Dreams by Jean, Mary and Aideen, and these women worked tirelessly to get our products on display in the

Showcase crafts trade fair at the Royal Dublin Society (RDS), held every January for buyers who come from all over the world to place orders for the tourist season. Margaret, Katherine, Lily and Mary took turns minding the Weaving Dreams stand. The sales exceeded our expectations – and the business was born!

When the orders started to come in, the women agreed to be 'hired'. Lily went to the Office of Social Welfare and filled out the forms to determine if she'd lose out in any way if she earned £3.25 per hour. They told her to get a letter from her neighbour to prove that her son was being minded, and in that way she could keep her 'book' – but, then she was told that she had to pay tax on the combination of her salary and social-welfare benefits! In spite of this, she took a leap of faith and accepted the job. Why did Lily do it? 'I wanted to get back my independence and self-esteem. I took the long-term view that by all of us taking a job – even for very little extra money – we could eventually get the business off the ground. I was determined to fight the obstacles they put in our way; you just put your head down and overcome them.'

Another single parent with four children felt the same way. She wanted to be free; she hated going to social welfare during crisis times: 'It was degrading to sit there and wait for your name to be called and to discuss your business at a window where others in the room could overhear what was going on.' She didn't go to social welfare after she was hired, though. She was just too afraid, and, with four children, she didn't want to take the chance. We were not aware of this at the time, but we learned later that, after two years' working, she was found out and ordered to pay back the tax for those two years.

The women coped with these day-to-day realities, building a community of trust between themselves and with us, weaving dreams to build a business that traded successfully on the domestic and international markets. Over the course of the next six years, the community enterprise employed two full-time and eight part-time people. When we travelled around the country, we'd often stop at a craft shop and see a Molly doll or a Jacob slipper. The business won a number of awards from FÁS and the Irish Heritage Council; our wall hangings adorn Office of Public Works' buildings and the Xilinx Corporate headquarters in Citywest near Tallaght. Lily Ward, on being promoted to Assistant Manager, gave back her 'book' to the Government. The other woman, after four years of carding and sewing, bought her council house. Their stories, their determination enabled us to 'keep on keeping on'.

*   *   *

Whenever a great artist and a great theme unite, one usually encounters a fine piece of art. Reading Aleksandr Solzhenitsyn's novel *Cancer Ward* as an undergraduate, Ann Louise recalls being riveted by both the quality of the writing and the topic addressed. Learning that Solzhenitsyn himself had a tumour removed unsuccessfully in 1954 and endured debilitating cancer until he was cured some years later, was hardly surprising – how else could he describe with the insight reserved to insider experience the graphic detail of this illness? Although frightening, the topic of cancer in one's early twenties remained in the realm of academic discussion. Ann Louise knew no one then who had suffered with this illness.

This was to change, change utterly. Her departure from religious life in the early seventies coincided with the revelation that her father had been diagnosed with cancer of the oesophagus. The following two years unveiled, in chilling detail, a personal cancer journey. Ann Louise used to brace herself each time as she entered the cancer ward in Mercer's Hospital, where the veneer of normality, the attempts at light-hearted conversation, couldn't dispel the gloom, the depression that hung in the air, anticipating death. After two years, when the illness had depleted everything but his consistent graciousness, Arthur died as he had lived, with calmness and courage. If such matters can be graded, Ann Louise's mother Imelda's diagnosis with pancreatic cancer a few years later was even more traumatic. She entered the cancer ward of St Vincent's Hospital via the emergency room, in agonising pain and, after a brief series of tests, her specialist told her she had a very short time to live. Upon hearing this news, she asked that the curtains around her bed be drawn and that she be left alone. A day later, she pulled back the curtains and, although still in excruciating pain, stated simply that she had had a wonderful life and accepted whatever was to come. She resumed an attentive and caring interest in the lives of the other women in the ward. They all wept when she died, with dignity, within a matter of weeks. Most young people expect that they will have their parents for many years, and to have neither who made it through their sixties left its scars, not least psychically.

With this background, Ann Louise greeted with angst the discovery of a small breast lump in 1992. Over the following two years, two doctors, two specialists and two mammograms all concluded that this was nothing to worry about. Eventually, a deep intuition signalled that all was not well, so our new female GP, Moira Slevin, sent Ann Louise to a further specialist. While saying that he really didn't think this was anything to worry about, he agreed that for Ann Louise's peace of mind he would biopsy the lump. As she waited that day for the initial procedure, she was reading a new book of poems by Eavan Boland. Suddenly she turned the page and read a bleak poem titled 'Mastectomy' – and a sense of foreboding filled the cubicle.

Although all the other patients in the day ward were released by lunchtime, Ann Louise was asked to wait back as the specialist needed to speak to her. By late afternoon he still hadn't turned up, and so, finally, she was discharged. Katherine arrived, all smiles, full of energy, carrying a bunch of gerbera ... but quickly read the atmosphere, and we both left anticipating the worst.

We were hardly home when the phone rang. It was the specialist apologising and telling us that, contrary to his anticipation, Ann Louise was right: this was a cancerous tumour and had been sent for analysis. Furthermore, they needed to do a lumpectomy to remove the surrounding tissue within the week. We just held each other, wept and absorbed this life-changing news. After a while, Ann Louise went to put the hens away and just walk quietly in the paddock. It was a beautiful June evening. Suddenly, there was movement in the long grass, and there was Whitie, our missing hen, gone for a number of weeks and presumed eaten by a fox. She was attending to eight chicks in her open-air nest. Surprised by joy at this apparition of new life within minutes of hearing such shattering news, Ann Louise's energy changed, and she experienced a glimpse of hope – surely this was a positive omen? The words of the mystic Julian of Norwich filtered through the shadows in her mind: 'All will be well, and all manner of things will be well.'

That evening, Ann Louise's sister June and a number of close friends arrived. Among them were Kay Conroy and Mary Paula Walsh, who in 1986 had founded Turning Point, an organisation that offered every support to those who faced serious illness, especially cancer. We had both participated in the beginnings of this organisation and had been part of the first strategic planning group – indeed, we continue to be patrons. Little did we know that we would personally become the beneficiaries of their wonderful expertise, generosity and care. Both Kay and Mary Paula have medical training and vast knowledge and experience, so the evening was spent planning Ann Louise's path to full recovery. Sitting on the couch that evening was a strange experience, being present to the extraordinary outpouring of unconditional love and solidarity, but also in some strange way being absent and removed. Serious illness makes you both the subject and object of your own existence. We were both acutely aware that the elemental moments of life are in essence lived alone – birth, death and the moments in between when life is interrupted with existential happenings that bring us back to the core of who we are and call us to decisions as to how we will go forward. In that sense, one walks the path of illness on one's own, feeling an outsider, a recipient and observer of people's goodness, all the while, in Ann Louise's case, dealing with memories and images of what a cancer journey can mean. As people chatted, our eyes met across the room, and we held a gaze of love, terror and searing pain.

The conclusion of the evening's discussion was that Ann Louise should get a second opinion, and Kay knew a breast-cancer specialist in Harley Street, London. So, with her usual élan and unstinting generosity, she arranged everything and allowed us to pay for nothing as the four of us set off for the consultation. This visit was calming, as the eminent professor stressed that there was no need for a 'fire-brigade response' to this news. In other words, there was time to think, to make one's decisions carefully. He also stressed that while people speak of cancer using a singular noun, there are many kinds of cancers, and that people with a similar disease and treatment have very different responses. This obvious information was strangely consoling. His only advice was that Ann Louise should have a bone scan to assess if the cancer had spread. On returning to Dublin, this suggestion was shared with the Irish consultant. He became instantly defensive at the news that Ann Louise had sought a second opinion and asked her to leave as she obviously didn't trust his expertise. Startled by his reaction, Ann Louise reminded him that this was *her* body, she was the one with cancer, and that she hoped that if he ever got the disease he would follow a similar course of action. Not used to such forthrightness, he paused, reassessed the situation and rallied. Following that moment of tension, her relationship with him was one of healthy respect for each other's opinion. The return to our GP, Dr Móira Slevin, was an utterly different experience. She held Ann Louise and empathised, expressing her deep regret that she had cancer and offering every support for the road ahead.

Entering the cancer ward of the Adelaide Hospital required a steely determination that hope, not fear, would reign. Katherine's unbounded love embraced each different moment of this terrifying experience. As in Solzhenitsyn's description, the ward contained every type of personality. The day after surgery, the old women lying limply in the corner bed offered her first gem of wisdom: 'Listen, love, take it slowly; you can't rush the river.' The young woman opposite, dying of lung cancer, saved her breath for the visits of her twelve-year-old daughter each evening, when she would instruct her on how to run the household after she was gone; one evening, the instruction was on buying firm vegetables and the need always to feel the fruit before purchase. These exchanges were so poignant they were almost unbearable.

Once the trauma of surgery was over and Ann Louise returned with her beloved Katherine to our Shanty, spirits lifted, and, although we had to endure a waiting game for the final results of the nature of the tumour and the degree of the cancer, our shared sense was that the worst was over and the healing journey had begun. We started to dream again. Anything we discerned together that could contribute to healing we undertook with a rigour and discipline that many might find daunting. Katherine got the recipe book from the Bristol Cancer Centre, a centre founded in 1980 by Penny Brohn and Pat Pilkington to offer 'a unique combination of physical, emotional and spiritual supports using complementary therapies and self-help techniques'. The diet was strictly vegetarian, which proved no difficulty as Ann Louise was already a committed vegetarian, and Katherine's rendition of each recipe was simply delicious. Dry white wine was permitted, which was a relief as wine-tasting and wine-drinking is one of our hobbies!

The results arrived, indicating that this was a tiny tumour at the earliest stage. This news added impetus and optimism to our efforts. Waiting to begin radiotherapy in St Luke's Hospital provided an opportunity for Ann Louise to read and understand as much as possible about breast cancer and all recommended therapies. The literature at the time indicated that a broad palate of factors influence healing: our beliefs, attitudes, thoughts influence our health. This was not new information – Plato held that to treat the body of a person while failing to treat the mind was foolish. However, the advances in scientific research could now *prove* the power and influence of the mind and emotions for the cure of cancer. Put otherwise: love heals.

Armed with a list of questions for the first meeting with the oncologist/radiologist in St Luke's, Ann Louise was greeted with a benignly patronising attitude. Querying the advisability of taking the drug Tamoxifen, as then recommended, he answered, 'Put it this way, if my wife got cancer, I'd have it on her breakfast tray every morning.' This was hardly the rational argument that she required. On the return visit the following week, to be marked up prior to beginning radiotherapy, the said specialist arrived surrounded by a bevy of white coats, young trainee doctors. They all peered as Ann Louise was being painted with a dye that would indicate the areas that the rays should target. She popped the question to the specialist: 'What do you think of the developing theory of psychoneuroimmunology?' Stunned silence. Eventually, he broke the silence with a confession, 'Truthfully, I know nothing about it, but let's ask the young people here.' The response was further silence, and as they all shuffled on to the next patient, some noted this strange question on their pads.

It was clear by now that broader, more holistic understandings of illness and healing hadn't impacted on the world of conventional medicine, so we were on our own to design a programme that would enable the positive outcome we imaged. The five weeks of daily radiotherapy were eased by the wonderful kindness of Ann Louise's cousin, Mary Hogan, a radiologist in St Luke's. The night before the first session she came to our home and described the whole process so there would be no surprises, and she also assured us that she would have one of her colleagues look out for Ann Louise during every visit; this happened and was such a gift. Also, a rota of family and friends was formed so that Ann Louise would never go alone for treatment. Always believing in the power of the imagination, Ann Louise spent the minutes under the machine each day imaging golden rays entering her body, killing unhealthy cells and revitalising the healthy variety. Also, since childhood she has always had a deep connection to her 'guardian angel', a devotion she inherited from her mother, who, when she would kiss her goodnight as a child, would remind her to pray to her angel. While understandings of this presence have changed and altered, there remains a sense of metaphysical connection – and for Ann Louise to sense presence rather than absence as one lay under this mammoth apparatus eased the terror.

The work of healing required easing the fear of inherited cancer and its possible outcomes. So, moving through deep-seated resistances, Ann Louise decided that if she could find a psychotherapist who would appreciate and match her intellectual development, and have an openness to the spiritual dimension of life, she would go into therapy. Her search led to Dr Ruth Doherty, a surgeon who had left medical practice to train as a psychotherapist and who was also a practising Buddhist. For the following two years, these bi-weekly sessions proved wonderfully reassuring. Ann Louise was open to learning from Ruth the techniques of mindfulness, quiet awareness and simple meditation practices that taught the wisdom of concentrating on the now.

The narrative of any healing journey is not prescriptive – if it were, one could end up blaming the victim for failing to heal themselves. Rather, illness is part of the mystery of life, and the restoration of health is a gift beyond compare and outside our control. Furthermore, Ann Louise had the privilege of availing of every healing resource she read about, going to the much-respected acupuncturist Patricia McNally, and learning and practising Tai Chi and autogenics, buying and consuming Chinese herbs and every recommended vitamin, all the while aware that money enhances the chances of survival from illness. Some years later, she watched, appalled, a woman in Jobstown wait for months to have a breast lump biopsied – and die soon after of breast cancer.

Above all, being enveloped by love helps to heal. A love relationship means that both partners live through the journey of illness, albeit in different ways. Katherine recalls vividly her fear at hearing the initial news and yet needing to shield Ann Louise by keeping her own terror at bay. Ann Louise had so often been the positive one, especially through Katherine's post-Trinity despair. Now it was time for Katherine to dive deep into her soul that at its essence held the joy of being caressed by Ann Louise and to surface with the power of peaceful, positive presence.

There were many times during that year when Katherine would need to transmute feelings of growing apprehension to sanguine expectation. She recalls the loneliness of the hospital waiting room where she sat during the hours of surgery and, when finally permitted, dashing up the stairs, not knowing what to expect. As she approached the bed and saw Ann Louise hooked up to an IV machine, asleep but in recovery, she felt the surge and fullness of years of faithful love; a sense of calm and strength descended as she waited for those green eyes to open. Some of the toughest times were experienced in St Luke's. As Ann Louise walked through the huge steel doors of the treatment room, Katherine sat outside watching the red light come on, signalling the blast Ann Louise was receiving, and feeling vicariously the impact of this invasion.

To accompany Ann Louise through this first year of healing, Katherine decided to take a year out of the MBA programme. Together we chose to make this a very special time. Katherine committed herself to looking after all domestic matters, including cooking (not her natural domain!). Ann Louise designed and had built a Finnish log cabin, with a wood-burning stove, located in the paddock, to ensure a restful environment at a certain distance for the ever-growing activity of the project in The Muse behind our home. She also sought and received six months' sick leave from work. The year before, she had stepped back from holding the Chair of the department, becoming a lecturer again, as the five-year period of her agreed term was now complete. She was aware that integral to her healing journey was the letting go of those years of unbearable work stress. She needed distance to discern a way forward.

At the end of this first year of healing, to celebrate Ann Louise's July birthday, Katherine held a surprise birthday party in the home of our dear friends Mary Paula and Kay. She had prepared a birthday ritual and invited all friends present to participate in a meditation called 'Three Jewels of Wisdom', which she adapted from Diane Mariechild's work. Some of the men present had never done anything like this before, but for Ann Louise they all entered the moment as best they could. It's a meditation that calls on each person to discover three gems of wisdom in their own souls: a yellow topaz symbolising right action, a ruby for compassion and a diamond for clarity of mind. The meditation concludes:

See ourselves within a circle of light. Our thoughts are seeds of action. Our words become reality. Speak of peace and love. Free from illusion, realise that our thoughts create. Free from illusion, let us not hesitate. Turn the anger into love. Transform the doubt into wisdom.

Let us live in peace.

From *Crystal Visions*

Ann Louise's birthday present from Katherine was a gold ring with the three jewels; we called it her 'healing ring'. It was to remind her that she was embraced by love as she used her own powers to imagine full health. She still wears it today.

Katherine resumed her MBA study in autumn 1994, pleased – even happy – to be back. She belonged to a new group of students, her former class having completed their degree the previous summer. This turned out to be a high-powered, yet gratifying year, thanks especially to her study group: Conleth O'Reilly, Gerard Moore and Brendan Healy. What she didn't know in finance or marketing, they did; what they didn't know in political economy or organisational psychology, she did. Following the Harvard-type groupwork model of business study, they spent endless hours together writing up collective assignments and case studies. These men were mighty; she learned so much from them. They approached – and crossed – the finish line together, and this time she decided to attend graduation, held in the grand O'Reilly Hall on the Belfield campus of University College Dublin. Her father's pride in her achievement considerably influenced this decision, and both her father and mother took the long journey from Seattle to Dublin to be there. There were now two MBAs in the family!

Katherine's mother – with an Irish-born grandmother – had something else to celebrate too. Katherine's application for Irish citizenship had finally been approved by the Minister for Justice, Nora Owens, and her mother stood proudly by her side as Katherine solemnly declared her fidelity to the Irish nation and her loyalty to the State in a courtroom of the Irish Four Courts. They held a great party after the court ceremony, taking over the Westbury Hotel's lobby for music and drinks,

Katherine having sent an invitation to family and friends that quoted a famous line from Mary Robinson's inaugural presidential speech: 'I am of Ireland, come dance with me!'

We celebrated until early morning, filled with massive relief as well as joy. We had lived with enormous insecurity since Katherine left Trinity because she did not have permission to stay in Ireland indefinitely. She was terrified that if she travelled out of the country the authorities might not let her back in. We faced the genuine possibility of being separated, not being able to live together for the rest of our lives. No words can be found to describe the fear and anger we felt.

Of course, had we been a married couple, acquiring citizenship would have been a matter of simply filling in a few forms. Katherine's route was filled with uncertainty and a deep sense of powerlessness. After sending her application for citizenship into the Department of Justice, a letter came back by return post, the gist of which was, 'Don't call us, we'll call you.' Twelve long months passed before she heard another word. Then a phone call came from the Department to say that they had arranged for her to be interviewed by a garda sergeant in the Harcourt Street Aliens' Office on the following Sunday morning. We were thrilled to hear something, yet exceptionally nervous about the interview. What would they ask? Why Sunday? She put on her best professional outfit, grabbed a Shanty newsletter – the front page of which had a photograph of President Robinson attending the Shanty fifth anniversary – and set off for the meeting. One of her primary thoughts that morning was: what if I were black? Or poor? I wouldn't have a chance. As it turned out, the interview went very well, and our hopes soared. Again, however, another twelve long months passed without a word. There was nothing we could do; the process was designed to keep the power on the side of the State. Then one day Katherine answered the telephone to hear: 'The Minister is preparing to approve your application,' and the letter came through, almost three years after posting the application. And we are the lucky ones. As we write this, we think of our friend Eoin Collins (Director of Policy Change for GLEN, the Irish Gay and Lesbian Equality Network) whose partner, Josep, does not have permission to reside with him in Ireland. They, like many other lesbian and gay couples, experience deep discrimination on a day-to-day basis, hoping that some day prejudice will be swept away and the law changed. We hope so too. This is one of the many reasons why we have put ourselves and our most intimate, private affairs into the public domain.

At the same time as Katherine resumed her MBA studies, Ann Louise returned to teaching in St Pat's, resolute in her determination to create a stress-free work environment. However, despite the application of every technique in the book and a faithful daily meditation practice in her log cabin before leaving home, it became clear that the only way forward was to try to move from the Department of Religious Studies. She could switch to the Department of Education, she thought. Holding an interdisciplinary doctorate in education and religious studies, she hoped that the move could be facilitated easily. She requested a meeting with the then President of the College, Fr Clyne, and respectfully requested that he consider this proposal. Due for a sabbatical, she applied and was granted the first six months of 1996, so she and Katherine decided to return to Boston. Wellspring House Inc. was to celebrate its tenth anniversary and had grown exponentially in the interval since we first worked there as volunteers in the early 1980s. By sheer coincidence, Nancy Schwoyer and Rosemary Haughton, the directors and our good friends, had received funding to undertake two pieces of work. They had recently built a large adult-education facility and wanted Ann Louise to advise on programme development and to work with the initial set of adult students from the local community in Gloucester. They had also been grant-aided to undertake a piece of participatory action research (PAR) in the local community to inform their work into the future. Aware of Katherine's recent training in her MBA, they invited her to lead that research project.

We arrived in Boston and settled into our delightful home in Rockport. How wonderful to return to this quaint little town on the

Above: Katherine at three years of age.

Right: Ann Louise, ready for school, aged four.

Below: Katherine playing at Mass at the Church of the Holy Spirit, Seattle University.

Above: Ann Louise as Sr Imelda, with a class of pupils in Loreto Abbey, Rathfarnham.

Below: On the porch of our first home together, in Gloucester, Massachusetts, 1982.

Above: Ann Louise enjoying time with theologian Mary Daly at Easter Point beach, north of Boston.

Right: Katherine with Rosemary Haughton and Nancy Schwoyer at one of our favourite restaurants, Tom O'Shea's in Essex, Massachusetts.

Below: Ann Louise, Revd. Flora Keshgegian and Katherine after our life-partnership ceremony in Rockport, Massachusetts, 16 October 1982.

Above: The Shanty, built in 1889, with our beloved dog Julian of Norwich (called after the mystic) in front.

Right: Ann Louise bringing back the Better Ireland Award from the AIB to the Community Centre in Jobstown.

Below: Katherine accepting the AIB Better Ireland Award for The Shanty Educational Project, 1992, from Peter Sutherland and Taoiseach Albert Reynolds at the AIB Bank Centre.

Above: Bob and Kathie, Katherine's parents, and Ann Louise celebrate with Katherine on the steps of the Four Courts after she received Irish citizenship in 1995.

Below: The opening of The Muse, a new community education centre six feet from our back door!

Top: American Ambassador Jean Kennedy-Smith at the tenth-anniversary celebration of The Shanty Educational Project in the garden of The Shanty.

Above: Taoiseach Bertie Ahern and Tánaiste Mary Harney celebrate with us at the opening of An Cosán 1999.

Left: An Cosán – a centre of Learning, Leadership and Enterprise in Jobstown, Tallaght West, Dublin 24.

Above: Our wedding day, 13 September 2003, with Canadian marriage commissioner Ann Moore.

Below left: Katherine signing the legal civil marriage register.

Below right: Cutting the cake at a family gathering the next day.

Left: The Midsummer Ball –
Labour LGTB fund-raiser for
our case.

Below: Going to the High Court to
receive the judgement on our case,
15 December 2006.

North Shore. The next morning we drew back the curtains to a winter wonderland. While we were sleeping, New England had soundlessly experienced one of the heaviest snowfalls in history. The snow had already covered the front door and spread a blanket above any distinguishing landmark. There was nothing for it but snuggle up for this opening week and enjoy our confinement to the full!

Once work began, the parallels between the lives of women living on welfare in the state of Massachusetts and the challenges encountered by the women in West Tallaght were all too evident. While there was a vast age range in the initial class, all the women here had also left formal education early; but they shared a common thirst for learning and took up this new opportunity with enthusiasm and commitment. We met each day for four hours, and, despite the challenges of childcare for some and ill health for others, attendance was excellent. While ill, Ann Louise had prepared a new course in Women's Studies, and she proposed that these ideas might form a backdrop to our classes. Despite the radical feminist content, there was no resistance, and we had wonderful debates. A number of the women started to dream about continuing with their education and getting a new life for themselves and their children, when suddenly all that hope turned to despair. Overnight, President Bill Clinton passed a draconian measure called 'Welfare to Work' which meant that contributions to those living on welfare would be stopped after eighteen months and they had to get a job. These measures were non-negotiable, and the anxiety among these women was palpable. The distance between federal policy-makers and the lived experience of women in poverty means that those in power seldom touch, feel or see the impact of their decisions. This is perhaps why Mahatma Gandhi exhorted that before we ever make an important decision we should pause and allow an image of a person living in poverty fill our senses – then and only then should we discern a way forward.

In directing the research project for the Wellspring community, Katherine knew that its success depended on including the perspectives of as many people as possible, especially those women who faced the recent harsh changes in US welfare policy. These were tough times for others, too. Gloucester town, where Wellspring was located, was a fishing village which faced soaring unemployment rates because of changes in international fishing policies. Forty residents worked with Katherine, learning the skills of action research to examine the problems they faced and to imagine a set of actions that could support the sustainability of their region. Families on limited income, business people, fisher-people, ecologists and educators worked tirelessly together to come up with a set of actions to present to the townspeople of Gloucester. The report they produced, 'We Love This Place', kick-started a process of community action that continues today. We learned, once again, that by building relationships of trust and care with people from diverse backgrounds, the energy to shift social and economic trends can be sustained. It demonstrated that the work we were doing in Tallaght was part of a global movement within civil society that enabled ordinary people to participate directly in shaping the future of their communities.

This blissful sabbatical was periodically and ruefully interrupted by letters and calls from St Pat's, narrating the latest set of obstacles blocking any suggested move between departments. Eventually, the college President told Ann Louise that he would put it to a vote of the education department to see if the staff wanted Ann Louise to transfer into their department or not, and we'd await the outcome. In an institution not prone to democratic gestures, this was a highly unusual act and one without precedent.

To conclude the sabbatical, we decided to hire a dormobile and take a five-week trip through the western states of America, starting in Seattle. Katherine's family came out in force to wave us off in this enormous machine. We must have looked terrified as we drove out of the car park – many of them later shared they expected us back by nightfall. Our anxiety wasn't eased when we saw a similar vehicle to our own in an awful crash about ten miles down the motorway. The deposit we had paid was hefty, so it behove us to keep the vehicle intact. After a few hours, we were fine, enjoying the freedom of having our house on our backs for the next five weeks. This turned out to be a holiday of a lifetime and one we have frequently recommended to our friends. We visited ten states and stayed in four different national parks. People sometimes collapse their image of the United States to cities such as New York or San Francisco. But experiencing the wild, vast expanses of prairie and desert allows an appreciation of a continent that includes extraordinary diversity and breathtaking beauty. That first glimpse, for example, of the Grand Canyon leaves a memory that can never be erased. The excitement of walking down the switch-back path to the blue-green Colorado river that snakes its way through the glen below, could only be matched by flying through the valley the following day in a light aircraft. The latter took a bit of persuasion, as Katherine wasn't too keen – but Ann Louise adores flying and had taken flying lessons for a number of years, and so managed to persuade Katherine of the safety of this undertaking!

The only cloud that hung over these idyllic weeks was the stress of not knowing whether Ann Louise would have a job in September. High in the Rockies in mid-August she found a phone booth symbolically located beside a rubbish dump. After many unsuccessful attempts, she finally got the President on the phone. At that very moment, a huge lorry arrived and proceeded to tip mountains of waste into the bins at her side. Through the din she heard the President pronounce the word, 'No.' No, the majority in the department didn't want her to transfer, and no, there wouldn't be a job for her in September.

10

RETURNING TO IRELAND (AGAIN)

Coming through a life-threatening illness offers a searing clarity about the essentials in life. The buoyant, carefree, 'I can cope with anything' attitude is altered permanently. There is no longer time to put up with intolerable situations and no longer the luxury of living within a stress-reactive cycle at work. While Ann Louise could have returned to her position at St Pat's within the Department of Religious Studies, for her this was no longer a viable option. The difficulties, conflicts and strains of working within that department were no longer tenable. Aware that her request to move departments was unusual, but given the backdrop to the situation, she hoped that in time a creative solution could have been found, even within the constraints of the university structure. With the growing numbers of students coming into the college which would require a corresponding growth of staff in the Education Department, she trusted that a flexible resolution could be sourced. She had also pointed out that resolving this matter in this way would cause the least hurt to all parties involved, something she desperately wanted. She recalled Emily Dickinson's beautiful lines:

'Hope' is the thing with feathers–
That perches in the soul–

However, and unfortunately, any creative resolution was resisted, so negotiations were at an impasse. Ann Louise asked Mary Redmond, an eminent employment lawyer, to step into the breach. Her empathy, her intellectual clarity and her sense of justice guided the process forward. However, after about three months, she indicated that she had exhausted every avenue and the matter might have to go to the courts. While she was more than willing to take a case, she wanted to be assured that Ann Louise understood the gravity of this next step and the stress that it could incur. Ann Louise gave permission, realising that the matter had to be resolved. Twenty-four hours later, a compromise had been reached, and Ann Louise could make the transfer as requested. The compromise resided in the President's insistence that she would only be appointed to a half-time position. This, of course, led to loss of earning and for the next two years contributions to her pension were also halved.

As in all difficult periods, new relations are formed. Shortly after acting on Ann Louise's behalf, Mary Redmond decided to establish a new national organisation for the community and voluntary sector, named The Wheel. Ann Louise was asked to form part of the initial steering group and to become one of the founding directors of the company. And within St Pat's, many colleagues extended a hand of friendship. Throughout the negotiations the Head of Education John Canavan and Joe Dunne, a philosopher in the department, were compassionate, generous with time and practical in the support they offered. Also, Fr Tom Woods, a Vincentian priest and her dear friend and colleague, never faltered in his support and loving concern. It must be said their kindness, each in their very different way, remains an overriding memory of this very difficult period. For the rest, perhaps the virtue of forgetting needs to be applied.

While Ann Louise never spoke to colleagues about the details of the work difficulties she had lived with, as she distains gossip and cliques don't interest her – furthermore, she didn't wish to divide the staff – still she often wonders if she could have done more to neutralise the President's initial resistance to her request. She also questions the non-relational style of leadership that marked the manner in which this matter was decided. It seems to her that effective leadership is governed by a few simple principles, ones which we have tried to live out in our work in Tallaght West. Holding a position of leadership is an opportunity to stand at the helm and offer a vision; it calls for articulate clarity on ethos and values, and, above all, offers opportunity to know, to affirm and to encourage those who work with you. Such an understanding of relational leadership seeks to build a flexible organisation where the focus is on ensuring that people find meaning in their work, and have the opportunity to make their own unique and creative contributions. Shifting departments in a university setting need not be seen as a negative request that could lead to chaos but, rather, could reasonably be understood as an opportunity to contribute to a new, dynamic energy for the benefit of all.

Both of us now shifted our professional energies towards re-engagement with happenings at The Shanty. While Katherine did begin her search for a job, armed with an MBA yet with little business experience, she knew that it would take a lot of time to find what she was looking for. Indeed, part of the difficulty centred on finding something that would utilise her particular skill set. There were days when that was hard to imagine: how does one combine training in theology and education with a qualification in business and find a job in the real world? So here we were, Ann Louise with a half-time position in St Pat's and Katherine looking for a new career – what a pair!

The mood in the country lifted us somewhat, though. We returned to Ireland with the 'Rainbow Coalition' – Fine Gael, Labour and Democratic Left – arching the possibility of combining economic success with genuine social change. The three parties oversaw the first period of unprecedented economic growth, job creation on a massive scale and Ireland's first budget surplus in over twenty-five years. In October 1996, the Taoiseach, John Bruton, invited the widest range of social partners to Dublin Castle – including representatives of the 'community sector' – to participate in discussions on the development of a new national partnership agreement to steer Ireland's development for the following three years. The previous time Katherine had met John he was at Kiltalown House in Jobstown, West Tallaght, with Pat Rabbitte (Labour) and other local politicians, listening to residents describe their desire for community education in order to get back to work. With the presence of Labour and Democratic Left, the politics of the Left, rather than the politics of the pragmatists, appeared to be in the ascendant, so maybe politically led transformation of poverty would become a reality.

Plans for the tenth anniversary of The Shanty Educational Project had already started while we were in Boston when our management team decided to host a community forum in West Tallaght. Katherine joined the team and worked closely with Carmel Habington, now The Shanty administrator, to figure out how such a gathering could genuinely reflect the voices of the people themselves and what they imagined as their future and their children's future, rather than what anyone else imposed upon them. If the political direction of the country really was changing, it was time for 'the people' to speak. We wanted to find a way to engage a wide variety of residents, to tap their imaginations and to envision positively how we could bring about change together. Informed by Katherine's work in Gloucester, Massachusetts, we decided to conduct a type of participatory research as one of the most unique features of the planning process. Katherine and Carmel set up 'house meetings' in the homes of eight residents throughout the four communities served by The Shanty, and at these meetings we invited the people to identify key problems they and their families faced and to analyse the causes and effects of these problems. Most people told us no one had ever asked them these questions before; no one had ever been prepared to listen to their reality. Katherine still remembers Joyce Cahill, one of the resident leaders who opened her home, spending quite some time persuading her neighbours to attend because they didn't really believe people like Katherine wanted to know.

As the planning progressed, it became apparent that another key marker of success would be the extent to which those of us working in the community – as distinct from those living there – cooperated in sponsoring the forum together. What had started as a Shanty event needed to be opened to other voluntary groups, otherwise the competitiveness between organisations could kill its potential. Development work, whether it is at the national or local level, is often filled with competition *between the workers,* the vision for justice and equality diminishes, and the potential for change is lessened as a result. We took up this challenge as best we could in the five months of planning. We had to negotiate the inevitable conflicts that arose between groups, and it was through the practice of working together that we learned how to share the responsibilities as well as the power. The practical experience of sharing a common project taught us how to negotiate in the midst of our different interests and unevenness of resources. We remembered often the old battle cry of 'divide and conquer'. We learned in a new way that paying heed to what divides us is *the* secret ingredient that keeps things the way they are or, in fact, makes them worse.

The day of the forum itself marked a turning point in our work in the community. Parents, young people, children, politicians, community workers and national media were present that day. During the morning, we analysed the problems as a whole community, and in the afternoon we heard about the positive things that were happening, followed by taking part in an exercise of the imagination that Ann Louise facilitated. She asked all of us to imagine what West Tallaght could be like in ten years' time if all our dreams were to come true. She said, 'On a large sheet of paper, draw, write or colour a statement for the year 2007 and make a list of the changes you expect to see by then.' The *Irish Times* editorial the following day covered our event: 'An experiment currently under way in Tallaght West in Dublin deserves attention and support. The idea is to take a vision of the future, created by local people, and to turn that vision into reality in ten years.' That same day, June Kelly, a Jobstown resident, wrote: 'I've only been living in Tallaght for the last three years and I hadn't really got a good opinion about it. I have two children ages three and five, and my feeling was that when, and if, I got the opportunity, I was going to move anywhere else in order to give my children a chance to grow up in an environment without drink or drugs ... Before yesterday, whenever I heard of a meeting in the area, I would just decide straight away that I wasn't going because it was nothing to do with me. I felt the problems were just too big and couldn't be sorted out anyway. I suppose I just didn't care ... Now, I'm not saying that I'm totally reformed, but I've decided I'm going to stay and make the best of it. To start with, I've decided to tidy up my street. I went out and bought a yard brush, and I'm going to go out and sweep the rubbish up off my street, and although I know that doesn't sound like much of an effort, I feel it's a start.'

As we write this, it is 2008, and when we look over the list of what people imagined that day, it's true to say that the vast majority of it has come to pass. June Kelly still lives in the area, working privately as a trained acupuncturist and part-time chef at An Cosán.

Not long after the forum day, Katherine interviewed for a job that, in all likelihood, offered an opportunity to bring her energy and feminist commitment to the national arena. It seemed the advertisement had been written for her: the National Women's Council of Ireland (formerly known as the Council for the Status of Women) was looking for a chief executive, part of its Herculean effort to revive the relevance and impact of an organisation that had been at the forefront of women's issues in the seventies and eighties. The Council had been established in 1973 as a direct result of the Government's report from the first Commission on the Status of Women. These were the heady days of the Irish Women's Liberation movement when feminists agitated for reforms in the welfare system for single mothers, for access for women to equal jobs, pay and education and for legal divorce and contraception. The night they launched the movement in Dublin's Mansion House, two thousand women showed up. One of the women's first actions was to board the infamous 'contraception train' to Belfast in May 1971. Contraceptives, while legal in Northern Ireland at the time, were not so in the Republic. Forty-seven women travelled from Dublin to Belfast and bought large quantities of them, which they openly declared at Irish customs on their return. Media coverage and additional lobbying efforts led to their eventual legalisation. During the subsequent twenty years, the Council had visible public presence, yet sporadic impact. In the mid-nineties, Noreen Byrne, a leading working-class activist, was elected to take over the Chair of the Council, holding a mandate to rebuild its effectiveness and bring about positive change across the equality spectrum for Irish women.

Katherine met Noreen for the first time across the interview table. She, along with Gráinne Healy (another leading feminist activist) and Maureen Lynott, former Chief Executive Officer (CEO) of Focus Point and Director of BUPA Ireland, grilled Katherine intensively about her feminist vision and her practical capacity to build a new organisation out of one with a worn history. If anything, their direct and tough approach pressed Katherine to respond with vigour and confidence, pushing away memories of the Trinity defeat. Ann Louise waited in a hotel around the corner, having bought a magnificent bouquet of flowers for Katherine, regardless of the outcome. As so often, Katherine felt overwhelmed by Ann Louise's fidelity and optimism – what a wonderful gesture of unbounded love. This time, though, Katherine approached Ann Louise with a magnificent smile. They had given her the job.

Katherine threw herself into the work, on the one hand, applying everything she had learned about management, strategy and finance, and, on the other hand, developing a practical blueprint out of an ideal feminist vision for a country where all women still were constitutionally oppressed, with one-third living below the poverty line. Noreen's working-class culture was not unfamiliar to Katherine, and both women knew that if they were to succeed they would have to find a way to get on together. Mutual respect between a Chair and Chief Executive, while not the most common phenomenon in statutory or non-governmental organisations, demands honesty and commitment to dialogue through the good times and bad. They taught each other how to do this, and it was perhaps the single most important ingredient that enabled swift organisational change.

In the first year, Katherine often felt like 'the new girl on the block' and that she would be tested. Soon after taking up the post, word reached her that the Secretary General of the Department of Justice, Equality and Law Reform was looking to audit the Council's financial records. Katherine remembers phoning her good friend Dara Hogan, a qualified accountant, and asking if he had anything – guidelines, formulas, whatever – to help her prepare for this unfamiliar task. Dara met with her, left her a huge handbook and promised additional support. This somewhat eased the feeling of terror! As it turned out, during her first meeting with Bernard McDonagh from the Department some months later, the issue didn't get raised. Instead, a most remarkable thing happened, brought on by the presence of Sylda Langford, newly appointed Assistant Secretary General in charge of the Equality Division of the Department. Katherine started by talking to both of them about her passion for childcare in the country, saying that if there was one thing that Irish women in all their diversity agreed upon and sought, it was state support for the care of their children. Katherine's strength of feeling came from years of working in West Tallaght as well as Ann Louise's current drive to find government monies for our much-hoped-for Rainbow House. She knew, from the inside and from the ground, what it was like for women, especially those living on social welfare, to be without any form of childcare. Without it, poverty would not be beaten. Sylda's face relaxed and energised simultaneously. She had a vision about children, a big and practical vision. The newly accepted national agreement, Partnership 2000, contained a commitment to establish a national working group that would create the first-ever childcare strategy for the country. Sylda was to be its Chair. She asked Katherine to join her steering committee, and that was the beginning of the Council working with Government in a new way.

This straightforward businesslike approach did not mean that the more traditional campaigning style was swept away. By hiring Anne

O'Donnell, one of the founders of the Rape Crisis Centre and former Director of the 'Pro-Choice' campaign, as the Council's Communications Manager, Katherine ensured that political lobbying and mobilising grass-roots members would form another part of the Council's tactics to effect change for women – and for children. As it happened, Anne and the rest of Katherine's team devised the Childcare 2000 campaign, inviting other national non-governmental agencies to join the Council in pressing for substantial change. This was a period when childcare was not on the lips of every politician, nor were they hearing about it at the doorstep. Determined to change that, the Council planned for one of the first marches by women (and supportive men and children) in Dublin for years. Explaining to a newspaper journalist why they were marching for childcare, Katherine said: "This past Thursday a group of women were taking a break from a women's studies course being run in West Tallaght by the Shanty Educational Project. The tutor of the course had been talking to the women about our Childcare march to the Dáil today. One of the women reached into her bag and took out a photo of her beautiful daughter at her debs'. She said to the other women gathered: "My daughter has a five-month old son. If she can't get childcare for him, her life is over. I'm going on the march, for my daughter and for her son.""

On a cold, crisp Saturday morning in mid-November, Katherine drove up to Parnell Square (the traditional place where people gather to march through Dublin) in her decorated RAV4 Toyota jeep and led the parade of five hundred-plus – women, buggies, children, men – with placards that read 'Every day is Mother's Day – we want childcare!' to the front of the Dáil where a band was playing, politicians gathered and microphones ready for the speeches. Katherine jumped up on the platform and shouted: 'If the State can provide grant and employment supports to other emerging industries, surely they can also invest in the future of its children? We're marching for childcare! Can anyone lose?' Well, the Government fudged the childcare issue on budget day that year, providing no tax reliefs to parents or other forms of government subsidies for families on social welfare. Interviewed that night across the street from Buswell's Hotel in Dublin (where lobbyists gather on budget day to hear the news), Katherine railed against the Government in an uncharacteristically fierce manner. The following year, after persistent campaigning by the Council and other childcare organisations, and after astute leadership by Sylda Langford within the system, the Government delivered a budget that initiated investment in a national childcare framework that continues today.

Equally challenging yet immensely satisfying work was Katherine's involvement in the social partnership process of negotiating national strategies and policies. In her capacity of representing the Women's Council, Katherine consistently criticised the Government's view that equality and social inclusion could only be paid for subsequent to an increase in Ireland's competitiveness. She insisted that there exists a *reciprocal* relationship between competitiveness and inclusion, not a *cause–effect* relationship. More than once in Dublin Castle she put forward the view that Ireland would lose its ability to be competitive if it did not become a more inclusive society. She drew on the research of Michael Porter, USA business guru and author of the highly influential *The Competitive Advantage of Nations,* who demonstrated that sustainable competitiveness and competitive advantage, at national and global level, results not from incessant cost-cutting measures but from a nation's ability to differentiate its products and services at the highest level of quality. 'Our nation's ability to differentiate,' Katherine maintained, 'is dependent on its promotion of the differences among its citizens. Thus, our ability to be competitive is dependent on a strong growth rate for mechanisms of social inclusion and equality.' Katherine and her dear friend Peadar Kirby (now Professor of International Politics and Public Policy at the University of Limerick) had a running battle in *The Irish Times* with Tánaiste Mary Harney who argued that the choice was between a 'liberal economy or a leftist economy'. They argued instead that the choice was between an economy that served the interests of a just and equitable society and an economy that made society subservient to its needs.

Gradually, however, Katherine's spirit wearied. While the public-policy work envigorated her, she felt like Sisyphus – the Greek king compelled to roll a huge rock up a steep hill, but before he reached the top, the rock always escaped him and rolled back down to the bottom, and he had to begin again – in her efforts to rebuild an organisation that adequately represented the views of a diverse and conflicted membership of 300,000 women. Some members of her board were not satisfied with her efforts, and Katherine perceived jealousies and conflicts of territory between the Executive and the Directors. This was an era prior to the 'science of corporate governance' that abounds today. During a couple of board meetings, some members raised issues about her performance without speaking to her beforehand, and Katherine's feeling of being undermined increased. Ann Louise kept telling her that she was looking pale and worn and that her idealistic spirit appeared beaten by the huge demands of the job. Katherine struggled to survive but was terrified that the stress would make her ill – she had seen it happen to Ann Louise. Surely there was something else she could do? She also felt torn between her yearning for the academic life, something she had trained for most of her life, and the adrenalin rush of operating within national and European circles. Perhaps she could have hung on longer, but she decided to conclude her work with the Council after negotiations for the national agreement in 2000. Most people were shocked at the news of her intended departure as the Council appeared to be reborn and performing well. Katherine's soul search, however, concluded with a choice to opt for a new role as an independent public-policy researcher. The draw of the intellectual life had won out, for now.

Simultaneous with Katherine's professional journey of representing 'the women of Ireland', Ann Louise boldly, yet always graciously, she hoped, led the realisation of a big dream. Throughout our work we have always seen a strong connection between social activism and the power of the human faculty of the creative imagination. At critical junctures in our work we often exercised our imagination in the belief that images of the possible would call us forward to unexpected horizons. As mentioned earlier, during the People's Forum in Tallaght West, imaginative exercises allowed us to glean insight into the vision of the community for their future, and that informed our work together. It was becoming ever more clear that we needed to take a leap of the imagination in order to respond positively to the growth of our organisation. The Muse was now being used at every hour of the day and evening. We had also started renting space in the new community centre in Jobstown, which was not entirely suitable for our purposes but allowed us to meet new demands. For example, Marie Moran, who was Chair of our management committee, held an open education morning every Wednesday on the indoor basketball pitch! Well-known speakers from around Ireland were invited to address topics chosen by the community, from drug addiction, to suicide, to every theme related to child and adolescent development. Women packed into these sessions as childcare was available. Their freedom to re-engage once a week with ideas and with others from the community spawned another large group who wanted to take the road back to education by attending year-long courses at The Shanty. Our work was at a crossroads: either we responded to the need to grow and change, or we stagnated. As Brenda O'Malley Farrell, a member of the management team stated, 'We are simply victims of our own success.'

In dialogue with all sections of the organisation the image became clear: we needed a large, multipurpose building, one that could house all three operations: The Shanty Education and Training Centre, the Weaving Dreams enterprise, and a new early education and childcare centre, Rainbow House. In the meantime, the management team continued to oversee the expanding operations of the different programmes. One night as we met together, we decided to name the new centre, and Imelda Hanratty came up with An Cosán, the Irish for 'The Path'; the metaphor was accurate, and we loved the language. The development team also stepped up to the plate, confident that we could raise the necessary funds while cognisant that this new venture was different in scale to anything we had ever attempted before. Ann Louise, still consigned to a half-time position at her college, was privileged to be able to take the role of Executive Director and drive this new phase forward. Katherine at this time was still in her more than full-time job at the National Women's Council. It was also agreed that we required a full-time development manager for the project, so funds were raised and we were blessed in the appointment of Phil O'Hehir. Although a lawyer and previously a nurse, her father had been a builder, and she had all the natural flair and talent to lead the operational development of the organisation towards this goal. It was decided that we would divide our fund-raising efforts into three categories: the corporate sector, contributions from grants and foundations and government monies.

Much was needed if the move from The Muse in Brittas was to be realised, and top of the agenda was the acquisition of a site in Jobstown. Eileen Durkan, a faithful member of the development team since the beginning, arranged a meeting for Ann Louise and herself in the offices of South Dublin County Council. This was the first of many. We were gracious in our rejection of all the initial sites on offer and explained that they were far too small to meet our ambition for change. Gradually, over many months, we convinced the officials that we had the track record in the community and the capacity to raise the money required, so finally they offered us a prime location – an acre of land in the newly planned village centre for Jobstown. At this stage, we had formed strong relationships with the council officials, and they seemed as excited as we were with this coup. Without even requesting it, they gave us, for no fee, the services of two of their finest architects, Mick McDonagh and Anne Golden. Indicative of the partnership we had established over the months, they insisted that they would draw their plans in dialogue with our suggestions for the multiplex building; the concept was entirely new to the Council.

This was our fourth building project: The Muse, the log cabin and, more recently, the restoration of an old cottage we had bought in Kerry. Up to now we had never had the luxury of an architect, not to mind two of them. Furthermore, previously we had been the project managers, and Ann Louise, who has a natural gift for imaging space and design, had drawn the plans, along with a little help from our friends. This proposed 10,000-square foot building was in a different league. However, we did intend giving our input. Anne Genockey, a participant in the development team from Jobstown, and Ann Louise headed off to visit some new early childhood education centres around the country and fed Mick some of the more creative ideas they encountered. He always loved to see them coming and never rejected any idea, however challenging to his plans. The same process was followed as the plans for Weaving Dreams and the Shanty Education and Training Centres were drawn.

The only proviso for South Dublin County Council as they gave us this prime site for £1 a year over a ninety-nine year lease, was that *we* had to raise the £1million required to build, and this within eighteen months or we'd lose the land! While they trusted us, they were understandably nervous as it was highly unusual that an independent organisation would attempt anything this large. There was no time to lose.

The philosopher David Hume stated that 'a powerful imagination has the ability to turn ideas into living impression', so we commissioned a young architect, Niamh Hogan, to make up a large model of Mick's drawings in the belief that the three-dimensional image would bring the project to life. We also commissioned a very talented commercial artist, Derry O'Connor, who at the time was designing the covers for Mary Black's albums, to develop a set of promotional materials and a video. While Derry had his studio in Rathfarnham about eight miles away, he had never been to West Tallaght. Following his first visit to the area, he was so distressed by the images of poverty he encountered that he insisted on doing this piece of work as a contribution. Armed with these excellent resources we began a campaign, with the slogan inspired by Hume: 'What is possible for the imagination is possible to be.'

The launch of An Cosán to the corporate sector took place at the Allied Irish Bank in central Tallaght. The Manager of the bank, Gerrie

Ross, who was a member of our development team, did a magnificent job ensuring that all the key players from big business in the surrounding area were present on the evening. Ron Bolger, Chairperson of Telecom Éireann and husband of Jenny – also on the development team, ran the evening, leaving none of the assembled gathering in any doubt about their corporate social responsibility to make this dream a reality by contributing hard cash. Mary Harney TD, Tánaiste and Minister for Enterprise, Trade and Employment, spoke with intensity and passion, stating that this work 'should inspire and challenge us all; this project needs practical and moral support.' In an area still blighted by 70 percent unemployment at the time, she then made a prophesy: 'This new development will create 31 jobs – 11 full-time and 20 part-time.' As an aside, it's always satisfying when the realisation of a dream surpasses the dream itself. Today An Cosán employs 40 full-time staff and a further 70 part-time; over half of the employees are from West Tallaght.

On behalf of the development team that evening, Ann Louise reflected on the learnings from our work over the previous eleven years: 'We know now, as we never knew before, that people who live on social welfare don't want handouts. They want opportunities. People living on low incomes don't want charity. They want the possibility of sharing as full citizens in the development of this state. We know now that the key to the eradication of poverty in this society is education, above all for those who have been failed by the State up to this point in their lives.' Anne Genockey, who many years later became the Manager of Rainbow House, used the economic argument in the understanding that financiers are most convinced by figures: 'The amounts we are trying to fund-raise here are small when one remembers that it costs £50,000 per year to hold one person in a detention centre. If An Cosán helped prevent, through adult education, training, enterprise opportunity and early childhood education in any one year fifteen people from getting into trouble with the law, it would pay off.'

Somewhat later, another corporate evening with a difference took place, this time in Auburn House, the beautiful home of Mary and Ulick

McEvaddy. Mary had the idea of hosting a grand ball in their recently renovated ballroom. This was a fairytale evening, with hundreds of people dancing the night away, the men in tuxedos and the ladies in magnificent attire. Mark Zappone, Katherine's brother and a costume designer in Seattle, designed and made our dresses – and connected with one of Ulick's planes to get them to the ball on time! A highlight of the evening was the auction conducted by Mark FitzGerald. Mary Harney had managed to get a signed copy of the Belfast Agreement – the hammer came down on that item alone at £38,000! After events such as this, reaching our target seemed achievable.

Once the land was secured, we did a maildrop to all the houses in West Tallaght asking for their responses to the proposal for An Cosán in the new village centre of Jobstown. We were humbled by the response. People expressed excitement and willingness to help the idea become a reality. This was our cue for a 'turning of the sod' celebration. The fact that it was a mid-winter frosty night didn't deter the local community from coming out in celebratory mood. Katherine's parents flew in from Seattle, as they so often did for big moments in our journey together. Aware that 'what you image is what you get', we all paused in silence and imaged the building that would be on the site in eighteen months' time. The local Minister for State Chris Flood officiated and opened the ground, and Fr Val from the parish gave his blessing. The local youth brass band then marched us all up the road for hot punch, food and speeches in the local school hall. Reflecting back, it is amazing the level of emotion that the memory of that evening still evokes. There were lots of children who ran across the site that night yelping with joy. Uninvited, they came in droves back to the school, and, when asked to sit until the speeches were over and the party began, they did so with a sense of occasion unusual for children so young. It was as if they sensed that this was about their future and was something that would help their parents – maybe they glimpsed a better chance in life if this actually happened.

The following March, Anne Genockey decided to form a local stakeholders' association; all past and present participants were invited to join, along with people from the local community who were interested in the goals and objectives of The Shanty and its aspiration to build An Cosán. With a small team, she organised a maildrop in Jobstown, and when she called to collect the forms, 560 people wanted to become members and paid their subscriptions. Their first meeting was with all the elected local politicians, and the message was clear that any politician wanting a vote in the next election needed to help procure government funding for An Cosán.

There was no doubt that the corporate sector in the area was on board along with the local community. To assist with raising money from foundations and among Irish Americans, it was agreed by the development committee that Katherine and Ann Louise should accept an invitation to go to Chicago over the Easter break. The well-known theologian, David Tracy, knew of our work and had extended this invitation. As a professor in Chicago University he had many contacts and upon our arrival gave us an extended list. We worked unbelievably hard for ten days making two presentations every day, some to significant businessmen, others to Irish-American foundations. All our efforts were in vain, and we raised almost no money – only $1,000 in a single contribution towards the end of the trip from a woman who clearly felt sorry for us as she sensed our weary spirits. While there was great interest and many questions asked about our work, the response was always the same: we give all our donations to Ireland now through the American Ireland Fund. We returned home disheartened. Not only had the trip been a dismal failure, but we had given a lot of valuable time to it.

Meanwhile, our efforts to extract money from the Government were proving equally unsuccessful. As each month passed, the estimated cost of building the facility increased. It had jumped from £550,000 to £740,000 in a few short months. Writing in *The Shanty Newsletter* of spring 1998, Phil O'Hehir expressed frustration with the fact that 'there is no clear system in place to deal with applications for capital funding. There is no one place where such an application can be sent. As a result, we have seven applications with seven different government departments.' This was particularly disconcerting and disingenuous from a government who had launched a National Anti-Poverty Strategy (NAPS) one year previously. The commitment of NAPS was to reduce poverty and social exclusion in our society by a concerted approach right across different government departments. While we applauded the excellent policy recommendations in the strategy, our experience was that there was no inter-departmental collaboration to implement these policies and little intra-departmental conversation or any joined-up thinking about concrete ways to create a more equitable society.

Tension was mounting as the deadline of June approached, when we would either have to pay up or lose the land. In May, the development team met in Mary McEvaddy's home. We had a crisis, and we needed a way forward. It is at moments such as these, which are normally never written about, that the hidden goodness, the moral fibre and the generosity of people are in evidence. Not one of these seventeen women had ever lived with poverty, yet every one of them, due to their practical engagement with the project, had a real empathy for the challenges facing people in West Tallaght and were determined that we would deliver our promise. As Mary's husband landed his helicopter on the front lawn, taking the tops off her roses – a matter to be dealt with later – we women plotted and planned. We could do it, we would do it. A number of the women stated that they could raise the money through their banks to create a bridging loan and allow the building to commence in June. We would tell no one of this plan until the last minute and keep up the pressure on Government.

Tension was also mounting in the local community. People organised various consciousness-raising events to keep up awareness that our time was running out. Nell McCafferty arrived to address a public meeting: 'It is the God-given right to develop as a whole person and thereby contribute to the well-being of family, community, society and the universe,' she stated. 'Give them half a million quid by next Wednesday, and the women of Jobstown will conquer the world.' Her words, as always, got great media coverage.

As there now seemed little hope, desperate measures were planned. We decided we would march on the Dáil the day after The Shanty graduation in June and then return to the site and camp out until funding was granted. That same evening, which was the day before the graduation ceremony, Ann Louise was at a function for Boston College held in the National Art Gallery, a few yards from the Dáil. The Minister for Education, Micheál Martin, was addressing the august assembly, which included the President of Boston College and many donors for the American Ireland Fund. After the speeches, the Minister moved through the crowd, and when he approached Ann Louise she quietly informed him of upcoming happenings. He became agitated – this was neither the time nor the place to inform him of such matters. Remaining calm, Ann Louise stated that as we had no success using the official channels of his department we thought out of courtesy that he might appreciate being told directly of the situation rather than suffering a political embarrassment. He wasn't impressed and moved away.

Next day, 16 June, we held our annual graduation ceremony in the community centre. Two hundred women and two classes of men filled the hall. Pat Rabbitte, local Labour Party TD, was speaking when the door at the back of the hall suddenly burst open. Without a by-your-leave, Minister for State Chris Flood walked up on to the stage. He took the microphone from Pat and stated: 'You have your money. The Cabinet Subcommittee on Social Inclusion, chaired by the Taoiseach, met this evening, and it has been agreed to give the necessary government contribution to build An Cosán.' Everyone rose to their feet and began to cheer; people wept and hugged; this was indeed a victory against all the odds for a community who held tenaciously to a dream.

One year later, when An Cosán was opened by Taoiseach Bertie Ahern and Tánaiste Mary Harney, they stated publicly that in the end the Government *had* to fund this project, as they and every minister in government was being approached from all sectors of Irish society about it. In the end, this was a victory for democracy at work.

As An Cosán rose three stories into the sky in Jobstown, West

Tallaght, the new President in St Pat's, Dr Pauric Travers, kindly and effectively resolved Ann Louise's situation there. She would be reappointed as a full-time member of staff, and included in her new duties would be to establish and direct a new educational disadvantage centre for the college, along with her work in philosophy and the philosophy of education. For those who believe in providence, this was truly a providential sequence of events. The two years' part-time employment had allowed her to avail of amazing opportunities, one of which was to join a team of researchers on the National Women's Millennium Project and travel the country teaching research skills to women in the most remote rural areas, so that they in turn could investigate the views, needs and concerns of women in their areas. Of course, the most significant work of the period was leading a team of people to achieve what most people said was unachievable: a large community-based centre owned, in every sense of that word, by the local community. While our work had taken us both in different directions over the previous two years, no day ever went by without us sharing the details of our different projects and offering each other mutual support; all achievements were shared in the realisation that without our relationship neither of us could accomplish our dreams.

Many years later, in June 2004, an article appeared in *Business and Finance*. The author Pádraig Ó Móráin wrote,

Back in the 1990s, before we spotted the Celtic Tiger leaping around the place, the *Irish Times* sent me to cover a seminar in Jobstown, Tallaght. It was organised by a community group called 'The Shanty' who had been running training courses for the local women for years. Their dream was to have their own purpose-built education and training centre. They didn't have speeches or PowerPoint presentations. Instead, they engaged in an exercise in 'visioning' in which the participants worked out, with crayons and markers, their vision of the future. And whatever all you power-suited people might think of that, the whole occasion had a remarkable strength to it.

Recently, I visited the new centre, now called An Cosán, which is the embodiment of the vision worked out that day. Now, An Cosán doesn't exist just because somebody had a dream or a vision about it. It took blood, sweat and tears, fund-raising, drawing up business plans and proposals, and all the rest of it. The point is, however, that none of that would have happened if the people behind it hadn't the dream in the first place.

So dream!

At this point in our journey, again each for different reasons, we realised that our relationship with the Catholic Church had ended. Some people talk about 'leaving the Church' in language that suggests that the moment of exit was abrupt and the door was slammed behind the decision. Reflecting on her own dawning realisation that her relationship with the Catholic Church was over, Ann Louise would name a gradual waning of a connection that had been so strong in her earlier life. She had grown up in a country that George Bernard Shaw accurately described: 'In Ireland, the people is the Church, and the Church is the people.' The Church, with all its ritual, filled up her senses and satisfied the longings of her soul. However, even as a young woman, she started to question the arrogant claims of infallible truth and the abuses of power in the name of the unknowable divine. There was little humility practised by the officials of the Church, and yet, in her study, she was aware that the doubt-filled or apophatic tradition was as much a part of the history of the teaching Church as the one that took precedence and called for absolute and unthinking credence.

In his study of the demise of the Catholic Church in Canada, the Jesuit Michael Paul Gallagher talks about a 'quiet revolution' – gradually and without any fanfare, a Church that held majority rule awoke one day to find its churches empty and its congregations missing. Many would offer a similar account of the changing fortunes of the Church in Ireland. Ann Louise didn't simply drift with the crowd. Her going was exacerbated by a number of personal experiences, already outlined, with leading authority figures of the Church. These ultimately shattered her ability to identify with this Church. There was nothing easy about this letting-go. Like any relationship that initially is rooted in love and deep connection, and that has consumed years of one's life, there is a mourning, filled with memory, in the final movement away. Her journey from organised religion was not a step into a void or a spiritual vacuum, however, as it is for many; rather, a new and rich spiritual engagement, informed by feminist spiritualities, ecological insights and a daily meditation practice continues to nourish her soul.

So, too, for Katherine. Movement away from Catholicism, and indeed Christianity itself, was as much about a movement into new spiritual territory as it was a letting-go of an old identity. Katherine's relationship with the divine shaped her early childhood and her adolescence. She described this in a prose-poem prepared for a public lecture delivered in 1996 in Vancouver, British Columbia.

> Upon coming into this world
> She was swaddled in the belief and devotion
> That was the central passion of her parents' lives.
>
> As she grew into childhood
> Her every sense was touched and stimulated
> by Catholicism:
> the incense of benediction
> the bells of consecration
> the wafer of Eucharist
> And the changing colours of vestments with each season.
>
> Every morning before school
> She would grace the parish church
> with her presence.
> Quietly paging the little blue prayerbook;
> At peace in the pew;
> Gazing at the tabernacle
> Enveloped by the *real* presence . . .

Katherine spent her young adulthood teaching and living Christian feminist theology, discussing at length, in writings and public lectures, whether a feminist ought to stay within or leave one's inherited religious tradition. Amidst all the heated debates, though, she remembers being affected most by the remarks of two feminist spiritual thinkers. In her book, *Laughter of Aphrodite: Reflections on a Journey to the Goddess,* Carol Christ says that 'the reasons each of us has for continuing to work within inherited traditions or leaving them are complex and not reducible to intellectual, logical argument.' And towards the end of her text, *The Journey Is Home,* Nelle Morton raises what Katherine always considered to be a prophetic question: 'If we take our tradition (Jewish, Christian, Buddhist, Islamic, humanist or what have you) with dead seriousness and remain faithful to it, will it push us beyond itself or draw us inward, separating us further from one another?'

Katherine took Christianity with dead seriousness, and she had remained faithful to it since her earliest days of childhood. When Christians 'put a bullet through her soul', and when she witnessed her beloved Ann Louise suffer at the hands of Church leaders, the spiritual grip of the Christian God dissolved, and slowly Katherine, with others, began to chart new territory for faithful feminists. In her visions and meditations she is brought to the edge of a clearing. The clearing, not unlike a Celtic stone circle in a low-cut grassy field, is space outside ordinary time, so one is bound to be transformed upon entering it. It takes a significant amount of courage to step in, and if you don't want to be changed, don't enter the circle. Katherine meets sacred presence now, uninhibited by the ongoing male mediation of a Father and Son God. The most likely place for her to experience sacred essence is in her love partnership with Ann Louise.

11

LET'S TALK
ABOUT LOVE

Love is the time and space in which the 'I'
assumes the right to be extraordinary.

Julia Kristeva

Once word went out that we had been asked to write this book, the most
frequent response from friends, colleagues and even acquaintances,
took the form of a request: 'Speak to us of love; tell us what has
sustained your clearly loving relationship over all these years,' or, as one
young lad asked with great hope, 'Will it be a love story?' So at this point
we have decided to linger on love, to pause and, in this interlude, to
reflect on our graced experience of love, its fragilities, vulnerabilities
and, above all, its joys.

To accept such a challenge is, of course, a daunting task. Initially, it is
important to state that the language of love is metaphoric. A metaphor is
both the richest form of language and the most humble, for it admits that
any attempt to state the meaning of something resides in the gap
between 'what is' and 'what is not'. It is impossible to talk of love in a
manner that would claim we have said it all, or that there is a final,
definitive description of love in general, or even of our own particular
experience of love.

Twenty-six years ago, we had the words 'God is Love' inscribed on our rings. This familiar phrase from St John can be passed over so easily, its meaning simply not noticed. For us, however, they highlight the newness – the forever newness – of love. John's words place on the horizon of human becoming an image of the possible – calling, cajoling, challenging us forward. The philosopher Julia Kristeva argues that this identification of God with love is truly revolutionary – it is dependent on a new, unprecedented, scandalous, insane attitude that forms the ideal of Christian love. Why 'insane'? Why 'scandalous'? Because love is the unknown, the future as well as the present and past, the forever changing. We commit ourselves to the unknown when we commit to love. It was because of this revolutionary understanding that we chose those words for our rings, to mark our 'forever love'.

To find appropriate language to speak about love is further complicated because the experience of love involves so much more than what goes on in one's mind. Love engages all aspects of the human: the emotion of the heart, the mystery of the thinking mind, the soft physicality of human attentiveness and the spiritual longing in the now for the eternal continuity of what is and what is to come. Here, more than in any other context, emotions inform our knowledge of love. Howard Gardner talks about the 'multiple intelligences' that we all possess; these are not limited to the narrow assessment of ability measured in standardised IQ tests. He draws attention to our emotional intelligence, our interpersonal and intrapersonal intelligence and our spiritual intelligence. We agree. To speak about love requires finding language that evokes our many intelligences, capabilities and imaginative abilities.

Despite these challenges, we stand with those who believe that we *must* speak about love in this society, not simply in the private reaches of our intimate relationships but also in public, in a way that engages and informs civic society. This would be a welcome antidote to the incessant public debate about economics and monetary matters that almost exclusively preoccupy this nation at this time. Furthermore, the narrative about relationship in recent Irish history has been heavily burdened with descriptions of the abuses of love. Many people commented to us that our talk about love, most especially our love for each other, as we emerged recently from the High Court, was refreshingly new and much needed. But that reflection is for a later chapter.

Like others, we read and enjoy philosophy, discussing ideas together. We try to think out our lives following Socrates' dictum: 'The unexamined life is not worth living.' Sometimes, this reflection and reading provides us with the language in which to reflect on our own life and love; sometimes it, too, leaves us short. Back in 1970, Iris Murdoch lamented that 'contemporary philosophers frequently connect consciousness with virtue, and although they constantly talk of freedom, they rarely talk of love.' And, more recently, Luce Irigaray reflected: 'If Western philosophy has tried to be a love of wisdom, it has neglected or forgotten to become a wisdom of love.' Thankfully, in recent years, a number of renowned female philosophers have broken the silence and, as already indicated, have published significant and acclaimed works on love. We have been shaped by many of these reflections, and no doubt they shape our thinking here as we dialogue with our own experiences of love.

Our story of love has a beginning. We met in 1981 and spontaneously 'fell in love'. This metaphor, used so lightly and naturally among heterosexuals, takes on a different hue when applied to a love that dares not speak its name. The intense, involuntary emotional attraction and desire is no different for opposite-sex or same-sex couples, the difference lies in the negative social construction that some within the majority of the population who are heterosexual impose on homosexual love. As our love and desire for each other grew in private, we were convinced of the rightness of our relationship, despite the lack of any public acknowledgement of the possibility of such love. In fact, Ann Louise was informed on several occasions of the affection for her of two male graduate students – various overtures were made but graciously resisted, as by now we were spending more and more time together and were privately enjoying the excitement and the joy of this new, intense love.

There are markers in any relationship that most couples can remember as turning points, moments of transition, the crossing of the threshold beyond the initial opening phase of attraction and connection. Such moments embody the realisation: we are in love with each other. And with that dawning and acknowledgement a new phase commences. The involuntary feeling of 'falling in love' now calls for choice, the will to love and the free, ethical decision to allow this emotional relationship to flower. For us, one such moment was an autumn evening in Boston; Bette Midler was giving an open-air concert on the Boston Commons. Katherine was over the moon as Bette was and is one of her favourite artists. We drove into the city in Katherine's orange Volkswagen Beetle, chatting excitedly all the way. Upon arrival, we parked and took with us all the necessities for the evening concert – a picnic, a rug and a bottle of wine. The concert was Beth at her best, singing songs we loved, which included, most appropriately, 'I Love Being Here With You' from her album *I Know, You Know*. At the end, she tootled on to the stage and with feminist panache burst her boobs (balloons) with a pin, to uproarious applause from the crowds. When it was all over, we lay on our rug gazing at the stars, chatting for hours and then rose to go back to the car – at which point we both realised that we had absolutely no memory of where we had abandoned the Beetle, in all our excitement of being together. It was time to name the obvious, at least to ourselves. We were women in love.

We both acknowledged a new intensification of life, a fullness of joy, a heightened sense of meaning and purpose and a discovery of new aspects of ourselves in this relationship. Little by little, we knew love in new ways. Already we were imagining together the creative possibilities of a shared life of love. It was uncanny: here we were, the two of us from the far reaches of the world, and yet we shared so many values, ideals and concerns. It was magical. There is a rhythm between lovers, a synchronicity, which confirms the truth of this romantic phase of relationship. Against the odds, we knew we would manage the miracle of this unexpected gift of love.

The author and philosopher bell hooks, writes: 'To love fully and deeply puts us at risk. When we love we are changed utterly.' This is generally true, but neither she nor the other female philosophers ever addresses the risk faced by same-sex couples as they choose to deepen and develop a relationship. To love fully always involves risk, the vulnerability of letting go and trusting the gift of love offered and to open and return that gift mutually and unreservedly. Loving someone of your own sex fully is tinged with an extra cloud of unknowing, the uncertainty created by homophobic prejudice and fear of our love. The taboos, the hate created by others from their blinkered ideology of love that excludes all but their own kind, poisons the air and stifles public celebration of love's diversity – often in the name of Christianity, which is utterly baffling. This was very true in Boston in 1981.

We didn't have the courage in that formative period of our relationship to announce publicly in Catholic Boston College that we were a couple in love, who at this stage had moved in with each other to our little house in Gloucester. We didn't share the excitement and magic of what went on behind closed doors. We didn't mention rising in the morning and dancing to Dan Fogelberg's, 'Good Morning to the Morning' or driving sixty miles home in the evening, north on the 127 motorway, singing along with Cris Williamson's lyrics or Meg Christian's 'The Road I Took to You'. We didn't talk of the risks we took to ensure that we could get back to our own place just to relax and freely express our love, driving in that first winter through freezing fog or skidding along icy roads.

However, while we didn't speak out, we learned from and admired those who did. We recall the evening that Claire Lowery and Ann Morgan, both Sisters of the Sacred Heart at the time, invited the poet May Sarton to join their community for dinner. As a well-known North American author, she was to address the student body in Boston College later that evening. The dinner progressed without incident, and we all made polite conversation as we ate our way though various courses. Suddenly, at dessert, and in response to an innocent question from one of the more frail nuns, May responded, 'Well, as a lesbian woman, I–' It was as if an electric shock went through the collected guests. The awkwardness never lifted, and May was manoeuvred out of the convent back to the college, with some mutterings that coffee would be served elsewhere. After her lecture, we waited for her and expressed our admiration for her openness and told her of our own relationship. In her next book, *At Seventy,* she makes reference to the two doctoral students who drove her home!

Telling May about our relationship and gradually speaking about our love with a growing number of friends was indicative of an increased confidence and a deepening outrage that prejudice and ignorance were imprisoning us in silence. We are not naturally secretive; rather, we tend to speak out and share our thoughts and feelings without hesitation. Around this time, we travelled to Quebec for a weekend break. Upon arrival, we found a quaint restaurant, chose a lovely table by the window and ordered a drink. Within minutes, two guys who had been standing at the bar came over, pulled over extra chairs and sat down: 'We see you're alone, so may we join you?' 'No,' we answered in harmony, 'actually, we're together.' It was a quintessential moment of triumph as we watched the men stand, reposition the chairs and walk backwards from our table mumbling some unpleasant response. This incident sowed the seed of an agreement that we would never deny our relationship if 'outed' or if greeted with heterosexual ignorance that presumes that we couldn't possibly be in relationship. This continues to happen even when we deliberately book a double room with a king-size bed in a hotel – only to arrive at the reception desk and observe a flurry of activity while they move us to a room with two single beds, without checking with us! At this point, we have talked to many hotel managers, begging that training of staff include consciousness-raising in relation to sexual identity and diversity.

Many couples in an active sexual relationship neither desire nor deem necessary any sort of commitment. Such freedom to choose the nature of one's relationship is part of the healthy diversity that marks our society today. We, however, hold with those who aspire towards a formal commitment. Here we agree with the sentiment expressed by Margaret Farley in her new book *Just Love* (2007):

> Commitment in sexual relationships that are just need not stifle either life or sexual love and desire; it may instead nurture, sustain, anchor, and transform sexuality. Its aim, at least, is to give a future to love and to a shared life, holding in continually ratified free choice what is otherwise fleeting and fragile. Commitment, or especially frameworks for commitment, are means, not ends in themselves. But they are means to the affirmation of persons as ends in themselves and the endurance of love that is an end itself for those who want their relationships to hold.

As mentioned previously, very soon after meeting each other we discerned that we wanted to commit our lives to each other and one year later had a formal ritual and celebration to mark the event. The day after this graced occasion, when all the guests had left, we walked the beach hand in hand, savouring the memories of the liturgy and the meal and the affirmations of the friends who had honoured us. As we walked, we hummed Placido Domingo's 'Perhaps Love', the theme song that had been threaded through the ceremony. We were now committed to a life of faithful love, a commitment that we have never broken.

This claim of faithful love is not made with any sense of arrogance or judgement. We simply have been blessed that our love has deepened with time and has continued to nourish and sustain us as individuals and in our togetherness. But personal commitments, the exercise of the imaginative faculty to make and keep promises, happens in a social context, and that context can either intrude negatively or support the freedom to love. For both of us, our families were the primary school of love. We both grew up in contexts of loving parental relationships that weathered the years and were lovingly faithful to the end – this has, without doubt, supported our freedom to love. Nobody disputes that one's early experiences of love have a fundamental effect on the kind of person one becomes. The philosopher Hannah Arendt stated, in one of her letters: 'Ever since I was a little girl, I have always known that love was the only thing that could give the feeling of truly existing.' As children we both reached a similar insight. Such schooling in love is an amazing grace for any child and shapes the creative imagination of love's possibility.

As our years of togetherness have advanced, our own distinct patterns of personality have become more evident. While we have much in common, we are also very different personalities – and perhaps respecting the otherness of the other has saved our love. Ann Louise is fiercely independent and couldn't imagine living in a possessive, suffocating relationship. Katherine loves her own space, and she has an unquenchable thirst for reading and reflection, time that our relationship protects. At times, as Katherine reads, Ann Louise potters – she adores to cook and garden. At other times, Ann Louise, who is a bit of a monk at heart, wants nothing more than a day of quiet reflection and writing in her log cabin. Katherine, on occasion, takes to the kitchen and assumes the persona of an Italian chef, cooking like her great-grandfather, who hailed from Campabassa, west of Rome. Of course, one mustn't overstate the harmony that reigns as we exercise our different talents – there are moments of tension too as Ann Louise plans yet another dinner party while Katherine expresses anxiety about the next work deadline! But, in general, it works, and fundamentally we have a love that respects our differences without any need for either to control the other.

We have always striven for, and often spoken about, the importance of respecting the otherness of the other. The awful alternative would be a fusion, a reduction of the other to oneself. We have shared friends and different friends, we have shared hobbies and different hobbies, but above all we have a core commitment to live a respect for each other at all times which is lived out in honouring our different female subjectivities. We have resisted, with our eyes wide open, growing into patterns of complementarity, where there would be a rigid division of labour and an expectation that one or other of us would always look after given aspects of our life together in some fixed arrangement.

Luce Irigaray reflects on the importance of remaining two – two different selves in relation. 'Sexual relation could be a path to becoming more aware and attentive, above all to intersubjectivity, and to approaching each other instead of appropriating one another,' she writes; in other words, developing respect for each other rather than controlling each other. Irigaray believes that being and remaining two is necessary for keeping love alive, and we absolutely agree. Regretfully, she restricts her discussion of love to that between opposite-sex couples. This burdens gays and lesbians with the chore of simultaneous translation as we read her work. In conversation with her, in Chez Papa, one of her favourite restaurants in Paris, we offered a strong critique of this lacuna in her work and look forward to a more inclusive discussion of relationship in her work in the future.

Celebration has consistently formed part of our lives together. Important and significant events have always been marked by time dedicated to naming and focusing on memorable moments. So, when the tenth anniversary of our life-partnership commitment came along in autumn 1992, we decided to celebrate not for a day but for a week, and not alone or in private but with a group of significant friends, some from the United States who had been at the original commitment ceremony and others representing our ever-growing community of friends in Ireland. Over thirty were invited, and some twenty arrived in celebratory mood. We suggested a structure for the week whereby every morning we would meet in The Muse, and one person, a couple, or small group would give a prepared presentation of some key ideas from their professional background that were of interest. For example, Reesa Vaughter, Professor of Psychology in Fordham University, and her partner Zola Golub, a nurse in charge of a large unit for premature infants in Columbia Presbyterian, one of New York's largest hospitals – both strong feminists – reflected on current issues facing women in their work in New York City. Unfortunately, on this occasion, their beautiful daughter Sarit couldn't come to the event, but they interwove their refection with illustrations from Sarit's life – a happy adolescent who contributed so much to the joy of their family life. The afternoons were spent outdoors in the mountains or walking by the sea. One strong image of nature that remains a vivid memory was the walk down to Lough Dan in County Wicklow, through the Guinness estate, with banks of heather in full bloom on either side of the path and clear blue skies up above. Each evening, a different team cooked a delicious meal, which was followed by a *siamsa* of song, dance, poetry and storytelling. On the last day, the group had prepared a special ritual celebrating our ten years; it was deeply moving, and we both felt truly nourished as the occasion drew to a close. One contributor joked that most relationships celebrate their tenth with a card, or at best a meal out, but this week-long celebration of relationship and love was eligible for entry in the *Guinness Book of Records* – in fact, it should be bottled and marketed, she remarked!

Many years later, reflecting on that special time, Dr Gail Grossman Freyne, one of the participants, wrote:

The word 'Ceremony', the dictionary says, is a formal occasion celebrating a particular event or anniversary. It sounds a heavy word, ceremony. It smacks of gold braid and trumpets, of processions and banners, of ermine tails and crowns, of medals pinned on chests or swords placed on shoulders. It is a man's word to mark men's achievements and their rights of passage. Even at wedding ceremonies, a man 'gives away' his daughter to another man.

Fifteen years ago a group of women were formally invited to come together to celebrate the tenth year of the union of Ann Louise and Katherine. A ceremony, a week of ceremony, is precisely what it was. It was a party, a feast, a hooley, a *fête*. We danced and we sang, we ate and we shared loving cups.

We shared memories, some funny and some poignant, so we laughed and wept together. We offered our experiences as mothers and daughters, both lesbian and straight. In place of being 'given away' we gave away special parts of ourselves to each other. As our reward, we took away not medals or knighthoods but bright, new insights and courage freshly polished. It was a celebration of love found and a healing for love lost.

No, there was nothing heavy about these days of ceremony and celebration. We didn't know it at the time but it was a preparation, a forerunner of the celebration that is to come when Ann Louise and Katherine have their marriage formally entered into the public records of the Irish Republic. That day may not be soon but that day will come and it will be their shining gift not only to the few but to the many across the generations, forever.

There is an unspoken but agreed ethics that respects the privacy of the intimate details of sexual relationships, and certainly our memoir will not breach the norm in this regard. However, artistic expression can be a midwife to appreciating the intimate lives we live. Such work illustrates that the dominant passion of the human is love. Erotic heterosexual love frequently finds expression in various art forms, from poetry to fine art, literature and music; this is less true for gay and lesbian love. Thankfully, this is changing, and in more recent years the voices of lesbian poets and novelists are reaching a general audience and, through the poetic imagination, giving metaphoric expression to such love. The black lesbian poet, Audre Lorde, is one such poet; her work has enriched our lives:

A Lover's Song
Give me fire and I will give you morning
Finding your heart
And a birth of fruit
For you, a flame that will stay beauty
Song will take us by the hand
And lead us back to light.

Give me fire and I will sing you evening
Asking you water
And quick breath
No farewell winds like a willow switch
Against my body

But a voice to speak
In a dark room.

Love Poem
Speak earth and bless me with what is richest
Make sky flow honey out of my hips
Rigid as mountains
Spread over a valley
Carved out by the mouth of rain.

And I knew when I entered her I was
high wind in her forest hollow
fingers whispering sound
honey flowed
from the split cup
Impaled on a lance of tongues
on the tips of her breasts on her navel
and my breath
Howling into her entrances
through lungs of pain.

Greedy as herring-gulls
or a child
I sing out over the earth
Over and over
Again.

While the celebration of our twentieth anniversary wasn't a week-long event, it was a landmark moment in the public proclamation of our love in an Irish context. Earlier celebrations had happened in the privacy of our own home, but on this occasion the chosen venue was the Clarence Hotel, in central Dublin. We loved this ambiance not only because of its association with U2, but because, over the years, we had had many happy evenings there. The invitations were clear:

20 Years

1982 – 2002

You are invited to

A Celebration of

Our Life Partnership

We invited seventy-five guests, family and friends from a rich diversity of backgrounds and ages, and felt badly that we couldn't include everyone. All who received an invitation responded in the affirmative. As part of her RSVP note, Liz Waters, CEO of An Cosán, wrote: 'The grace of twenty years of loving active partnership shines through all you do and supports and touches all of us who know you. Also it supports my own belief that loving partnership can be found, shared and last.'

The party was our gift to each other, so when the morning of 16 October arrived we didn't exchange gifts, but we did share cards. Katherine, who is a wonderful archivist and keeps everything, can take credit for saving our words to each other on that day.

Oct. 16, 2002

To my beloved partner

for Life!!

Thanking you for all the years,

for the event of a lifetime,

for your courage

and for your eternal gift of love.

It doesn't get better than these 20 years.

All my Love,

Kay

16· Oct. 02.

My dearest One,

The memory of that beautiful day in Rockport 20 years ago

is as fresh as ever. The reality we shared then has deepened,

matured in ways that only 'living love' can allow.

The excitement, the wonder I was filled with that day, I'm filled with again

today as I long to be with you this evening for our special celebration.

Thank you for <u>all</u>, for being who you are and sharing that being with me so

beautifully, so generously, so kindly – always.

My love to you, beautiful one.

Annie

That evening, everyone arrived in celebratory mood. From the beginning there was a great energy, and it was clear that we were in for a special night. Most of those invited knew we were a couple, but for some we had never spelt out the nature of our relationship. However, the invitation had made that very clear. The plan was to begin with a champagne reception in the downstairs drawing room and then move upstairs to dinner, which was to be served in the long room with guests seated at round tables overlooking the river Liffey. As we moved around the periphery of the room, greeting everyone, Ann Louise spotted a waiter in a black tuxedo at the far side of the room who looked awfully like Mark Zappone, Katherine's youngest brother. Suddenly, the said gentleman approached with two huge bunches of red roses – it *was* Mark Zappone! As Katherine embraced and hugged him, a sudden hush came over the crowd – there in the doorway stood Katherine's father, Bob. At eighty-one years of age he had flown through the night with Mark to surprise us, his daughters, and to celebrate with us. (We are jumping ahead of ourselves slightly here; in the next chapter we tell of our 'coming out' to Katherine's parents.) There are images one will hold forever – this, without doubt, is one of them. He carried a card from himself and his wife Kathie, as she wasn't able to travel. It read:

We are proud of both of you for your faithful and generous commitment. We applaud both your personal and professional lives and will always support you in whatever you do. Twenty years of commitment is truly something to celebrate.

All our love
Mom & Dad, Kathie and Bob

Before dinner was served, we formally welcomed everyone, and we spoke of our love for each other which had been resourced and nourished by each person in the room, not least by our families, who were now, much to our joy, both represented. Once dinner ended, dancing began to a wonderful jazz band, the Cole Porter Song Book. Many wrote after that night of the wonderful celebration, and Meriel Kilroy wasn't alone when she commented, 'There weren't too many dry eyes when you both spoke so movingly of your love.'

Thankfully, there is no conclusion to this interlude on love. Loving fidelity to life together has allowed us to live time in three dimensions: the present, the past and the future. We remain excited in each other's presence in the now. We often comment on the genuine joy we feel when we meet up again even after the briefest absence. As the years go by, the present is enriched by an ever-fuller stock of memories. Twenty-seven years on, we have built a history together peopled with a community of family, friends and events – memories that nourish and from which we constantly learn. Respecting the mystery of the other always allows that anticipation of the new in the future. As we see it, the work of love is to allow that creative possibility. We hope to remain surprised by love.

12

'DEAR DAUGHTERS'

'Dear Friend. A letter always feels to me like immortality
because it is the mind alone without corporeal friend.'

Emily Dickinson

Because we have been together most of our twenty-seven years (except
on the odd occasion of a professional trip by one or the other, or when
Katherine visits her parents in Seattle without Ann Louise), we do not
have a collection of 'love letters'. We do not regret this, at all. The grace
of minutes, hours, days and years of physical presence far surpasses any
sense of loss in this regard.

Katherine's parents, however, have been wonderfully faithful
letter-writers over the years and, when they became aware of our
memoir project, produced two boxes filled with almost forty years of
correspondence that travelled between the two coasts of America and
across the Atlantic. Ann Louise wrote to them often, telling them the
daily stories of our lives as one way to thank them for allowing their
eldest daughter to live in a land so far away from them. Katherine kept
them informed too and used letters to express gratitude for their constant
support and unconditional love throughout her life.

Some letters, however, are extra special, and here we select four of
those. Our selection reflects our choice to convey some of the
intimacies, deep feelings and careful thinking that happen between

children and parents when parents are told that one of their beautiful daughters or sons is lesbian or gay. The first letter contains Katherine's 'coming out' to her parents, written when she was thirty-eight years old. As it happened, her youngest brother's earlier disclosure to their parents that he is gay prompted her to take up her pen. She remembers feeling that the time had finally come, that somehow she had to summon the courage to reveal what her parents might hear as a defective or even abhorrent side of herself. She was their darling daughter; she knew she had made them so proud. Would this revelation take all of that away? And if it did, what then? On the other hand, she wanted to be faithful to her brother and not let him 'hang out there' on his own. She admired his courage and felt that in some way by his action he had stepped into, even superseded, her usual role within the family as the initiator, caretaker, leader. Though not intended, he had laid down the gauntlet for her.

So, she sat down one immensely cold winter Sunday morning and started to write. Telling a parent that you are lesbian or gay consists of two events: first, that *you* are telling them, and, second, that *they* are hearing this truth. In writing the first letter, Katherine attempted to communicate what Gertrude Stein called 'the inside' of herself to the 'outside' world of her parents. In her book *Narration*, Stein talks about letter-writing as an act where your audience is inside you; you write and listen at the same time, and then there is 'recognition'. What does it sound like to hear yourself engaged in this revelatory act? Does it give you a new sense of self? Indeed, Katherine experienced it as a deeper form of knowing herself, of pushing the emergence of a more positive sense of self, of securing acceptance in her own soul. This came slowly, over time, but it did begin in a new awareness that can only happen through the event of a child telling a parent.

One can tell a thousand million friends, colleagues or other family members, but the recognition of self – that one is a person who chooses to love someone of her or his same gender – is solidly sealed, in a unique way, through this exchange between child and parent.

The genre of letter-writing may be particularly suited for this type of conversation because it necessarily puts some space between the writer and reader. It is, in effect, a conversation at a distance, and the person or people that the writer is talking to cannot break in. So we had the space and the time to craft language in letters with loving sensitivity, straight honesty and careful logic that reflected years of feeling and thought. As for Katherine's parents, they too had space to digest, to reflect on their own beliefs and to feel the variety of emotions that would most likely erupt for any parent. A letter meant that an instantaneous response was not demanded, something that physical presence would require, even if that response were silence or simply to walk away. With a letter, nothing more is demanded of the person at the other end than that they are there, listening. With space and time, Katherine's father, then seventy-one years old, wrote his own letter back. Such was its content and tone that we both felt compelled to continue the conversation through two additional letters, one from each of us.

Here they are, then, in sequence and without interruption, a conversation between daughter and parents, parents and daughters.

Sunday
12 January 1992
The Shanty

Dearest Mom and Dad,

I have been thinking about writing this letter to you for almost a month, ever since Suzie told me on the phone that while in France this past time, Mark told you he is gay. Needless to say, that came as a surprise to me since we had no discussion about it while you were here. I suppose, though, that above all I was relieved to hear that he told you and you – as I would expect – have accepted the explicit revelation with abundant love, though not without a mixture of other thoughts and feelings too.

My relief stems from the fact that not only do you know about Mark, but that it also challenges me to tell you that I, too, live a sexual orientation that is counter to our culture. I have never been happy with labels, so I'm not going to use them now. Perhaps that's part of my own protest to the stereotyping and judgements of our society. It's also part of my own inability to identify with anything publicly identified as homosexual or lesbian.

I have many feelings and thoughts that I want to tell you now, but it's very difficult to know where to begin and, of course, impossible to put it all in a letter. I have, of course, wanted to tell you for years, and in many implicit ways I tried. I presume this is not a surprise to you, though I am quite clear about the difference between my telling someone, and they knowing without my telling. I want you to know how much I appreciate your not asking – perhaps it was prompted by fear, like the fear I always carried whenever I thought about telling you. But I also believe that it was because you accepted me and love me and respected my choice to remain silent.

Ultimately, it's not good for one to remain silent about the heart of one's identity. And so, I've lived with the effects of that and often think that I ought to have more courage and let the whole world know. But then I think that I fight so many battles of injustice, I just don't want to take one more on – and as for so many others – being publically 'out' can jeopardise so much, especially financial security and all that we've built at The Shanty. So, this is just a trace of the kinds of thoughts and feelings that I carry every day because of oppression.

Much more personally, of course, there's a part of me that feels guilty that I never told you. We are so close on everything else – I've really told you absolutely everything else about my life as the years have gone on. And I sometimes felt so dishonest with you – especially on a couple of occasions that I still recall. That really was the worst part – the dishonesty when I was so honest about everything else. I also feel badly that I've been able to tell many other people before you. But you two were the greatest risk. I loved you the most, so I would fear most losing your love, respect and acceptance. I remember one day that I told you Mom, that I would live with Ann Louise for the rest of my life. That was the closest I ever got, and I took great solace in that I really felt you heard and understood.

So, those – and many more – are the negative, difficult feelings that I have carried for a long time. There is, of course, an extraordinary positive side to it all. In fact, many more positive dimensions than negative ones, and I believe that my life – how I live, love and work – is a testimony to that. I believe that I was born oriented more towards girls and women – I never felt there was any real choice, though of course I tried to go out with boys and men. But this orientation has provided me with infinite richness, happiness and incredible energy to live as I have lived. Though my life has always been filled with struggles, challenges, anxieties and pressures, the love of my family and friends has always given me more than I need. My friendships with women have filled me up – provided me with what I needed to make something of my life. And so, what society rejects and judges as immoral and abnormal in fact has empowered me to be very moral and better than the norm. This I believe, and this is why amidst all the difficulties, I live with consistent happiness and richness.

The positive dimensions of my lifestyle were sustaining me fairly well before I went to Boston College. Katie was very central but eventually I decided I needed to move on. Little did I know then, that going to B.C. would change my life forever because of meeting Ann Louise. I had a pretty good life up to that point, but never had I glimpsed before how rich, full and amazing life could be. Meeting Ann Louise has been the greatest grace/gift of my life. One year after we met, on 16 October 1982 we gathered a few friends together for what we called a 'commitment ceremony' and started our life partnership. We believe that we have one of the most extraordinary partnerships that we've ever seen – and we both feel that our respective parents provided great models.

Ann Louise has helped me to find and love my real self. Because of that, together we have been able to do things I never would have dreamed possible before. I think that she really unlocked something in me. The fundamental peace and love I feel with her – amidst many of the ongoing struggles – provides a stability and security that fuels my love for life and ability to meet its ongoing challenges. I often say 'Heaven couldn't be better than this.' To touch such contentment – every once in a while – is rare I think. What else is life about?

So, this is just a beginning, a start, to do some catching up. I know that you will have – as I do – many mixed feelings. I do hope that your overriding one will be of acceptance and happiness. I hope it won't cause you too much pain. Let me just say for now that I believe that my relative 'success' is *because* of who I am, not in spite of it.

I think you are the *best* parents in the whole world. I love you with all my heart and hope that we have many more years together.

I will be coming to Seattle in the summer with Ann Louise. I am so looking forward to being there without any pressures of work. We can have, if you like, long conversations about all of this. There's so much more to say. Please tell Suzie I wrote and thank her for prompting me.

All my love as always,

Kay

11 July 92

To my daughters –

Kay and Ann Louise

I've wanted to write you now for quite some time concerning your sexual orientation. I also don't particularly like labels, but for lack of better words, sexuality and sexual orientation will have to do.

In some respects the thinking, meditating or praxis has been very beneficial for me. This letter among other things is part of the actions from that meditation.

Both Mother and I expressed our heartfelt support to you immediately [by a long-distance telephone call] and that will never change. You are first and foremost our daughters, and God gave you both to us as a very special gift.

You have given us much pleasure, excitement, true enjoyment and enriched our lives. Yes, we know that you are good in heart and mind. We have always felt that you have led and are leading exemplary role-model lives – and for all of this we truly thank God as we have been singularly blessed. Also, you are part of our family, and they too support you in your sexual orientation.

Yes, it was a little disconcerting to receive this news from both Mark and you at almost the same time. Our support for Mark was also immediate, and his explanations to us too were intelligent and well thought out. I guess when we came home it was a little like waiting for 'the other shoe to drop'. Mom was the hardest hit by your news.

Yes, we've all had to change our thinking and our feelings and have become acutely aware of the circumstances of sexual orientation and also the difficult and agonising situations that you must have gone through and particularly because the world and even our own Church does not accept anything that they do not believe is according to their current standards or norms. Yes, it is a very forefront area of discussion in the United States at this time and particularly since it is an election year. However, more and more we see astonishing evidence and support of public stands on the right of sexual orientation.

Generally speaking, when I am confronted with a problem, I try to get all the facts possible coupled with a lot of research and study and then try to reach what for me is a reasonable conclusion. However, I have not researched homosexuality, and I am not sure that I ever will. For me it is enough for my children and my personal physician to tell me that it is not a matter of choice and that it is no one's fault and that people with a different sexual orientation than mine are good people. Also, my family and my daughters are still my family and my daughters, and that will never change!

Yes, we will discuss this when you are home, but suffice it to say that Mother and I have already made our decision, and yes we will stand up and be counted with you. All through history men have loved other men and women have loved other women and have lived together and taken oaths of fidelity to one another even to the death. However, if I have a problem with homosexuality, it is not in accepting the sexual orientation but it would relate to the sexual practices just as I have always felt about some of the sexual practices of heterosexuals and primarily because of my education in the natural law. Perhaps you may enlighten me in this regard.

However, this I must insist upon, that both of you do not have any feelings of guilt for not having told us sooner. You are completely absolved in this, and, in God's good grace, this was the right time.

Remember that I have a prayer in front of me every day that says –

> God grant me the serenity
> To accept the things I cannot change
> Courage to change the things I can
> And Wisdom to know the difference.

Welcome home daughters –

With all our love,

Mom and Dad

25 July 1992

The Shanty

Dearest Dad and Mom,

When I saw the large envelope in the post from Seattle, I must admit that I felt some anxiety as I opened it. I know that you support me and love me, and that you love Ann Louise, but I wasn't sure if I felt ready to hear your more extended reflections on my sexual orientation and life partnership with Ann Louise.

So, perhaps you can imagine my sense of relief, more importantly, my profound gratitude for your huge embrace of us across the waters. I hope that you have some idea of the way in which your response is so healing, so inspiring and so real. It is more than I could have imagined, though not untypical of the ways in which you both – in your very different styles – have offered a kind of parental love that continues to build me up from the inside out. This is such an enormous gift. I am reminded now of all the times growing up when I felt so proud to bring my friends home, especially to our dinner table. I knew that you, Mom, would demonstrate an affectionate and warm interest in my friends. I knew that you would be able to talk to them on their level. They appreciated that and often told me how smart you were and how included they felt in conversation with you. My friends were equally impressed with the ways in which you were involved in my life, whether it was through being President of the Mother's Club at St. Luke's (remember those days??!), by your presence at my softball games or by always being there when I sang in the choir or participated in a speech tournament.

And you, dear Dad. Your energy, your intellectual capacity and your interest too in whatever was going on, at my school or in other parts of my life, made my growing up an easier journey than it seemed so many of my friends and aquaintances had. One of the highlights, of course, was when you stepped in to lead Holy Names through one of its first major financial crises and put together a successful business plan for them, as well as took the Chair of the first-ever lay board of the school. One of my proudest moments was when you were the guest of honour at my graduation – as a way of Holy Names acknowledging your leadership and generosity – especially as you handed out the diplomas to all of my classmates, including, of course, myself! I remember, too, the article Sr Marianne Therese wrote about you after that period in order to express her appreciation as principal of the school. She titled it, 'A Man for All Seasons' – how apt.

Coming back to the present, I am, of course, distressed Mom that this news is difficult for you. I appreciate your honesty, above all. I wonder if you might be able to talk to me, at some point, about some of the things that you find upsetting. I am hoping we will have time for this during our visit next month.

Dad, I want to say to you that I was especially moved, and grateful for, your words regarding the fact that – for you – this news is not akin to other problems you have faced and, as such, you have no need to 'research it' in order to find a 'solution'. Instead, you accept the reasoned views of your children who have first-hand experience and the wisdom of your doctor. Underneath this response, I think, lies your willingness to privilege the interpretive viewpoint of those of us who are in the minority, or those of us who have not had access to influence the viewpoints of those in authority, especially the men who make up what is called the 'teaching magisterium of the Church.'

Your willingness to do so, in my view, is comparable to those theologians in Latin America – like Gustavo Gutiérrez – who had the courage to say to the Church, 'you should listen to the views of the poor. They are interpreting the gospel in a different way than the rich and educated have done down through the centuries.' Or it is similar to those feminist theologians who are arguing that 'women's experiences and viewpoints' provide us with new insights on the nature of the human person, as well as how humanity experiences the divine or how we should remember the stories of women in the Scriptures as well as the stories of men.

What I am saying here is that new knowledge is being discovered every day about what it means to be human, and this is not coming simply from the scientists. It also comes from the reflected experience of those who – for whatever reason – have not had similar opportunities to influence or contribute to the 'accepted' or 'traditional' wisdom on what it means to be a man, or what it means to be a woman, or what 'normal' love between two people is, or how we ought to make ethical decisions in our lives.

This brings me to the question you raise in your letter, Dad, about the natural law. Let me express my gratitude, first of all, that you are open to hearing my views on this issue. To me this demonstrates once again your vital intellectual curiosity, your willingness to learn new things and your commitment to being a reflective Catholic as an *expression* of your fidelity rather than as a challenge to it.

I count it a blessing in my life to have had a Jesuit education, following in your footsteps. I am humbled by your request that I 'enlighten' you. As it happens, I am reviewing some of the philosophical and theological literature on the natural law as part of my preparations to teach an ethics course in Trinity, so let me try to outline some of the key issues here and how they relate to the ethical question of sexual practices, be they – as you say – heterosexual or homosexual.

I suspect that when you studied philosophy at Gonzaga in the forties, you might have learned that the natural law tradition had its roots in the Roman Republic from thinkers like Cicero. They proposed that the natural universe is governed by laws or moral principles that can be discerned by reason. They then argued that ethical decisions could be made by reflection on human nature. Their view of human nature was derived from understandings of anthropology or philosophy in their day. So, the crucial question was – and still is – what *is* human nature? If we can know what is natural, this we can choose as good, and it also tells us what is unnatural or evil, and this we should avoid.

What you may have learned, too, is that the natural law has been understood in a variety of ways down through history. Aristotle was a big proponent of the natural law as a source for ethical judgement, However, some of Aristotle's judgements regarding the nature of some human persons is now considered by most modern people as inaccurate and unacceptable. For example, Aristotle argued that, according to the natural law, women are inferior to men and that barbarians, slaves and women are naturally incapable of independent moral judgement and, therefore, are justly subject to the authority of male citizens. There were other philosophers at the time who disagreed with him, on the basis of their understanding of the human person. These natural lawyers insisted that *all* human beings are equal in their ability to make moral decisions.

One of my points here, Dad, is that there are different understandings of the natural law even at one point in time, and the basis of these differences reside in how the question, 'What *is* human nature?' is answered.

As you know, I think, natural law was reinterpreted again by Thomas Aquinas in the thirteenth century, and his views still largely determine the ethical pronouncements by the Catholic magisterium today. Aquinas's theory of natural law is rooted in Aristotelian philosophy and the fourth-century understanding of physical science that underpins much of Aristotle's notions of human nature. This is a critical point to remember, I think, when we come to our contemporary period. Why do I say this? Well, if Aquinas's theory of natural law dictates that certain practices are unnatural, then we must be sure that we *accept* his understanding of human nature before we accept his ethical analysis upon which it is based.

So, what were his views on sexual practices? He believed that a sexual act – of any kind – violates nature (or is 'unnatural') if it is *unreproductive*. So, any sexual practice other than sexual intercourse between a man and a woman is unnatural (because it is not procreative), and sex outside marriage is wrong because only marriage provides the moral context within which a child can be conceived. The purpose of marriage in his natural-law theory is procreation, and pleasure without procreation is meaningless. (I don't know how he would advise an elderly couple who wish to marry – this may point to an area where his, and the Church's, rationality breaks down.) Most moral theologians today, Dad, reject this exclusively biological understanding of human sexuality because the relational dimension is absent. Most moral theologians would argue that the nature of the human person is centred in our ability to love, as well as to reason, and that human behaviour that expresses or supports love between two individuals – especially within a sexually intimate relationship – is good and natural. They do not view that it is essential for every sexual act to be procreative in order to be good.

There's so much more to say here, Dad. I could also talk about the fact that the Catholic Church's teaching on the immorality of the use of artificial contraception (contained in *Humanae Vitae*) is rooted in the same natural-law principles as is its teaching on homosexuality. If one uses artificial contraception, it prevents the biological procreative possibility of heterosexual intercourse. That's why they still deem it to be wrong. How many Catholics (or Catholic theologians) today accept the Church's teaching on this? Most argue that there is nothing wrong with its use, that the nature of sexual intimacy is not essentially and only about having kids. If we apply the same logic to sexual intimacy between gay people, then it stands that these practices may also be good and natural.

In conclusion, Dad and Mom, I do believe in the use of moral principles to assist us in making good choices and in living an ethical life. I also believe in the power of the Christian story to teach us the meaning of love, fidelity and God's creative activity within our world, especially as it is expressed in the lives of those who choose to be life partners. I accept the Church's teaching that our own conscience – as long as it is informed and I am faithful to doing so – is the final arbitrer in the making of ethical choices and that the '*sensus fidelium*' (the common sense of faith-filled people) is equally important to the teaching magisterium in these issues, it offers the necessary checks and balances.

These are some of the reasons why, then, I know that my love for and my life with Ann Louise enables me to live as God intended and that I am surprised by joy, daily, in my life with her. I hope you will find these reflections helpful. It means the world to me that you asked.

I love you both with all my heart.

We'll be home, soon.

Kay

The Shanty

25 July 1992

My dear Bob and Kathie,

Although I don't wish to intrude in any way on the correspondence between yourselves and Kay, however, as your response was to both of us, I will send a short note.

Initially, let me express my deep appreciation for your naming of me as your 'daughter'. I always recall that moment during my first visit to your home in 1982, when you stated that I would be your 'adopted daughter'. I felt embraced by such a generous gesture; it meant so much, especially as I was still grieving the recent loss of my own parents and in some strange way had felt, even in adulthood, 'orphaned'.

Your response to Kay's letter contained few surprises; rather, it confirmed you as the people I have come to know, love and respect over the years. Your commitment to family has always been unequivocal, and your unconditional love of each of your children has always been evident, despite their different personalities. I have observed when I'm staying in your home that on most days you talk to each one of them, which, I surmise, is not the norm even in close-knit families. I've observed especially Kathie's delight when the phone rings and it's one of the children checking in.

The voice of affirmation in your letter is reflective of a quality I have come to know in you both. Your ability to affirm and appreciate, to focus on the positive and to encourage has enriched and supported our life together. I often think that affirmation is a virtue and you both certainly exemplify its practice.

While Kay will address your questions in her response, I just want to acknowledge and state how much I admire your reflective approach to the issues our sexual identity has raised for you. Your attitude of openness and your willingness to consider other arguments as they present themselves is exemplary. I do believe that there would be a lot less fear and prejudice in the world if all people were willing to adopt this rational, reflective approach to matters related to sexual morality.

I think we all agree that there is no life worth living but 'the examined life'. Over the years we too have had to reflect on the teachings we received and place them in dialogue with our conscience. From our perspective, the Catholic Church teaches that love is its highest value. Our own experience of a life together full of love and happiness dissolves any lingering doubt that some abstract man-made teaching from times past holds greater authority or authentic truth. Thankfully, there are a growing number of theorists, including philosophers and theologians, whose teachings concur with our own reflected experience – that there are many different ways of being sexual and living in loving relationships.

It will be good to meet up soon again and continue this conversation if you so wish. Until we meet take good care of yourselves and of each other.

My love to you both,

Ann Louise

13

JUSTICE FOR OURSELVES

We planned an exciting trip over Christmas and new year, 2001–2. Our close friends Toni Ryan and Peadar Kirby were on sabbatical in Santiago, Chile, as Peadar was lecturing in the Pontifical Catholic University there. They were well used to the South American continent, and Peadar had written a couple of books comparing socio-economic developmental approaches of Latin American countries with Ireland's. They wanted us to come and see; we accepted the invitation with enthusiasm. Our membership in the Bootleggers' Club in Dublin added a special excitement to this opportunity – we could try our luck at climbing the Andes!

Two years previously, Ann Louise had returned to a full-time position in St Pat's in the Department of Education and, in addition to lecturing, had set up the Centre for Educational Disadvantage. In mid-2000, the Minister for Education had also appointed her to establish and chair a state board, the National Education Welfare Board, so her professional hands were more than full once again. Katherine had worked on several public-policy research projects, recently completing a major one for the Equality Authority of Ireland. The Minister for Justice appointed her as a commissioner for the newly established Irish Human Rights Commission in 2001, so Katherine's workload was also ample. An Cosán, with a professional staff of thirty-five people, developed an independence of our direct involvement as it built new programmes, courses and services for growing numbers of adults, young people and children. We felt it was an opportune time for an extended break.

The prospect of taking such a long flight and being in such a faraway land prompted us to prepare for the trip in a way we had not done before. Our 'last wills and testaments', drawn up after purchasing The Shanty, noted the co-ownership of this as our family home, so we assumed that the surviving partner's ownership would be protected without any inheritance-tax liability. The wills did not include, however, the farmhouse we had purchased and reconstructed in County Kerry, and so we thought it time to update them, just in case anything might happen to us. We telephoned Phil O'Hehir (who had decided to return to lawyering after overseeing the brilliant completion of An Cosán) and set up an appointment. While we weren't that bothered about money, we had acquired the Kerry property to provide for Katherine's pension. Because she had only part-time appointments in Trinity, and the National Women's Council had no employee pension scheme at the time, Katherine had few financial resources reserved for the future. How shocked we were, then, to discover that this property, which we also co-owned, would be taxed differently than if we were a married couple. We were informed that, regardless of how the title was held, tax was payable on the survivor's half of the inheritance. This would not apply to a married couple because inheritance tax between husband and wife had been abolished. In our case, or for any non-married couple, the survivor was allowed €15,840 and would then be taxed on the balance of one half of the property. For us, the financial implications of this law meant that the survivor would, in effect, have to sell the property to pay the tax. What we thought was our financial security went up in smoke that day. We felt extremely distressed and angry. It simply wasn't fair.

We went off to Chile feeling greatly unsettled, and, though our visit was marvellous in so many ways, it was an ongoing challenge for us to leave aside thoughts about how we should respond to these new-found revelations when we returned home. This blatant denigration of our lifelong love and partnership and simultaneous denial of the inherent dignity of our very selves, gnawed away at us so much that by the end of

January we decided to take stock regarding the best route forward. We talked at length about whether or not some kind of legal challenge to these laws would help to change things. We thought long and hard about the fact that, though we were 'out' to a wide circle of friends and colleagues, we had not participated in any form of lesbian and gay activism in Ireland. We admired the courage and political astuteness of people like Ailbhe Smyth (lecturer in UCD and founder of the Women's Education Research and Resource Centre), Ursula Barry (lecturer in the School of Social Justice at UCD and lesbian activist since the 1980s), Joni Crone (arts consultant and first lesbian to appear publicly with Gay Byrne on 'The Late Late Show' in the 1980s), Senator David Norris (whose fifteen-year legal battle resulted in the decriminalisation of homosexuality in 1993), and Christopher Robson and Kieran Rose of GLEN (the Irish Gay and Lesbian Equality Network that supported Senator Norris's case). They, along with many others, had put their professional and personal reputations at risk by advocating gay and lesbian rights in the public domain where homophobic prejudice – supported by Irish domestic law – was rampant.

Perhaps our turn had come.

To be perfectly honest, though the origins of our activism in this regard had to do with tax and inheritance laws, the issue of money was never going to be the primary motivating factor. We had lived lives that reaped relatively little financial resources, given our professional education and middle-class standing. The status quo rarely rewards the critical or creative voice. We're not trying to say that money is not important – in fact, our financial security is extremely important, and we do not want anyone else, not even the State, to have to provide for us in our later years (especially if the reason is that the State blocked us from providing for ourselves). The deepening of our desire to do something that could bring about change had more to do with the fact that our lifelong partnership was being denied proper legal recognition. We knew that many had fought for anti-discrimination legislation in relation to sexual orientation and had been relatively successful with the introduction of the Employment Equality Act in 1998 and the Equal Status Act in 2000. However, little had been done for the recognition of life partnerships. As we looked around at what was happening in other countries, we discovered that Denmark had legalised same-sex civil unions in 1981! Norway did the same in 1993, and Sweden followed in 1995. The Netherlands, Germany and France trailed the Scandinavian countries soon afterwards.

By continuing this research, we observed that in these countries – and many others, including the United States, Canada, South Africa, Belgium, Spain – public debates between civil society and the law-makers about the rights of same-sex couples filled their newspapers, other media outlets and academic journals. While the Equality Authority of Ireland had established an advisory group on lesbian, gay and bisexual issues in December of 1999, the public silence about these issues in Ireland depressed us. If one were to review the *Irish Times* archives today, one would discover that the first time there is any mention of rights for Irish same-sex couples was *December 2002* when the editorial commented on the fact that the British Government intended to extend to gay couples the property and inheritance rights afforded to married couples and that the Equality Authority's group had endorsed similar changes in Irish law. Over the next two years, you could count on one hand the number of articles published in that same newspaper on this topic. From where we sat, in early 2002, and with the knowledge we had about the very tenuous relationship between recommendations in policy documents and subsequent, substantive change, we discerned that little was going to happen unless there was a grass-roots mobilisation to bring pressure to bear on law-makers or some kind of legal challenge within the courts. This is how things had been changed in other jurisdictions, and so we assessed that the same would be true for Ireland.

So much for what was going on in our heads! For the next couple of months we talked endlessly about how we felt and what it might mean for us to do something in the public arena. This talking helped to deal with a myriad of conflictual feelings (Freud was right about talking!). Ann Louise's cultural upbringing did not encourage putting oneself out there; she was, and is, an extremely private person. While Katherine's American origins supported an ease in public directness, she was surprised to discover that cultural homophobia in both the United States and in Ireland had seeped deeper into her sense of self – more than she had realised. Feeling these emotions, living with them, analysing them filled our days. The personal journey of what we later called 'consciousness-raising in ourselves' had begun. We were shedding, in a much deeper way than before, and ever so slowly, the negative conditioning from both our cultures that there is only one real way to be a sexual, relational human being. And, of course, one's relational, sexual identity is at the core of who one is as a human being. It's in the centre, it's in the heart, from which every choice, action and loving invitation flows. It makes us who we are. So, we had to come face to face with the fear of simply saying who we were and how we loved, knowing that there was and still is a societal context – fuelled by religions that are not free – that shouts 'No' or 'Evil' or 'Abnormal', often with professional or socially negative consequences. In *Coming Out: Irish Gay Experiences,* a collection of forty-one stories of lesbian and gay people, the editor, Glen O'Brien, refers to these feelings:

> In many of these stories there is the journey, sometimes over half a lifetime, to come to perceive ourselves to be 'beautiful' and to allow ourselves trust our instincts as to our 'rightness'. Unless you are gay you don't experience the awful weight of history, both secular and religious, both past and present, that works to convince us that in the very depths of our being there dwells no 'rightness'.

The reader may ask: But didn't you have all that sorted by then? Well, we thought we had! But shame and cultural disapproval are powerful tools to keep people who are 'different' down, more powerful, perhaps, than most realise.

Maybe that is why freedom lives on the other side of fear.

At the beginning of April, Katherine telephoned the Equality Authority to say that we wanted to find a way to legalise our life partnership of twenty years, and that we were willing to undertake the necessary journey in order to achieve this end. A gentleman in the legal section responded by sounding quite excited about what this could mean and asked us to send in a letter with a formal request for the Authority's assistance. This we did the next day. We stated clearly that our primary desire was to challenge the denial of our human right to have our life partnership acknowledged in law. Second, we declared that we wished to contest the inequality and discriminatory practice of the current inheritance-taxation laws as applied to those who are a non-married couple.

Two weeks passed slowly with no response from the Authority. Katherine decided to phone and was told by the same gentleman that he would get back to her. Two more weeks passed slowly. Katherine phoned again, this time to be told that, no, the Authority couldn't do anything for us and we should go to a solicitor if we wanted to proceed. What had happened over the course of the month? Surely they could at least have invited us in to discuss the matter? How distressed and angry we felt after that exchange. Having put ourselves out there, still with strong feelings of tentativeness and fear, a door that was supposed to be friendly and supportive slammed in our face. That's what it felt like, and it required considerable inner strength to recover from that first of many, many barriers at personal and professional levels to regroup and consider what to do next. It mystified both of us and, indeed, made us feel quite alone, that the statutory organisation established to promote equality could do nothing for us.

Still in a quandary some weeks later about how to proceed, Katherine happened to meet Niall Crowley, CEO of the Equality Authority, for a drink in the Stephen's Green Hotel at the end of the work day. She cherished his friendship; they had fought many battles together when both worked in the social-partnership domain. While feeling awkward about raising the issue with him, Katherine decided that she would. At least he might be able to offer some personal advice as to what to do next. When Katherine told Niall what had happened, he responded with surprise and embarrassment. His honesty and humility marked the strong leader that he is. He asked Katherine if he could consider this as an 'official complaint' and if she would send to him a copy of the letter that we had written to the Authority. He promised to investigate the matter and to ask Eilish Barry, head of their legal section, if she would agree to meet us. If they couldn't help us by taking a case, they could at least assist us in figuring out what other options might be available to us.

Late in the summer, we met with Eilish in the Equality Authority offices. She explained that the Equality Tribunal (the sister agency that conducts legal investigations) could take up our case only if there were issues that related to the equality legislation because the statutory remit of the Equality Authority and Tribunal are limited to ensuring enforcement of the Employment Equality and Equal Status Acts of the Irish Government. These pieces of legislation prohibit discrimination in employment, and in the provision of goods and services (including education). So, on the face of it, our claims with regard to discrimination in taxation issues and discrimination in having no legal opportunity to recognise our life partnership might not be under their remit. However, given the Authority's responsibility to promote partnership rights for lesbian and gay couples and the possibility that provisions related to pensions might fall within the legal category of 'services', she took our full details and agreed to a first step of investigating our claims by preparing a legal brief for a junior counsel to conduct research and to prepare a legal opinion. Eilish's expertise, warmth and sensitivity made such a big difference to us. We thought that something might finally begin to happen. She told us that we had several years ahead of us, though, if we really were determined to see this through. We only half-heard this prediction; our optimism shielded us from the time barrier.

Months and months went by with little word from the Authority. Their legal section was swamped with work, given its limited resources. We wondered if there was anything else we could do, especially if the legal opinion – when it finally did come in – might find that the Authority could not help us to pursue the primary issues of our case. We started to inquire about other routes to progress our case. Katherine telephoned Ailbhe Smyth, long-time friend of ours and Co-Chair of the National Lesbian and Gay Federation, and she agreed to meet Katherine in the Westbury hotel for a pre-Christmas drink and to hear what was on our minds. As always, Ailbhe was warm, supportive and strategic in her advice. She recommended that we speak with Christopher Robson (of GLEN) because she knew that he was working with David Norris on a 'Domestic Partnership Bill' that David wanted to introduce into the Seanad (Senate).

Later that week, Katherine talked to Christopher, and he outlined the nature of the Bill they were working on and asked if we might consider putting on hold our desire to take a case in the light of their efforts to get legislative change. The Bill, however, described 'domestic partnership' as a relationship for the purpose of organising a couple's life (mixed gender or of the same sex) and that, similar to a commercial partnership, its duration was a matter for the partners to determine. This didn't sound at all like the nature of our life partnership; it sounded, instead, like a business contract between two people who co-habit. Further, it was not apparent from the conversation if the ideas for the Bill came from a few individuals or if they represented the wishes of a large number of gay and lesbian people. There appeared to be no grass-roots mobilisation behind this effort. And, of course, David's independence as a senator, as distinct from being a member of government, did not place him in a strong position for getting such a Bill enacted. Katherine and Christopher promised to stay in touch on the matter.

We decided not to stop our own efforts to find a legal route. We continued our wait for the Equality Authority research; at this stage, it was May 2003, a little over a year since we had first contacted them. One evening at dinner with two good friends, Monica O'Connor and Mary Dorcey, we shared with them our desire to seek legal recognition of our partnership and expressed our frustration about the long wait for the research. They immediately recommended that we speak with Ivana Bacik, barrister-at-law and Reid Professor of Criminal Law at Trinity College. Ivana was well known for her progressive views on issues related to homosexuality and she is a strong, brilliant feminist. Maybe she could help us. Though swamped with exam corrections and a hundred other things, Ivana agreed to meet Katherine in a coffee shop on Dawson Street after lectures one morning. They spoke about the possible legal case and agreed to meet again when the research from the Equality Authority was completed. Two months later, having heard no progress from the Authority, Katherine met Ivana again, and she agreed in principle to take our case as junior counsel and to ask Gerard Hogan, her colleague at Trinity and Ireland's foremost constitutional lawyer, to join our legal team as the Senior Counsel. Ivana offered her services *pro bono* – without charge because of the huge public importance of such a case – and promised to ask Mr Hogan if he would join us on the same basis. With a mixture of elation and relief, Katherine went back to The Shanty to telephone Ann Louise (who was in Vancouver, British Columbia, giving a paper at a conference) with the news.

Ann Louise responded with gratitude and courage. We both felt overwhelmed by Ivana's generosity and decisiveness. We believed that – though we would be facing an enormous battle with the State and, possibly, the Irish public – Ivana's expertise, commitment to the issues and sensitivity to the personal impact this could have upon both of us put us in the strongest possible position to move forward. As we continued our long-distance conversation, though, we reminded each other of the potential risk that Ann Louise might face regarding her job. The Irish Employment Equality Act, 1998, provides protection against discrimination for people in employment, regardless of sexual orientation. However, there is a famous 'opt out' clause, as we call it, in the legislation. Towards the end of the Act (Section 37.1) it says:

A religious, educational or medical institution which is under the direction or control of a body established for religious purposes or whose objectives include the provision of services in an environment which promotes certain religious values shall not be taken to discriminate against a person for the purposes of this [Act, and that the institution may ... take] action which is reasonably necessary to prevent an employee or a prospective employee from undermining the religious ethos of the institution.

In effect, if the authorities of a religious institution deem that the sexual identity of an employee undermines its religious ethos, they can dismiss that person from her or his job and that person has no legal recourse to the claim of discrimination. Irish law, in this case, *allows* discriminatory treatment. The Roman Catholic Archbishop of Dublin was the official manager of Ann Louise's college of the university. In this capacity he held considerable administrative power. For example, he had to approve all academic appointments. Though formally a college of Dublin City University, the governing body of St Pat's still answered to the Archbishop and the ethos of the institution promoted Roman Catholic values. Consequently, it appeared to us that the Archbishop, upon coming to knowledge of Ann Louise's sexual identity through our pursuit of a case, could dismiss Ann Louise from her employment of twenty-seven years.

Ann Louise's position was not unlike hundreds, perhaps thousands, of other lesbian or gay teachers throughout the country working in primary and secondary schools and third-level colleges owned and managed by the Catholic Church. Over the years, this section of the (in)equality legislation has hindered countless teachers and lecturers from living open lives – they do not feel free to be themselves in public. They literally fear for their livelihoods, and their inner spirit must constantly fend off this denigration of themselves and their most intimate relationships. We do not exaggerate. We know many of them. This is the reality in twenty-first-century Ireland. People's sexual identity can cost them their jobs.

We decided to check out our concern with Ivana, and, by email correspondence, she confirmed our suspicion:

16 July 2003

Dear Katherine,

You have raised a significant and potentially serious issue! You are right in your reading of section 37 (1) of the Act ... Under this section arguably you don't have a right of protection against dismissal where it was carried out to uphold the religious ethos. So that is something you should consider. . . . Maybe now we have more understanding as to why this sort of case has not been taken by anyone else before ... Best wishes, Ivana

Katherine forwarded this e-mail to Ann Louise in Vancouver and went to bed filled with distress and fear once again. On 17 July 2003, she wrote in her diary:

This morning I woke up with a feeling of dread. Yes, if we go forward with this case, this jeopardises our financial security significantly. But then I worked through it and felt OK. Really, the weight of the discrimination needs to be challenged head-on. And, how can we possibly move beyond the bullying, violence and discrimination in the education system if teachers can be dismissed for being openly lesbian or gay? It's up to Ann Louise. I will do it, or I will absolutely respect her choice not to do it. We could have two big cases instead of one! What seemed mammoth but possible before – well the mountain to climb just got a whole lot higher.

As Ann Louise read Ivana's email six thousand miles away from her beloved Katherine, she thought about a lot of things: her own fierce protection of her privacy over the years, the current controversy raging within the Anglican Churches over the ordination of gay bishops (threatening the disbandment of the worldwide communion of the Churches), her two former legal battles with the Dublin Catholic Archdiocese and the college over her employment. She also considered the recent media coverage on a publication by the National Economic and Social Forum that advocated multiple partnership rights for same-sex couples, yet with no willingness by the Government Coalition to do anything about it. Foremost in her mind and heart, however, was her awareness of how much Katherine wanted to take a case. It had almost become an obsession with her, as she swung between naked fear and a passionate desire to push for justice for ourselves as well as countless others, especially lesbian and gay young people.

We spoke later that day, again by long-distance. Ann Louise said 'Yes. Yes, let's do it.' A deliberate yet slow sense of peace filled us both, our connection palpable across the many miles. We knew there was no turning back and that it was OK.

The next morning, Katherine emailed Ivana to confirm our decision and then telephoned Phil O'Hehir to ask if she would be willing to join our legal team as solicitor. We trusted Phil – because of our friendship with her and knowledge of her – that she would always have our best interests at the top of her priorities and that her thoroughness, intellect and strategic capacity would help us to steer a safe and accurate path through the stormy times ahead. Phil responded by affirming our decision with great respect and by saying, 'I would love to work on it.' She checked with Kevin Brophy, the owner and managing partner of her firm, and they both agreed to take the case on a *pro-bono* basis. We decided to hold our first meeting with Phil *after* the Equality Authority research was in as we had word that it would be ready by the beginning of September.

In early September we did receive the research brief and had a meeting with Eilish Barry to discuss its findings. The report from the Equality Authority came to some disturbing conclusions and some encouraging ones. First, it stated that the Equal Status Act of Ireland *could not be used* to support our case because discrimination with regard to same-sex partnership recognition and partnership rights *is based in domestic law*. Section 14 of the Equal Status Act declares that the Act cannot be used to challenge any forms of discrimination that are rooted in other domestic laws. So, for example, because Irish taxation and inheritance laws do not entitle same-sex couples to the same rights as opposite-sex couples, the Equal Status Act cannot be used to overturn these laws; it can be used only to follow up on breaches of laws that already exist in Ireland. Once again, we hit up against a serious limitation of the 'equality' legislation of Ireland! However, the report noted that in other jurisdictions equality and personal-rights guarantees contained in their constitutions *had been relied upon* to challenge discrimination against same-sex couples and to argue for a right to recognition in law for the status of same-sex couples, and, in many cases, these arguments had been successful. If judges in other jurisdictions had done it, was it not possible that Irish justices could do the same? Finally, it concluded that we *could* take a *constitutional* case – most likely to Supreme Court level – challenging legislation that discriminated against us on the basis of Article 40.1 of the Constitution which guarantees persons 'equality before the law' and also on the basis of Article 40.3 which protects the rights of privacy and dignity for all Irish citizens. In other words, the research argued that while we could not use the Equal Status Act to pursue a legal recognition of our relationship, 'good sound arguments can be advanced in support of the recognition of the constitutional rights of same-sex couples'.

On the basis of the research findings, the Equality Authority advised us that we should consider taking a constitutional case. We assured them that we were considering this action and that we would stay in touch. A week later, when we met with Phil O'Hehir in her office, she took instructions from us regarding our desire to take the case. During that meeting we discovered two significant things we were unaware of before. Phil outlined to us that, because we owned a second property in Ireland, upon the death of one of us, the surviving partner would be taxed not only on her inheritance of half the value of the holiday property (which we already knew), but that she would also be taxed on her inheritance of The Shanty, our family home. So, while we *thought* that, as the law currently stood, at least the surviving partner would not have to pay tax on the 'family home', now, because we owned a second property, this protection, or benefit, or right – whatever you want to call it – no longer applied to us. It did apply, of course, to heterosexual married couples. We were appalled. The bottom line for us, then, meant that upon the death of one of us not only would the surviving partner have to cope with inestimable grief, she would be forced to sell both our family home and our holiday property in order to pay capital acquisitions and inheritance tax. As we write, this massive unfairness and discrimination against us, and all other co-habiting lesbian and gay couples, *still* stands. This is the law of the land!

And if that wasn't enough, Phil also outlined another equally distressing reality. Should we decide to take the case, and should we lose, the possibility existed that the judges could order costs against us and we could be left with a bill of €250,000 or more! All she could give us was a rough estimate. She, and countless other lawyers and ordinary citizens throughout the land, would view this as a case of huge 'public interest', and often in cases of such public interest the judiciary would not ask for costs from the individuals involved; however, this did not always happen.

We took a long walk along the quays after that meeting, with much heaviness in our hearts. On the one hand, we had discovered deeper layers of discrimination against us and other lesbian and gay people than we were previously aware of and, on the other hand, we faced another hurdle, another financial risk. Not only could Ann Louise lose her job, we could be faced with a big bill at the end of it all. The darkness of the early autumn day came down upon us.

What was it, then, that lifted us beyond these deadly realities? Why did we choose – again – to face the fear and to keep moving in the direction we had chosen two years previously?

Once upon a time, in the town of Boston, one young woman met another young woman, and they fell in love. A magnificent energy was unleashed that only intimate love contains, and they believed then – and now – that they could do anything together.

We believed then – and now – that our relationship not only constantly gives birth to our best selves, but that our committed, lifelong partnership is productive of our best for those we love and work with. We believe that it is positive too for an Irish society – so it may be filled with more justice and more equality than it holds now. The public silence on the lifelong love of lesbian and gay people needed to be broken. And statements from the Vatican that have added to prejudice and heterosexism needed to be exposed. For example, in the document 'Unions between Homosexual Persons', Joseph Cardinal Ratzinger wrote: 'Those who would move from tolerance to the legitimisation of specific rights for cohabiting homosexual persons need to be reminded that the approval or legalisation of evil is something far different from the toleration of evil.' These are wounding words. We had a right to demand that our human dignity was respected, not undermined, in public Church documents. Furthermore, the complete lack of any kind of partnership policies for same-sex couples from the biggest political party in the land, Fianna Fáil, demanded exposure. We felt we had the health, the blessed relationship and the professional standing to be the ones to take this great risk.

14

WHY MARRIAGE?

There is an old-fashioned ring to the word 'providence'. We both can recall our grannies talking about a particular disposition of events that seemed to follow a special unanticipated sequence as being 'providential'. In their world view, the word indicated a divine foresight, a transcendent presence that guided the ordering of otherwise unrelated happenings. Reflecting back on a visit Ann Louise made to British Columbia, Canada, in order to deliver a paper at a conference in early July 2003, we both concur that there was a providential feel to the events that unfolded. Others, of course, would see this as pure coincidence; we, however, would agree with our grannies' interpretation in this instance.

During the conference, Mark, Katherine's brother, rang to say that he would be travelling to Vancouver to act as best man at a wedding. Some days later, as Ann Louise and he shared lunch, Mark revealed that the celebration was for two gay friends, David and Chris, who lived in Seattle. It transpired that they were one of the first couples to come over the border from the United States to avail of the new law in British Columbia opening the institution of marriage to gays and lesbians. Mark described how the wedding had taken place in a beautiful house right by the water overlooking Vancouver Bay. This was the home of the Commissioner of Oaths who performed the ceremony, a woman called Ann Moore. As Mark described the day, his face lit up with happiness. He narrated that the couple were overjoyed as they had reared a son together and now had their own union and their family publicly and legally recognised. In fact, it was their teenage son who had requested that they get married once the opportunity arose so that he could talk about his parents as married just like the other adolescent boys in his school.

It was interesting that it was another child, from Ontario, written about in the papers, who had been at the heart of changing the minds of the people and the legislature. As a lesbian couple were mounting the steps to the court to have their case for marriage heard, a journalist thrust a microphone in front of their nine-year-old son and asked him what it would mean to him if his parents could marry. He replied, 'I think after this no one will be able to say I don't have a real family.' This comment was shown on TV throughout Canada and published in all newspapers. Within days, the Ontario Court of Appeal ruled that the law denying marriage to same-sex couples was unconstitutional as it denied basic human rights and so gay and lesbian coupes were permitted to marry forthwith.

Ann Louise rang Katherine to share the glorious news, and we chatted excitedly, running up an enormous phone bill. Suddenly what we had dreamed of was now possible.

Back in Canada, once word went out that there were no restrictions to this legislation, that is, none of the usual requirements for residency or citizenship, gay and lesbian couples came in their hundreds over the border to get married, intermingling with equal numbers of natives. It was almost too good to be true! Suddenly, a community, which, in every country around the globe had suffered prejudice, abuse and even death, was acknowledged as fully human with all rights accruing. This was an extraordinary moment in our history. The focus now was not on the negative, not on decriminalising homosexual activity; rather, it was on positively honouring homosexual couples by acknowledging that we had as much right as heterosexuals to marry the person we loved. In the newspapers that week, editorial after editorial communicated the same message – marriage equality is not about *minimum* rights; rather, it's about granting gay and lesbian people full rights to choose how they wish to live in relationship. Now, in case anyone tried to change the legislation and block this opportunity for full equality, people who had wanted to get married for years wanted to exercise that right without delay in Canada. The memory of what had happened in Hawaii in 1993 lingered: back then, the Supreme Court agreed with a lesbian couple that on the grounds of sex discrimination it was illegal to prevent them from marrying, but, by 1996, due to a vociferous anti-gay backlash, the decision was reversed by the law-makers.

It is important to state that when we started the journey of seeking full legal recognition of our relationship, our mapped destination was influenced by the cartography of the period. We had been active observers of the gradual concession of gay and lesbian partnership rights starting with Denmark in 1989. Although there were now up to twenty-five nations that offered varying degrees of partnership rights to gay and lesbian couples, whenever we enquired there was always a clear stipulation that no one need apply unless they were either a citizen or a resident of the respective state. Those, like ourselves, who live their difference as a minority in society can sometimes assume the prejudices of the majority, even if that contributes to their own oppression – it's a classic example of internalised oppression. Thus, when lesser rights are offered, such as domestic or civil-partnership rights, many are willing to acquiesce and accept, with gratitude, any advance of rights. This position is often rationalised with a theory of incremental justice: let's be pragmatic and take what we can get now in the hope that '*they*' will give us the choice of full equality later. We understand this position because we were there.

But, as the years passed, we became aware that the claim for civil marriage was the only option that would offer us full equality with all other human beings. It was obvious, of course: separate rights are not equal rights. We would attribute the raising of our own consciousness and desire for marriage to the fact that we had remained careful students of the development of legal recognition of same-sex partnership rights and the more recent opening of the civil institution of marriage to all in certain countries. But Canada was the first country to confer the possibility of marriage without restriction, and Ann Louise just happened to be present for the joyous first week of couples availing of that opportunity – initially in two states, then throughout Canada. It was a time of huge excitement and positive energy. It became a talking point at the conference she was attending, the theme of which was, appropriately, 'Philosophies of Imagination'. This new legislation was, indeed, the outcome of legislators having the courage and capacity to image differently, and without doubt it would change people's image and concept of love and who is permitted to proclaim their love publicly.

Now that the choice to marry had become a reality for us, we felt the need to revisit our earlier conversations and articulate anew the reasons for our own wish to marry. After all, as some would remind us, as if we needed reminding, we did have a celebration some twenty years previously, and we did commit to a lifelong partnership back then, so why marriage? And why now? Perhaps Alice Walker explains it well in her book *In Search of Our Mothers' Gardens* when she advises to keep in mind always the present you are constructing – that it should be the future you want. In the present of 1982, we chose all we could with little realisation that the future would present the option we wanted: marriage.

We were, of course, aware that if we now exercised this option we would face various questions, resistances and critiques and that there would be consequences. For the following two weeks, we set aside time each day just to be together and reflect anew on the importance of this choice for our own relationship, to consider how it would impact on our family and friends and on the wider community within which we live and work. To marry is a public act, unlike our earlier partnership celebration among like-minded friends. We had to balance a desire to take time to pause and reflect with the very real sense of urgency we were both experiencing. We certainly didn't wish to miss this window of opportunity to marry in Canada. What if the legislation was revoked or the usual restrictions on residency or citizenship were suddenly introduced?

In all our deliberations, we were aware, as feminist women, of the current critique of marriage. Why choose to participate in an institution where women had often been treated as unequal partners? In the past, we had both given courses on feminist ethics and had discussed the distinctions between the ideal of marriage and 'patriarchal' marriage, marred by a history of male control and dominance. We'd know and indeed respect the reasons why many feminists feel that the very institution of marriage is irredeemable as it has been constructed by so many societies over the years in the service of male privilege and power and female inequality. We personally know women who have escaped from such marriages and have heard them speak of a life lived in an essentially dependent or self-sacrificingly supportive role that stifled, if not snuffed out, their own growth as self-identified women.

While cognisant of the critique, we remained steadfast in our belief that marriage is a living institution and open to change. We were confident too in our own choice to marry. Understanding the nature, purpose and consequences of marriage, aspiring to live as best we could the ideals of this time-honoured institution, we wished to avail of this opportunity, to celebrate our love and have full legal recognition for all we had nurtured up to this point in our relationship. When heterosexual couples announce that they intend to marry – and they still do in their droves – nobody ever says: But why marriage? Heterosexuals aren't asked to justify their desire to exercise their option as citizens to marry the person they love. They are aware that marriage is a legally binding contract publicly proclaimed. There is an innate acceptance that the institution of marriage is the only institution couples can avail of in this state that is protected under the Constitution with all its rights, responsibilities, duties and privileges. In fact, as all know, the contract of marriage is accorded a special status by our state in Article 41.3.1 of the Constitution, which begins 'The State pledges itself to guard with special care the institution of Marriage …'. As an aside, it is also interesting that nowhere does the Constitution define marriage or explicate which genders are eligible to marry. So, to those who questioned our choice to marry, we'd ask: Why not? Or politely enquire: Why did you marry? Following the usual response: We married because we loved each other and wanted to spend the rest of our lives together, we'd gently reply: Well, in this matter we are like you.

In choosing to marry, we were not setting out with some arrogant notion that we would redeem marriage; however, as two strong women who worked hard to live a relationship of mutuality and respect, we weren't overly concerned that our marriage, once contracted, would fall into the patriarchal trap. Rather, we hoped that we would simply join the number of happily married lesbians and gay men, in countries such as Spain, Belgium, the Netherlands, South Africa, Norway and the states of Massachusetts and California in the USA, and allow a new image emerge against which some institutionalised models of marriage could be measured! And this, of course, brings us to a key point: understandings of marriage have changed radically over time. The institution of marriage isn't a static institution and certainly isn't confined to any one social cultural or historical interpretation. In fact, the early history of marriage in Ireland, the *Cáin Lánamhna*, makes reference to as many as nine forms of sexual union that were recognised, as Fergus Kelly ably reminds us in his scholarly *A Guide to Early Irish Law*. While in some unions women held positions of 'joint authority' where they had contributed as much property at the time of marriage as their spouse, all were marked by hierarchical assumptions that conferred the power and control on males. In times past, marriage was clearly a legal institution negotiated between and among men for their benefit and to ensure their paternity. The very word 'matrimony' was understood as the opportunity for a man to acquire a '*mater*/mother' of his children.

In *Goodbye to Catholic Ireland*, Mary Kenny narrates that in more recent Irish history one issue of concern was the dampening of the desire to marry at all. By the mid-1950s, the decline in marriages was so drastic that it was lamented publicly from the pulpit by various Catholic bishops, including the Bishop of Cork, Cornelius Lucey, who stated that 'Rural Ireland is stricken and dying, and the will to marry on the land is almost gone.' Other bishops berated 'the bachelors for their selfishness and the "old-maids" for being over-cautious.' It was all a bit of an anomaly that bishops, themselves bachelors, were berating their flocks for not getting married while at the same time teaching chastity and control of sexuality with such authority and firmness that people were petrified about 'impure thoughts' – never mind 'impure actions', as they would then have been judged!

Recent history of marriage reflects a much more egalitarian understanding, although church weddings persist in promulgating the notion that marriage is about the reduction of two persons to a union of one. In fact, Ann Louise recalls calling a relation of hers aside before her marriage and pleading that they would not include the increasingly popular ritual in their ceremony where at the beginning the couple light two candles one on either side of the altar and then after the vows are shared these are blown out and together they light one candle. Any notion that two become one in marriage is dangerous; blowing out one identity at the start of a marriage is rather startling – and definitely a bad idea. It belies the question which one remains lit! Anyway, the intervention was unnecessary as this intelligent young woman had no intention of including this ritual; they'd begin as they intended to go forward, as two strong individuals in love and ready to commit to a life together with distinct identities and diverse needs.

Of course, once news of our own marriage became known, we anticipated that there could be resistance from conservative Church quarters, especially from the Irish Roman Catholic Church. But then we would not be looking for a Church blessing or requesting to participate in the sacrament of marriage, so we would not expect that the Church would intrude on our right to exercise our liberty and choose civil marriage. Although, upon reflection, we found it interesting that the Church we so loved in our youth would now, if we had remained members, excluded us from two of its seven sacraments, Holy Orders and Marriage, because of our gender and our sexual identity. Yet this same Church continues to preach that 'There are no more distinctions between Jew and Greek, slave and free, male and female, but all of you are one in Christ Jesus' (Galatians 3:28).

Following these few weeks of deliberation and confirming our desire to exercise our choice to marry, we set off for a break to our home in Kerry at the end of July. As a surprise, Katherine booked an evening in the Smuggler's Inn in Waterville, to celebrate Ann Louise's birthday. Later that evening we took a stroll by moonlight on the strand and agreed to marry. Who proposed first is irrelevant as we both have different versions of that story! But we were both clear we wanted to marry each other. It was an evening filled with joy, romance and infinite love. We were overcome with the genuine anticipation of what it would mean for our life partnership and in creating new possibilities for our lives together into the future.

The following day, preparations began in earnest. We settled on Saturday, 13 September as the date, in the hope that it would suit our respective families. We then called each one of them, putting the phone on loudspeaker so that we both could hear the different responses. Katherine called her parents first. 'More power to the two of you,' responded her mom, 'anyway what difference does it make in marriage, whether you're gay, lesbian or straight?' Her dad, listening on the other phone in their apartment, then spoke: 'I'm thrilled with what you are doing and I will be there to support you; you set an outstanding example. Is this going to be a "black tie" affair?' Then her mom said again, 'Let me get the calendar and put it in.'

Ann Louise called her brother, Arthur, in Canada. He was most accepting of the idea and expressed real excitement. As a Canadian citizen living on Vancouver Island, he spoke about his pride in Canada's Charter of Human Rights and mentioned that he had followed the progression through the legislature in British Columbia of the ruling in favour of opening marriage to all. This was not a conversation we had ever had before – in fact, apart from inviting him and his family to our twentieth celebration, Ann Louise had never talked openly to her brother about her sexual identity. Yes, he'd be there with his family for the celebration, was his immediate response. That evening, she got through to her sister June. Again, she too was delighted with our decision. Later that evening, Ann Louise realised in her anxiety to convey the news that she hadn't extended an invitation to June and her family to attend, anticipating that it was too short notice for such a long trip. Early next morning, June rang: 'By the way I'll be coming to the wedding. Michael won't be able to travel but I'll be there!' Katherine called each of her siblings in turn, and it was really touching to listen to each spontaneous response, each person positive and each response reflecting their different personalities – but all expressing joy and delight. Her brother Bob just laughed and laughed upon hearing the news and then said teasingly: 'Gee! That's great! It's about time! We will be there!'

Sharing with one's family that one is choosing to get married is 'coming out' *par excellence.* It is also, *ipso facto,* a public 'outing' of one's family. After all the phone calls and the open conversation that followed with each member, we were left reflecting on the capacity of family, and indeed friends and acquaintances, to make the transition to a different consciousness as they accepted and rejoiced in our decision. This was a proof, if one were needed, that where there is love and relationship, prejudice and fear dissolve. While we have been lucky in having families who get on with one another, there is a growing number of stories told by other couples whose extended families hadn't talked for years, but who, in their effort to show solidarity to brother or sister by coming to their wedding, have resolved differences between and among themselves. As two male gay friends of ours who experienced such a situation, quipped, 'Gay marriage is good for families – theirs and ours!'

We contacted Ann Moore, the commissioner who had officiated for Mark's friends, and, after various conversations with her and many emails, she confirmed our wedding for Saturday, 13 September at 1.00pm, in her home. She stated that after the formal ceremony she would like to offer a champagne reception on the front porch. Invitations went out to the family, and all twenty-five accepted by return of post. We ordered our rings at our favourite jeweller's, Emma Stewart

Liberty, in the Powerscourt Centre in Dublin, a simple band design with a weave of white, red and yellow gold. We celebrated each step along the way as the entry in Katherine's journal from 4 September indicates – this was the day we collected the rings. She titled the entry: *Different Identities; Same Rights.*

> What is this feeling that is growing in me, expanding my experience of the day, the now, the present? It is the experience of joy. And how it deepens as each moment passes. The joy that can only come as one prepares to marry the person one intends/wills to love forever. To deny access to a human *right* is often to deny a person one of the most profound human experiences – that is joy.

We flew to Seattle, then, together with Katherine's parents, drove to Vancouver on 12 September. The Granville Island Hotel, located on Granville Island, met all our expectations. Our room overhung the water. In the early afternoon, we set out, taking the False Creek ferry from beside the hotel over to the city centre and then walking to Robson Street where the Vital Statistics Office is located. Here we had to get our licence to marry. We waited in a long queue and could overhear as people registered births, deaths and marriages. As our turn drew near, we grew increasingly nervous. How would Ivy, the named official behind the desk, respond? Our turn arrived, and in a faltering duet we requested a licence to marry. She didn't even blink; rather, she reached under the counter and came up with a form and placed it on the counter before us. 'Who will be on the left?' she asked. Ann Louise, who had no idea what the question meant but was usually (politically!) on the left, answered, 'I will.' As we scrutinised the document, we discovered that the original form had not yet been changed to accommodate same-sex couples and so the left was for the details of the husband and the right for those of the wife! Nothing daunted, we carried on, filled out the required details and left the office relieved, licence in hand, ready for the next day.

That evening, we took Bob and Kathie to a lovely restaurant in Granville village. It was a beautiful warm evening, and so we chose a table on the sidewalk. Granville Island is an artists' oasis, home to the Emily Carr Institute of Art and Design and an area that supports a wonderful public market, many art galleries, quaint shops and cafés. So, while close to the Vancouver downtown area, it really is a world apart. We enjoyed some good Canadian wine and soaked up the ambience. Back in our room, we savoured the remainder of the evening together, watching the moon shimmer on the water outside our window as we sipped champagne and looked again with disbelief and joy at our licence to marry. Whenever we both say something at the same time, we entwine our little fingers together. Suddenly we both said, 'This is as good as it gets!' We laughed, locked fingers and wished for 'forever'.

Next morning, we anticipated a leisurely breakfast in bed and a calm few hours to prepare. But an early knock on the door interrupted any such expectation. Suzie, our goddaughter Kaitlin and Mark were all present, clamouring to get us ready. They entered the room with flowers, make-up cases and hair-styling instruments. Sue and Kaitlin did the face and bodywork, while Mark took over the hair. Kathie came and went from next door, enjoying the transformations. Posies of flowers were artistically assembled. We just laughed and relaxed, arriving finally at Ann Moore's residence greatly enhanced specimens. We wore long, simple cotton dresses that we had bought in France earlier in the summer. It was really emotional to watch the families greet each other with delight. June arrived in a wonderful, large black hat, which added real style to the occasion. Once everyone was present we went inside and were greeted by Ann Moore in her large, stately home. She had been very clear in all her correspondence that the formal part of the marriage would happen first, with strict adherence to the legal script. There was an appropriate tone of solemnity and quiet as each person present followed the service. As rehearsed, we both said our vows following the prescribed text. The only anomaly was that here again the formal text had not yet been changed, so each of us had to say, 'I take thee as my lawfully wedded "wife".' While we had requested to change the language to 'spouse', legally there could be no interference with the existing words. Following the exchange of vows, we then exchanged rings. At this point, the realisation that we were now married drew applause and cheers from all assembled. It was an extraordinary moment for us both, and, equally, it was profoundly moving to watch the gaze of affirmation that extended to us from faces aged from twelve to eighty-two years. Celebrating the ritual of marriage was confirmation, if one was needed, that symbols matter.

We kissed and held each other and then shared a few words that we had prepared to try and encapsulate our appreciation, our acknowledgement of all who had brought us to this moment and of our desire to live the privilege of married love. Ann Louise stated simply that this day was all about love: our marriage was a celebration of the life-enhancing possibilities of our relationship, lived for many years without recognition and now formally recognised. She said that this day brought a deep happiness, a sense of well-being, not only to both of us, but, as was evident in this room, to all our families. Katherine stated that this celebration evidenced that we lived by the same ethic as all other couples who choose to marry, and this moment was truly liberating; that the feeling that the struggle was over, the wait was over, was amazing after so many years. We then each signed the register for marriages in the presence of our witnesses, Mark and Suzie. All the symbols of the ceremony, publicly enacted – our exchange of rings, the signing of the contract – seemed to strengthen the words we had spoken to each other and give visibility to the promises we had made, signalling the intent of permanence.

The champagne flutes by the Irish designer Louise Kennedy that we had brought to Ann Moore as a small token of our appreciation were added to her own collection set out for the champagne reception on the porch. In the distance, the blue waters broke gently on the shore, the sun dazzled and glistened on this perfect September day. Back in the Granville Hotel a delicious lunch, served at a long table by the window, was accompanied by words of congratulation from all the staff. By late afternoon, all our guests had departed, leaving us alone to enjoy our wedding night, which we did to the full.

Next day, as we approached the border to cross back into the United States, we suddenly heard someone shouting on loudspeakers, 'Stop, stop immediately.' Our car was immediately surrounded by armed guards, one of them shouting to open the windows and put our hands up! While we were aware that not everyone was in favour of lesbians marrying, this seemed an overreaction! The shouting guard, with gun directly pointed at us, then leaned into the car and requested that we open the glove compartment; fumbling with terror, we managed to get it open. (This, it seems, was to check that we had no gun.) The next command was then issued through the loudspeaker, 'Leave the car and walk into the building on the left.' By this point, we were nervous wrecks but managed to make it to the required building where we were left sitting for what seemed hours as they examined all our papers, including our marriage licence. After an oral interrogation, the mood suddenly changed; it seems the registration of our car was similar to one they were in pursuit of – it was all a bit of a misunderstanding we were informed. Angry, but so numbed with terror that we didn't complain, we returned to the car and drove off.

Any lingering sense that this incident had intruded on our feeling of married bliss was quickly dispelled upon arrival at Suzie and Karl's home. Our first surprise was to find all Katherine's family assembled once again. At the hall door we were told to close our eyes and were led, blindfold, into the dining room. On the table, they had placed a three-tiered wedding cake, on top of which Kaitlin had placed a beautiful glass sculpture, which she had personally sourced. We cut the cake to cheers, and then Suzie spoke. She described how our wedding had transformed a pain she had lived with ever since she married Karl, over twenty-five years ago. She recalled how on that day she looked at her maid of honour, Katherine, her older sister, and thought, She will never know the joy and happiness of a wedding day. Yes, the cake was a celebration of our marriage and a prolongation of the festivities of the previous day, and it was also a symbol stating: Our rights are your rights, justice at last. Suzie wept as she spoke, and she and Katherine embraced.

Before leaving Seattle, we were able to put together a beautiful album of photographs taken by Arthur and Mark, both artists in their own professions. The pictures are stunningly beautiful, as they present through artists' eyes all the perceived beauty of individual moments captured in time. They have left us with a picture history of images that shatter any stereotyping or preconceptions of family wedding photographs. In other words, the camera reflects an authentic flavour of a new world. Although our own memories are etched in a virtually indelible fashion on the corridors of our minds, these photos allow us to see in an enhanced way and know in an enduring fashion even more about the importance of that day for all present.

As we flew home to Ireland, we reflected on Hannah Arendt's observation, 'The remedy for unpredictability, for the chaotic uncertainty of the future, is contained in the faculty to make and keep promises.' In marrying each other, we made promises in the present that we knew would sustain us into the future, a future that we sensed would be unpredictable as we resolved to have our marriage recognised in Ireland.

15

TO THE COURTS

Equality is not an abstract concept . . . The Court has an historic choice to make – a choice that commits our legal system to equality or one that entrenches and confirms prejudice and discrimination.

Fionnuala Ní Aoláin, *The Irish Times,* 2 October 2006

Democracy is not an abstract concept. When we decided to go to court, we believed that it was our right as citizens to engage with the structure of Irish democracy in order to seek justice for ourselves: the Irish Constitution proclaims that 'Justice shall be administered in courts established by law by judges appointed' (Article 34.1). At a personal level, we wanted to ensure that our fundamental rights were protected in the same way as other citizens. The judicial structure is there precisely to provide citizens with this way of practising democracy.

We believed too that the issues which our case would raise would go far beyond our own individual lives and would bring us into the realm of what is called 'matters of public interest'. The human, psychological impact of interacting with the legal structure, however, is profound, and there has been and continues to be a massive cost to our lives at all sorts of levels, and yet, this kind of action, we believe, supports a healthy democracy. But how many people are able to take such action? This question weighed heavily on our minds and hearts, and, while we clearly took this case on our own behalf, we also took it on behalf of those who might not be able to withstand the human cost – financial and otherwise – of engaging in such democratic action.

Later on, we heard from our senior counsel, Gerard Hogan, that the Irish Constitution is not 'permafrost in the period of 1937' (when it was written), rather, that it is a 'living document' that requires reinterpretation as society changes, as 'we the people of Éire' (from the Prologue to the Irish Constitution) evolve over time. How is this foundational document to maintain its life, we ask, if 'we, the people' do not engage with it?

Returning to Ireland from Vancouver brought us back to the real world of the Irish legal realm. We had stepped outside that realm to do what any couple does when they are in love and want to solemnise and legalise their partnership (except, of course, those who are barred by law). As we faced the next steps of the legal journey, though, we did feel changed. When one's marital or family status alters, something happens inside as well as outside – at least, it did for us. An interplay between social choice and personal identity begins and eventually melds into a new understanding and experience of ourselves as family, and so Ann Louise's family is now Katherine's and Katherine's family is Ann Louise's in that formal sense. Family shapes identity, and now we are people who have a wider network of relationships that we depend on and who depend on us. Kinship through law may not always deepen intimacies between people, but it did for us. June is Katherine's sister-in-law. Philip is Ann Louise's brother-in-law. Katherine's sister Suzie introduces her friends to Ann Louise as her sister-in-law. How proud that makes us both feel, how recognised and how affirmed on the outside for who we are now on the inside.

We wonder if all married couples go through this path of changing and unfolding self-awareness? We suspect that we are like them, indeed, we are like you the reader who is married – at least in this regard.

Towards the end of September 2003, ten days after we were married, Phil O'Hehir (our solicitor) and Ivana Bacik (our junior counsel) passed on the Equality Authority research to Gerard Hogan (senior counsel and constitutional expert) along with a statement about our circumstances and our desire to press ahead. We held our breath for his preliminary opinion, and it came towards the end of November. While Mr Hogan was quite cautious about predicting anything close to a clean win, he did write that we have a 'serious and stateable constitutional case' and that he would be willing to act on our behalf. Uplifted by his response, we met with Phil and Kevin Brophy (owner of Phil's firm) to discuss the implications of Mr Hogan's opinion and to plan the next steps. As we reviewed recent case law and parliamentary changes in other jurisdictions, we noted that the usual tack was for same-sex couples to present themselves to apply for a marriage license, be refused and, on that basis, to initiate legal proceedings in the light of that refusal. We also noticed that in jurisdictions where cases were successful in opening the institution of marriage to same-sex couples, several couples took the one case.

In light of this first review, we agreed to undertake a number of actions. We decided that the best thing to do would be to apply for a marriage license in Ireland (following the route of those in other jurisdictions), to seek out at least four or five other couples who would join us in this action and to begin to think about ways to raise money for the case. While Brophy's and our counsel were willing to take the case *pro bono*, there still would be significant costs for administrative and other types of outlay, and we still had the weighty threat of costs being awarded against us should we lose.

What strikes us now, as we record these memories, is that there was no previously charted course for what we would end up doing. Equally, as we took each step, we would discover unanticipated dimensions; barriers would appear from nowhere, and dead ends would litter the path. Every time these things happened, we would have to regroup as the Americans say, or take stock as the Irish say, and dig deep within our souls to keep on course.

Finding other couples to enter the legal action with us proved to be one extremely disheartening dead end. We put the word out through various formal and informal networks, and we held countless conversations with colleagues and friends. We hit a wall, time and again, mainly for two types of reason: most lesbian or gay couples we knew, while happy for us that we married, absolutely did not want to have anything to do with the 'heterosexual' or 'patriarchal' institution of marriage: marriage held a burdensome history of oppressing women; or marriage was too much like 'them'; or marriage lasted too long; or some had the experience of marriage already and it contained memories fraught with conflict, disappointment or torment. Second, the few couples who did not hold these views were not 'out' to their families or to their workplace or to the public; declaring a desire to marry would carry too great a personal risk. We realised, eventually, that we would have to go it alone. We tried not to pass judgement on anyone, though this was very tough to avoid at times. Once again, we felt immensely frustrated that, unlike other countries, no Irish national organisation was campaigning for civil marriage for same-sex couples. Our solitary position dampened our spirits some days, but our will never faltered. The road to justice simply lengthened.

In early December, we received a great gift, which we experienced like a blessing dropping from the heavens. Our friends Mary Paula Walsh and Kay Conroy hosted an Irish wedding reception for us in their beautiful home. It was a generous evening, which is the hallmark of all evenings in their home. Before the meal was served and the music began, they had prepared a ritual of blessing to celebrate our marriage. Everyone sat around in a large circle; some shared their reflections on love and marriage, and others played a piece of music or read a poem that summarised their thoughts. In conclusion, all present joined hands forming an archway down the long room, they then invited us to enter and to pass under as they each gave us their blessing. The old Irish word for marriage, *cétmuintir* – *cét* together' and *muintir* 'community' – summarised the event.

Some time later, in An Cosán, West Tallaght, a similar evening was held with many of our friends from the local community present. During the evening, Nuala Wood came up to us: 'I was so relieved when I heard that you two got married,' she said. 'You know, during the early days, when we used to go up to The Shanty, I'd look at you both and say to myself, I just hope these women can find two good, eligible men.' Then, warming the lobby with her hearty laugh, she added, 'Little did I know!'

Before the close of the year, we approached two friends, Patricia Prendiville and Éadaoín Ní Chléirigh, to discuss any possible avenues to raise funds. Together they had founded Meitheal, a not-for-profit highly successful organisation that provides technical support to the community and voluntary sector in Ireland. While they took up our cause without hesitation and met with a large philanthropic organisation to put our case (anonymously) to them, the answer came back with a negative. Another dead end. The year 2003 closed with our health intact and our personal happiness high, a legal team assembled, but a strategy that required revision.

By mid-Februray of 2004, the new strategy crystallised on Parliament Street in the offices of our solicitors when we met our junior and senior counsel together for the very first time. While Mr Hogan's reputation preceded him, we could not have anticipated how his graciousness (which reminded Ann Louise of her father Arthur), combined with his astute intellect and immense breadth of legal knowledge and expertise, could comfort us so much. We felt intellectually inspired and personally accompanied throughout the discussion and debate of the best way forward. Mr Hogan (or Ger, as we would now call him) believed that it was a good time to take the case. Once again, we were cautioned in relation to costs and further warned of the 'sensation' that the case would create within the media and the public. We must be aware that this would happen, he told us, we must know that our case would bring a spotlight on many aspects of our personal lives and be ready to withstand the unexpected as well as the anticipated. 'Yes, yes,' we said (with some trepidation it must be admitted), 'but why do we need to apply for a marriage licence here? We ARE married!' A pause in the heated conversation took place, but it was not long. 'The best thing to do in this case, then,' he said, 'is to apply to the Revenue Commissioners to recognise your marriage by requesting a change of tax status, and to apply to the Registrar General to recognise your marriage – as any married couple returning from a foreign land would do! If they accept your application, we will have completed our business. If they refuse, this constitutes grounds to seek a judicial review of their decision, and this will be the starting point of *our* case.'

We required only one thing, and that was an affidavit from a Canadian lawyer stating that we had had the capacity to marry in Canada and that our marriage was legally recognised in that jurisdiction. We knew no Canadian lawyers, but, through our friend Fionnuala Ní Aoláin (who sat on the Human Rights Commission with Katherine and had many international legal contacts), we were put in touch with lawyers Shelagh Day and Gwen Brodsky, both active in the Canadian movement for the recognition of same-sex marriage. They recommended Kenneth Smith, a barrister and solicitor practising in British Columbia and working in the area of gay and lesbian rights and the rights of same-sex couples since before his call to the bar in 1978. To this day, we have not set sight on Ken, though he responded to our request with enormous generosity, international solidarity and pragmatic swiftness. We owe him a huge debt of gratitude. By April of 2004, we had written to our local office of the Revenue Commissioners (based in Tallaght!), enclosing the affidavit and our marriage certificate, stating that we were married in Vancouver on 13 September 2003, that we were both Irish citizens and residents in Ireland and that 'we now request that we be able to claim our allowances as a married couple under the Taxes Consolidation Act.' Around the same time, Phil wrote on our behalf to the Registrar General of Marriages, requesting that they confirm that our Canadian marriage was binding under Irish law.

We received a speedy reply from the Registrar General telling us that the remit of its office does not extend to making a declaration on the validity of marriages that occur outside of the Irish State, and that it was a matter for the courts. The Revenue Commissioners were a different matter. Their very courteous letter, addressing us as 'Dear Ladies', stated that as they had never received a request such as ours, and as 'Irish taxation legislation caters for marriage only on the basis of the institution consisting of a husband and wife', they needed a legal opinion, which they now forwarded on to us, stating that, though 'the Taxes Acts do not define husband and wife, the *Oxford English Dictionary* offers the following:

Husband – a married man especially in relation to his wife

Wife – a married woman especially in relation to her husband.

So, on the basis of using the *Oxford English Dictionary* to interpret Irish tax law, the Revenue declared that they could not give us the allowances that any other married couple would get. While the negative response was not unexpected, the rationale certainly was.

We held another meeting with our legal team and formally agreed to apply for a judicial review of the Revenue's decision because we believed – and still believe – that it is unjustly discriminatory and in breach of our rights under the Irish Constitution. Our lawyers went to work immediately, drawing up all the appropriate papers over the late summer and early autumn. When all was completed, they simply notified the courts' office that we were looking for a date to go into the High Court to get permission from a judge to take the review. That's the way it works: one needs permission to begin the review process before a date is given for the case to be heard.

Phil rang us at the beginning of November. The date for mention (the technical term for 'date to seek permission') in the High Court was set for 8 November. A list is published, the judge knows only that Mr Hogan is coming in to seek leave to apply for a judicial review – there is no notification of the content of any 'mention'. The day had finally come! While this was not the date that the case commenced (we belabour the point!), it was the date that our intent would be unveiled to the Irish public. So, we decided that, out of courtesy or in friendship, we would get in touch with as many close friends as possible to let them know that they might be hearing about us in the news. In addition, Katherine rang the President of the Human Rights Commission, Dr Maurice Manning, as well as the CEO, Dr Alpha Connelly, to let them know. Both were immensely sympathetic and supportive. In fact, Katherine had discussed our intentions with Maurice a number of months previously, beginning with the news of our marriage. She will never forget his gracious and magnanimous response: during the meeting, he excused himself for a moment, and towards the end of their session, glasses of champagne arrived to congratulate Katherine on her marriage to Ann Louise. These are the memories that sustain us, even to this day.

Ann Louise phoned Eddie Ward, CEO of the National Educational Welfare Board, the statutory board she chaired, to tell him of our impending action. Eddie also responded sympathetically and graciously, and he made two eminently sensible suggestions: perhaps we should ring our respective government ministers (Education for Ann Louise; Justice, Equality and Law Reform for Katherine) on the morning of going to court and inform them so they wouldn't be taken off-guard if they were door-stepped for a quote; he also suggested we might get some personal assistance to deal with the media queries that undoubtedly would come our way once the news broke. On the weekend before the court mention (8 November was a Monday), Katherine phoned Edel Hackett, a public-relations consultant that both she and Ann Louise had worked with professionally in the past. After describing to Edel what we were up to, Katherine said, 'We think that there *may* be some media interest when we go to court – could you help us with that?' Edel responded with her characteristic good humour and generosity 'I think you may be right! Of course I'll do anything I can to help you out.'

Monday morning arrived, and Katherine was in her office telephoning the last few friends we hadn't got a hold of the night before, when Ann Louise burst through the door saying, 'It's on "Morning Ireland"!' (the RTÉ breakfast radio programme). They gave the whole story, based on a piece from Carol Coulter on the front page of *The Irish Times* – no names, but everything else! How did this happen? We had waited to phone almost everyone until the night before, swearing all to secrecy. To this day, we do not know how Carol got the information.

Needless to say, as we approached the courts later that morning, there was a swarm of photographers and television cameras. Phil advised us to be courteous, smile and say nothing and just keep on walking into the courts, which we dutifully did. When we arrived in the courtroom, barristers, solicitors and clients came and went as each stood before the judge to get permission for their case. At 12.55pm Judge McKechnie called on Mr Hogan to put forward our details. Ger stood up and said that his clients, Katherine Zappone and Ann Louise Gilligan, were seeking a change in their marital status for taxation purposes in the light of their Canadian marriage. The statement electrified the courtroom. The Judge immediately requested that all other cases be held over until the next day and further stated that he would be ready to hear Mr Hogan's submission after lunch. Mary Wilson, RTÉ legal correspondent, and other journalists literally ran from the courtroom to phone in our names to the various news outlets. Though we did not know it then, our names were soon going around the world – to Boston, New York, Canada, Japan, Australia, South Africa, Taiwan, Seattle – as journalists reported that Ireland would now have to deal with the issue of marriage and partnership rights for same-sex couples.

When we returned to the courtroom after lunch, Ger outlined the central issues of our case. Judge McKechnie asked numerous questions, including technical issues related to articles of the European Convention on Human Rights. The Convention had recently been incorporated into Irish domestic law, and so we were claiming that our convention rights as well as constitutional rights had been breached. An hour passed very slowly before Ger concluded his submission. To our complete amazement, Judge McKechnie declared that he would hold his judgement until the next morning! This rarely happens: standard practice is that a judge will decide then and there. Our legal team certainly did not expect that getting permission to take leave to apply for a judicial review would be a big hurdle. What could we do except leave and wait until the morning? Phil informed us that correct protocol prevented us from speaking about the details of our case once we had started the judicial process, so we pushed our way out through the cameras and journalists. We felt deeply unsettled. After all the planning, the facing of fear time and again, were we to be halted at the starting line? The night also passed very slowly.

At breakfast, we discussed the fact that as Ann Louise was interviewing candidates for a new doctoral programme in St Pat's, she simply had to go to work, which meant that Katherine would be in court to hear the judgement without her. We decided then that we wanted to make some kind of personal statement to the public, so that Ann Louise could be named even though she was unable to be present. We wrote a few lines together – with the anticipation of a positive outcome (and hoping that our words would not breach protocol) – and Katherine went off to meet our legal team at the courthouse, while Ann Louise went to St Pat's.

A packed courtroom greeted Katherine, Phil, Ivana and Ger. We all rose as the Judge entered. His judgement began with a recitation of the facts as presented to him, followed by an explanation of the 'threshold for leave', namely, that we must satisfy the Court that on the facts and the law as outlined, an arguable case was established. We were all on the edge of our seats – still no indication! Then finally he said:

> It is not necessary for the purpose of determining this application to outline in any detail the relevant cases or passages cited. This case is not simply about tax bands or allowances, or a comparative analysis between married and unmarried persons. The matters raised here transcend these individuals, and are of profound importance to society and to persons contemplating same-sex marriages. A number of deeply held values, and so on, are up for consideration. The issue of marriage itself is up for debate. The ramifications of the case will not stop there. If the Applicants succeed, a stream of consequences – legal, cultural – may follow. Far-reaching issues are raised. However, this is but a Leave application ... Having considered the documents and reread the case overnight, I have no doubt that the Applicants have met that threshold, therefore, as a matter of law they are entitled to Leave.
>
> (As noted by Counsel, Ivana Bacik, 9 November 2004)

We rushed from the room, jubilant. Katherine telephoned Ann Louise, didn't get her, but left her a voicemail with the great news. Katherine and Phil went towards the outside of the courts where the media were gathering in droves at the gate (they are not allowed inside the court grounds), and Katherine asked Phil to read what we had written, to see if she thought it was OK; she said, yes, the personal nature of the statement meant it was fine. The cameras flashed and Katherine could only think of Ann Louise as she said,

Ann Louise Gilligan, my beloved partner, and I are delighted with the outcome of the judgement this morning.

Twenty-three years ago we made a commitment of life partnership to each other. We have been exceptionally blessed by our unconditional love for and fidelity to one another. Yesterday and today are simply the first steps to seek legal recognition of our lifelong love and faithfulness. This case is about equality, fairness and human rights – as our legal team has so ably outlined in the court. For us, it is a case as well about equality and human rights in the context of love.

We wish to thank, at this point, all our family, friends, legal team and colleagues who have enabled us to get to this day and who have promised to walk the path ahead with us – four-square. We want to acknowledge as well the Equality Authority and all its important work in this arena. Our parents have provided us with exceptional models of love and married life, and we are inspired by them and grateful to them.

Today is a happy day. This is a happy case.

The floodgates opened. For two solid weeks, newspapers, magazines, radio and television shows carried our story. One of the best headlines proclaimed: 'Archbishop Backs Legal Rights for Gay Couples' (front page, *Irish Independent*, 16 November 2004). What Dr Diarmuid Martin, the Catholic Archbishop of Dublin, actually said was: 'I recognise that there are many different kinds of caring relationships and these often create dependencies for those involved. The State may feel in justice that the rights of people in these relationships need to be protected.' He was responding to comments made by Taoiseach Bertie Ahern, who had said earlier in the week that extending rights to gay couples in the areas of tax and inheritance was the 'fairest' and 'Christian way to deal with this'. While neither of these men got anywhere near declaring support to recognise our marriage, likewise neither of them had ever uttered such positive statements before about legal rights for same-sex couples. The public, political and religious ground started to shift during those weeks. A huge majority of the coverage was positive; very few voices were critical of our action, barring a few of the usual suspects. We declined all interviews – though we would love to have given a few! – as we thought it best during that time to stay quiet. We were just beginning to discern what we could say and what we couldn't, when it was the right time to speak and when silence was the appropriate response.

Our reactions to the public focus on our private lives differed considerably. Ann Louise returned to college with certain trepidation, wondering when or if she would get a knock on the door to deliver the news that she was being dismissed. Thankfully, this never happened. Also, she received nothing but support and affirmation from the majority of her colleagues. One staff member did feel the need to send out an email to 'all staff' reminding them of the Catholic ethos of the college and reiterating the negative Church teaching on homosexuality. This correspondence was short-lived as the College President intervened and called a halt. The said colleague met Ann Louise in the car park later that day and assured her there was 'nothing personal' in his stance, he just had to uphold Catholic faith and morals.

Katherine loved the coverage – finally the Irish public were debating the issues, and she didn't mind at all that her face and Ann Louise's provided the focal point. Our neighbours, on a quiet rural road in Brittas, delighted in our stance and surprised us by all sorts of kind gestures. One morning, we went to the post box at the end of our drive to discover a bottle of champagne from new neighbours we hadn't even met; congratulations cards also came through the box – some with euro notes to provide practical support – and our next-door neighbours on both sides (one a younger couple, another an older couple) said they would stand with us and support what we were doing. Friends, colleagues and people we had never met sent us hundreds of cards and letters with deeply moving expressions of encouragement. Ann Louise received a petition signed by hundreds of students in St Pat's declaring their admiration and approval. To this day, we have received only two letters with damning words and tone.

During the subsequent months, we worked with our legal team as they drew up the documents to submit to the High Court office, and we considered carefully the kinds of expert witnesses who would provide the necessary evidence for our case. We continued to be troubled, though, by the financial risk that we were embarking upon and so decided to host three dinners of friends and colleagues to discuss these concerns. Their response went beyond what we could have imagined: Grainne Healy and Denise Charlton agreed to found and co-chair a fund-raising and advocacy initiative on our behalf. Ailbhe Smyth and Orla Howard of the National Lesbian and Gay Federation, and Christopher Robson, Keith O'Malley, Brian Sheehan and Eoin Collins of the Gay and Lesbian Equality Network declared practical support for the initiative. Edel Hackett pledged her public-relations expertise, and at the request of Brian Kearney-Grieve, a staff member of Atlantic Philanthropies' human-rights programme, our dear friends Deirdre Hannigan and Anne O'Reilly agreed to develop a proposal to support extra-legal expenses that we would incur. Rachel Matthews-McKay and Richie Keane of the Labour LGBT (Lesbian, Gay, Bisexual, Transgender) group, Aengus Carroll, a professional editor, Senator David Norris, Maureen Lynott, Monica O'Connor, Olive Braiden, Ellen O'Malley-Dunlop and many others got to work on planning fund-raising and public affairs events for our cause.

On Friday, 15 April 2005, we appeared on the front page of *The Irish Times* yet again. The headlines read, 'State to Challenge Lesbian Couple's Legal Action' and the subsequent article outlined how, at a cabinet meeting, ministers agreed to contest our case. They could have chosen otherwise, but they did not. The full gravity of what we were taking on hit us hard. Imagine if you wake up one morning to read that the State, the Attorney General and all the Cabinet Ministers are against you? While we admit that we did not really expect them to do the brave thing, equally we did not anticipate that we would feel personally insulted and degraded, nor did we expect or anticipate our own feelings of rejection, denial and, yes, fear at what now lay ahead. It took several months to regain our energy and drive, but when we walked into a packed Mansion House on Dawson Street in late November for the first fund-raising event, and as we drank champagne with Senator Norris who was kind enough to MC the lunch, our courage and well-being returned. That is the enormous gift of solidarity; being accompanied by so many people from every sector of Irish society transformed us time and again. We owe a debt that cannot be repaid, and we are humbled by the experience and knowledge that our human achievement does not happen on its own.

At the beginning of 2006, we received an invitation to be interviewed by Ireland's premier television talk-show host, Pat Kenny, on 'The Late Late Show'. After considerable consultation with our lawyers and friends, we decided to rise to this personal challenge because we discerned that the Irish public might benefit from hearing our story. So much of the prejudice against lesbian and gay people happens, we think, because a substantial number of the population do not see the normal, everyday lives that lesbian and gay people lead. Yes, we are different from the majority in our sexual identity, but, as ordinary human beings, we are like them in so many other ways. We fall in love, we get sick, and we want to mind each other; we deal with the stresses of twenty-first-century living; we work hard and relish leisure. While we could not talk about our court case, narrating the story of our relationship and marriage might demonstrate the normality of a minority group.

Stage fright set in, however, several weeks prior to our 10 March appearance. A live show, in full view of the hundreds of thousands who often watch the 'Late Late', called upon every ounce of courage we could muster. We sought the assistance of our friends Michael Murphy, RTÉ broadcaster, and Terry O'Sullivan to help reduce our fear by working with us to develop a plan for what we wanted to say. Edel Hackett also provided advice and travelled from her home in Westport, County Mayo, to accompany us out to the Montrose studios for the evening itself. While Katherine fussed over what she would wear, Ann Louise struggled to overcome a cold and laryngitis. We met Pat Kenny in the hospitality room about an hour before we walked on the set. He seemed uncomfortable in our presence, and we did our best to make conversation. When we met each other again in front of the cameras and live audience, Pat appeared to be as nervous as we were. Once we started to tell our story, though, all three of us relaxed as the power of narrative took hold. When he turned to the audience for their questions to us, the first woman with her hand up spoke angrily, stating that we can't be married because marriage is between a man and a woman, that it has always been that way, and that if we take those rules away then she would cease to be married because she is married to a man! The depth of her paternalism evoked a collective gasp from the audience. Pat questioned her further, and she then continued: 'You may have minority rights, but *I* have human rights, and you ought to be eternally grateful to live in an Irish society where the law could change so you can get partnership rights.' Another woman shot up her hand and said: 'How can we know whether or not marriage between two women actually works? See how they love one another, love is shining in their lives', and after a big clap from the audience, she concluded with: 'I am straight and my marriage broke down. I haven't measured up in the way that they have measured up,' and there was another round of applause. Pat noted that Taoiseach Bertie Ahern had said earlier in the week that he would not embark on a referendum to change the law to allow gay marriage because the Irish people didn't want it. Pat then asked his audience, 'Hands up those who would vote to change the Constitution so that gay and lesbian people can marry here' – and all but a few raised their hand. He concluded the twenty-four minute interview with the words, 'Bertie, you were wrong!' Afterwards, in the hospitality room, the producer ran in to tell us that the phone calls and text mesages they received about our interview were overwhelmingly positive. Facing the fear, yet again, had been worth it.

Two days later, we received word that 'An Irish Tea' fund-raiser was being held for us in the Boston home of Liz Breadon and Mary McCarthy, two women we had never met. They read about our efforts on the front page of *The Boston Globe*, 30 December 2005, with the headline 'Same-Sex Couple's Lawsuit – a Test of Tolerance in Ireland'. The article began with: 'In a country that has had its share of revolutionaries, Katherine Zappone and Ann Louise Gilligan hardly look the part. They are smartly dressed, well-coiffed, middle-aged members of Ireland's burgeoning middle class. But in trying to get the Government to recognise their 2003 marriage in Canada, they are challenging the very notion that Ireland has become a less socially conservative, more tolerant corner of Europe' (Kevin Cullen, *Globe* staff). Then and there, Liz and Mary set about planning the fund-raiser, and it just so happened they did know one of our dear friends, Maura Twomey, another Irish woman who had moved to Boston. Their invitation to the Boston Irish and American clan read: 'Those whom we support hold us up in life. You are warmly invited to join us for "An Irish Tea" in support of Katherine Zappone and Ann Louise Gilligan.' They passed around a book for all who came to sign and send on to us. We include here two of the entries that reflect such extraordinary solidarity between Boston and Ireland.

> Katherine and Ann Louise, you would so enjoy the afternoon here in Oak Square. A lovely gathering of women and men, interested in justice, having tea and homemade scones, homemade blackcurrant (organic!) jam supporting your case. 'I thank my God, each time I think of you and when I pray for you, I pray with joy' ... The connections stay strong, and I am so proud of the two of you and of the friends here who are moved to support you. I look forward to introducing you to each other when you next come to Boston. Liz, Mary and Cathleen have done a great job here.
> Love, Le Grá, Maura.

Dear Ann Louise and Katherine,

We applaud your courage and determination in fighting for equality. We are very fortunate to live in the great commonwealth of Massachusetts where many of us have been able to get recognition for our relationships. The important work of letting people know who you are and building respect is essential to not only winning in the courts but winning in the court of public opinion which is ultimately more important. We love you both as our 'sisters in arms'.

Love, Cathleen Finn and Carey Cohley-Finn,

Married, 17 July 04, civil, and 18 September 04, church.

Overwhelmed and humbled by these human connections with friends, known and unknown, we continued preparations with our legal team for the High Court Judicial Review. During this period, Ger Hogan indicated that he would be greatly assisted by adding another senior counsel to the team. Michael Collins, well known for his work in commercial law, agreed to join us. At our first meeting, Michael impressed us greatly. In a relatively short period of time he had acquired a comprehensive grasp of the issues and brought to the table not only exceptional experience in the courts but also the crucial legal argument of 'liberty' to complement our foundational plea for equality. The principle of liberty – that all people ought to be free to make critical life choices – provided the basis for the eloquent contention that we ought to be able to marry the person we choose to love.

Finally, we heard that the case would begin on 3 October 2006, a date four and a half years subsequent to making our first telephone call to the Equality Authority. Our time had come. The Court set aside two weeks to hear the arguments of both sides. Michael Collins rose to his feet to deliver our opening submissions on the 3rd, and Gerard Hogan closed our arguments on the 13th. In between, of course, the State presented its arguments and rebuffed those witnesses we put forward to provide expert evidence on our behalf. Because we are writing now while the case is *sub judice* – that is, still in the courts – we do not think it appropriate to outline the happenings of those days. (May we recommend to the interested reader to go to the online archives of Ireland's newspapers which provided in-depth coverage of each day, and plenty of photos!) We note briefly, instead, fragments of feelings and reflections, recorded in our own court journals, alternating here between us.

I am moved deeply by Michael's opening – the impeccable rationale is matched by his oratory skills, and I am weeping by the time he finishes. His voicing our arguments publicly in a court of law seeps into the deepest part of my being and I feel acknowledged for who I am. I tried to explain this to him at the end of the day.

The courtroom is packed, with people we know and don't know. So many of our friends and colleagues took off work to be here; thank God, we are not alone. Anne Colley (Chair of the Government's Working Group on Domestic Partnerships, set up by Minister Michael McDowell in March 2006) just walked in, and we had a brief word – I am reminded of a winter afternoon in the Bridge Bar, a Portmagee, County Kerry, pub, where we met her mother with Lelia Doolin, and shared drinks and stories.

Ger told us that no matter what, only good will come from what we have undertaken. His kindness sustains our courage and confidence.

I wanted to sit next to Katherine, but she has got the court officer to agree to allowing her to sit up front – with the legal teams – because of her hearing loss. As my hearing is impeccable I watch and listen from the back bench. I am fascinated with law, it runs in the blood, and while nervous from time to time because this court scene is about *us*, I am enthralled with how it all works.

The State counsellors argue that it is not appropriate to have Professor Dan Maguire provide expert testimony (as a Roman Catholic theologian) about how the Church's understanding of marriage has changed through time, and that Roman Catholicism is pluralistic on the subject of same-sex relationships. Please say yes, Judge Dunne, please allow him to testify. He has flown from Milwaukee to be here. She calls him to the stand ...

We have just listened to two days of the State's arguments, and I feel so angry. Aren't these men free to marry? Why do they want to block us? I know their arguments are not personal, but it feels that way. As Michael said, there will be good days and bad days during the hearing. These have been bad days.

Phil and Jeanne (Boyle) have put in endless hours on our behalf. Jeanne mentioned that she works voluntarily on our case, after her own work day is complete! At every step of the way, they listen with great attentiveness to our concerns, our ideas, our frustrations and our hopes. We feel graced to be accompanied by them.

The last days are approaching. Ivana, Michael and Ger work overtime to prepare the closing submissions. As Ger stands to his feet, I glance back at Ivana who sits behind him. I have never seen her looking so exhausted and yet still working furiously on our behalf, handing up to Ger various texts of jurisprudence or articles with the most recent psychological and sociological evidence to support our arguments. Ger's power of speech spellbinds all of us. How could we lose? We are elated – and emotionally drained – as he closes the final big notebook and sits down.

On 15 December 2006, we arrived early at the Four Courts to hear Judge Elizabeth Dunne's judgement. Several friends and colleagues waited with us outside the courtroom until we were called in. Two members of Ann Louise's family (and now Katherine's) surprised us with their presence – Dermot McEvoy and Sally Kelly embraced us with love and hope. The court officer signalled to enter the courtroom. We rose as the Judge arrived and then sat down after her. While her written text is lengthy (138 pages), she kept us less than ten minutes, saying that, in summary, we do not have the right to marry here under the Constitution because that right is confined to the union of a man and a woman; consequently, our marriage in Canada is not recognised as valid here.

As we reread the media coverage now in writing this account, a lowness descends again, as it did that wintry morning. Nevertheless, we faced the cameras afterwards with dignity and an upbeat statement that, 'while disappointed at a human and personal level' we wanted to thank the Judge for her graciousness throughout the hearing, and that we would study her judgement carefully. We concluded our words with the vision we still have: 'We believe that Ireland will be a land of justice and equality for all human beings. We believe that the Irish Constitution does protect and promote our rights – as it does all others.'

Six days later, we walked back into the Four Courts to receive her judgement on costs. The State Counsel indicated that the Government would not be looking for costs on their side, though they argued vigorously that we should not be awarded costs for our side. Judge Dunne declared that, as this case was not a matter of public interest, there did not exist any rationale for her to award costs to our side. Ger Hogan jumped to his feet, appearing stunned by the judgement, and proclaimed that his clients would seek to appeal her judgement in the Supreme Court. He came over to us then, after the Judge left the room, and said once again, 'Only good will come from what you are doing.' Some two weeks later, we filed our appeal to the Supreme Court, the highest court in the land, where the case would be heard, probably by five judges.

We had lost twice, once on the case and once on costs. Our emotions reflected the season: it was the winter solstice, the darkest day of the year, yet equally the seasonal turning towards the light. Later that evening, we agreed to go on 'Drivetime', the RTÉ radio show, at the invitation of its presenter, Mary Wilson. We described our hurt, our disappointment to the nation. Ann Louise said: 'This judicial decision, its lack of recognition, means we are not equal in this country in one of the most critical aspects of our lives. You are either equal or you are not. We are not.' Katherine addressed a special group of listeners: 'I want to say something to the young people who right this very moment are preparing to marry, and I want to say it to their parents as well. Can you imagine what it would be like if you were not allowed to marry the person you choose to love? That is what the judge has said to us.' Ann

Louise concluded, reaching for hope we did not feel but knew would return: 'No family member or no stranger in the street has done anything but wish us well; they say they are so sorry this has happened to us and encourage us to keep going.'

And that is what we are doing.

APPENDIX

OUR METHOD FOR

PRACTISING SOCIAL CHANGE

SOULWORK IN PUBLIC

When we returned from Boston as a couple in the early eighties, the Irish culture of resisting oppression and striving for liberation was palpable. During this period, many brave and radical leaders pushed progress for justice, and law-makers enacted far-reaching equality and human-rights legislation in several arenas, including the decriminalisation of homosexuality. The generative creativity of our own life partnership found expression in establishing – along with many others – The Shanty or An Cosán, as it is now called twenty-two years on, and has been at the heart of our attempt to eradicate Irish poverty through empowering adult and child-centred education. More recently, we decided to extend this search for justice and equality to ourselves – and to those who share our minority sexual identity – and are currently in the midst of a 'long walk towards freedom' (to quote Nelson Mandela) so that our marriage to one another can be recognised in Ireland one day.

In light of these life experiences, we have formulated what we think is one effective method for achieving social change. It brings together the two primary strands of our pursuit for justice – spirituality and politics – what we now call 'soulwork in public'. What follows is an outline of the method, illustrated with stories from our life and work with others.

SOULWORK

1 Attention to Soul

We were both raised within a religious tradition, and this influenced us greatly, though, as we have described, each of us, for very different reasons, grew beyond this influence as a worldview or way of interpreting our life's meaning. So we do not think that religion is a requirement for soulful living but we do believe that the essence of our humanity or the uniqueness of each of our identities is sustained, refashioned and revivified through the power of the invisible energy of soul (our metaphor for 'the beyond in our midst'). From here, our yearning for freedom, equality, companionship, meaning and love ascends and returns. Here is where we experience our reach for each other, for those who are other than ourselves, and for the transcendent meaning of life together, in community and society and as part of the natural world. Often we experience this in our physicality: we literally feel the movement of be-ing human in our bodies, and those feelings have changed as we have aged. Some days they are stronger and more energetic than when we were younger. Other days, a quieting takes over the rhythm. Perhaps the difference can be explained by the ongoing ebb and flow of life creating new layers over the earlier years, akin to the developing age lines of a tree. Within every new layer, soulprints, building from the inside out, reflect the ways in which we resolve the tensions and conflicts of be-ing who we are – in relation. Was it Martin Buber, the Jewish philosopher, who said, 'to be, is to be in relation'?

Paying attention to soul or taking time for soul needs to be done on one's own as well as with others. Most mornings, Ann Louise lights a candle in our kitchen, moves to the centre of the tiled floor and begins her practice of T'ai chi. Through this physical, graceful movement, she rediscovers the power of her breath, her life force, and the various positions release any blocks in her energy or *chi* so that she is more ready for the day ahead. Katherine will be found in our conservatory that fronts The Shanty. She sits amidst the seasonal flowering of jasmine or geranium or amaryllis and begins her practice of mindful meditation, learning anew the habit of stilling the mind in order to reconnect with and acknowledge the essence and goodness of what is. There is always a book of poetry on our breakfast counter. Some days we read a poem aloud to each other; other days we reflect silently on the text. While there are periods when the busyness of our lives crowds out this soultime, we notice this lack of nourishment, and our day is more scattered, stress-filled and less productive. Myriad books, techniques and programmes are on offer today to assist the practice of be-ing or soul. These are just a few of the ones we engage to enable us to remember who we are, on the earth, at this time. People often ask us where we get and how we sustain our energy. This is part of our secret: the rhythm of stillness and attention to transcendence in the immanent present.

We find that sustaining soul or tapping the power of our human essence also requires words and deeds done together. Today, as we write, another group of people from West Tallaght gather in The Muse at the back of our kitchen door to experience an 'Isabel's Day.' As described in an earlier chapter, 'Isabel's Day', named after a holy American woman and dear friend of ours, provides an opportunity for women and men to come to the quiet peace of the Dublin hills and, in this environ, to be guided in meditation or ritual, to reflect on the meaning of their work together, to be nourished by poetry or music, to share a home-cooked meal and to walk in the fresh mountain air. If we are at home, we simply carry on about our own work as staff from An Cosán facilitate the quieting and cook for the day. It is such a simple formula, yet its impact lingers long after the participants return home.

We also share in the residual peace that such days of stillness generate on the grounds of our home.

Simple rituals and formal ceremonies offer additional opportunities to replenish the human soul through symbolic gestures and words that capture our efforts to live justly in relation to each other. For years we have had the custom of lighting a candle in our kitchen whenever someone asks us to remember them on a given day. Word of this has obviously gone out, and so now people often ring us and request that the candle be lit. Focused mindfulness of one another can also enable a particular group to express the meaning they seek, be that joyful transitions, conflict resolved, suffering or death itself. After Maria Macken, an extraordinary Tallaght West community leader and Director of the Board of The Shanty, passed away following a lengthy battle with cancer, participants in all of the classes at An Cosán emptied the building and stood at its entrance. When the hearse carrying her body passed on its way to her funeral, we sang together 'Amazing Grace'. The hearse slowed down and paused, her husband, children and other family members listened to several verses, and then continued on the journey. This was our way, in a simple ritualistic gesture, to honour her leadership, her courage and her contribution to our work.

In an earlier chapter, we talked about the central place that the 'opening circle' holds in An Cosán courses. Tutors and participants begin their time together with poetry, guided meditation, a brief reflection or sometimes simply a few minutes of silence to bring themselves into the presence of each other before they focus on the day's work. At the end of each academic year, graduation is held, and the hundreds of people who have achieved higher learning participate in a celebration that initiates with a lighting of candles, followed by a reflective reading, and continues with speeches and certificates handed out. At our Shanty table, we regularly begin a meal with an expression of thanks to those gathered or a moment of stillness to bring our whole being to each other and to the food. Ritualising our presence with one another, reminding ourselves of the 'bigger picture' or the values that we hold or the meaning that unfolds as we reflect on our common work almost always brings balm to the soul. Recently, we were invited to say a few words at the Irish celebration of the Canadian marriage of our friends Deirdre Hannigan and Anne O'Reilly. As part of a traditional Irish 'afters' (wedding reception), we offered a blessing, a song and a political reflection on the fact that our friends had to travel to a foreign jurisdiction in order to be free to marry the person they love. This is the blessing we gave to them:

> May you always wake to delight in each other.
> May each day be filled with the love energy between you.
> May you always live bravely, and with freedom.
> May your courage be a beacon for others to follow.
> May your creativity and imaginations be nourished by forever love, so that your partnership will continue to light up the path of your shared future.
> May your partnership nourish self-confidence in each of you, so that your dreams for your selves will rise with the sun each day.
> May you never go to sleep with anger in your soul.
> May the trust you have in each other melt the negativities that come your way.
> May your families be happy for you, may they delight in your courage, vivacity, playfulness and all the ways in which you care for them, stand by them, love them, regardless.
> May the gathering of your family and friends this evening become a memory that fills you with the grace to be together, through richer and poorer, through sickness and in health, until death do you part.

2 Practising Virtue: Habits of the Soul

Defining virtue has long preoccupied philosophers and theologians; indeed, the ancient Greeks almost always conceived the acquisition of moral virtue as directed toward public life within the community. Virtues

– dispositions to enable right living within the private and public sphere – carry us from the stillness of be-ing or mindfulness of being-in-relation, into the powers of the human person to make ongoing choices for an equal and just society. We call them 'habits of the soul' to indicate that they need to be capacities exercised often and to convey that they reside within the core of each individual.

We find that at least seven virtues are indispensable to maintaining our focus on societal transformation. While we do not claim to practise any of these in a consistent manner, in naming them we catch a glimpse of how essential they are to sustain the life we and others are attempting to live. Our efforts to develop these habits are informed as much by the ways in which others embody them as by our own agency from time to time. They comprise a moral agenda of sorts and are informed by the example of those we have had privilege to share our lives with – members of the West Tallaght communities, academic colleagues, friends, family as well as leading human-rights and equality activists. To name them as virtues signifies our belief that political work for transformative change can be an ethical act.

GENEROSITY The virtue of generosity – to give of one's self for the benefit of others – creates the possibility that things can change for the better. While paid employment drives the productivity of the economy, volunteerism sparks movement towards changing systems, services, laws and policies that seek to ensure just and equitable treatment of every member of society. Often this requires the creation of something new: a community group, an organisation, or a social movement for change on behalf of a group that experiences discrimination because of its identity or social location. Changing the status quo always requires generosity; there is little financial reward for this activity. Here we think of Denise Charlton and Gráinne Healy, Co-Chairs of the organisation MarriagEquality. Before, during or after their 'day job' they manage to find the time to lead a social initiative that seeks equality, fairness and freedom for lesbian and gay people so that Irish law is changed to open the institution of marriage to them and contribute to the common good of all citizens. Gráinne and Denise have been at it for three years now, both carrying family commitments, demanding professional jobs and both with the sanguine awareness that making significant change takes time.

PERSONAL COMMITMENT, loyalty of heart, is another virtue without which social change will not occur. We sometimes speak about this as a commitment to the long haul, a willingness to be faithful to the people, the community or the cause for as long as it takes to get substantial, empirical progress. Anne and Martin Genockey provide exemplary witness to the practice of this virtue. For over twenty years they have lived and worked in Jobstown, Tallaght West. During that period they have educated themselves and their families and have taken leadership positions on community councils, within An Cosán, on drugs taskforces, and on wider county initiatives. Both are now professionals in their own right and could choose to get jobs in any part of the country – many have chosen this route as the correct path for themselves. Yet Anne and Martin stay in Jobstown, in the same house and neighbourhood where they have raised their children. While the geographic region has improved considerably because of their leadership, and while they, along with other neighbours and friends, are responsible for the development of a proud culture in Tallaght West, they are free to leave but they choose to stay because there is more to be done and because they have rendered the loyalty of their hearts to this great venture of justice.

INTEGRITY Within the contemporary political climate of highly sophisticated public relations, the practice of integrity – particularly in public communications – confers a fairer chance to shift change towards the removal of inequalities because it creates space for reasonable debate rather than media spin to protect things staying as they are. Practising the virtue of integrity in public means that we tell the truth. We tell the truth of what we know rather than 'message' a view of social reality that clandestinely advances the interests of the powerful, the majority or the able-bodied at the expense of radical inclusive change. Living with integrity often requires fearlessness or a willingess to risk personal attack, withdrawal of financial or personal support in order to speak a truth that is at one with the self's experience. When a government minister and local political representative told Liz Waters, the Chief Executive of An Cosán, that her chances of future government funding were in jeopardy because the organisation was being run 'by a bunch of lesbians', she told him that she was proud to work with us and that he must stop using the language of prejudice. She would not be bullied. Recently, there has been substantial media coverage of the Irish Government's proposals to develop a 'civil partnership bill' so that same-sex couples can have some financial and other civil protections embedded in law. The Government coalition partners – Fianna Fáil and the Green Party – argue that this is a 'step toward equality', and journalists write about 'marriage-like' rights that will be contained in the forthcoming Bill. From the centre of who we are – as two women who had to travel to Canada to exercise our right to marry – we know that to speak about 'marriage-like' rights is to use distorted communication. That language spins a sense of 'equality-like' change when, in fact, what is being prepared is a Bill that will establish a separate institution to marriage and tell gay and lesbian people that 'this is for them' and 'we are doing our best, for now.' When is the time for equality, we ask? If it is not now, when is it?

OPEN-MINDEDNESS So much of the path of change is affected by how we perceive the roadblocks to justice and how we work together to develop strategies and tactics that will dismantle the barriers to freedom. This is why practising the virtue of open-mindedness is so critical: it challenges us to a presence of attentive listening in order to learn from the insights of those who hold an opposing view to our own. Without openness to such learning, arrogant righteousness can overtake us. We are not talking about the art of compromise here, though that is important too. Open-mindedness often precedes compromise, but its practice demands something far deeper than political pragmatism. We open our minds to the view of others because we genuinely believe that the angle of their vision can be a corrective to our own, that they see things we do not have access to otherwise. Open-mindedness provides a marvellous antidote to the temptation of arrogance or absolutism. During the past year, we have participated in intense debates at the board table of An Cosán. One of six directors from the community, Joyce Cahill, kept saying to the middle-class members that we needed to find a 'common language' to analyse the problems of their communities. 'Policy or management speak' – language crafted by the socially powerful – did not reflect adequately the reality of their lives. We have now agreed on various strategies to translate our language for each other, holding respect for the language of both worlds, so that they learn the tools of the system and we understand resilience and learn the strategies of survivors. Through this dialogue, we continue to strive for a 'living language' that inspires us all to keep acting for change.

HOPE Recently, at the celebration of An Cosán's twenty-second anniversary, a young Nigerian woman approached Katherine and spoke to her of her hope for a better future for herself in this foreign land. Later, reflecting on the encounter, it brought to mind a small green paperback that both of us used to teach from during the mid-eighties in our university courses on the theologies of liberation. *Hope and Suffering,* written by Desmond Tutu during the South African apartheid era, riveted the attention of our students as they stepped into his world and heard his narration of practising hope in the midst of social systems denigrating his own and his people's dignity, causing their poverty or death. The virtue of hope – imagining better times with a resilience that blocks despair – is truly a transcendent activity. We imagine ourselves and/or others in a place that we do not yet reside, and we manage to do that in spite of the weight of present suffering, injustice or prejudice. Soon after the publication of his book in 1984, Archbishop Tutu spoke to the American people on a national television station and said, 'I am not interested in picking up crumbs of compassion thrown from the table of someone who considers himself my master. I want the full menu of human rights.' Hope – fired by justifiable indignation – consistently invigorates the human spirit to reach for that which is her or his due in spite of the hard, slow slog of fundamental change.

PROTECTION Reaching for the Irish State's recognition of our marriage has required that we let go of a lot of the privacy of our lives together that used to be kept for ourselves and a few close friends. While we carefully discerned both the need and willingness to let go, we also realised that there would come times when it would be prudent to practise the virtue of protection. Political or personal activism for change can put people in places that may be harmful to their physical or psychic health. If possible, this personal risk should be complimented by physical or psychic precautionary activity. Dr Ruth Doherty, a psychologist and spiritual healer introduced to us during Ann Louise's illness with cancer, used to tell us that prior to attending a difficult meeting or before entering a conflictual situation, we should zip ourselves up in an imaginary suit of our favourite colour to keep us from emotional harm. While this imagery sounds light and humoursome, there is an essential wisdom in the counsel that one must strive to protect one's inner core and remain centred. The seriousness of clothing ourselves in mind-made armour usually prepared us well for the struggle on behalf of others or for the personal exposure of ourselves. Changing the world is risky business, and it is important to stay well and centred while doing it.

LOVE We have already written an entire chapter about the greatest virtue of all, that is, the practice of love. In this context, however, we offer a few words on the practice of love as evoked and sustained by memory. The power of memory as the faculty that can hold the past in the now and allow the stories of past lives to challenge present listeners to a renewed commitment to the good life is something that we have been privileged to witness over the years of work with the community of An Cosán. Nuala Wallace joined the first fund-raising team, having recently lost her beloved husband Bob. He had been a highly successful young businessman, an entrepreneur always committed to improving the ordinary in the everyday. As Nuala got to know and admire the entrepreneurial spirit of many people in Tallaght West, she decided that in her husband's memory she would establish the Bob Wallace Memorial Fund, to ensure that his memory would sustain and resource their courage. At the launch of this significant gift, she presented a beautiful copper plaque, still hanging in The Muse, carved with Bob's words: 'Let us appreciate the beauty in the ordinary.' The narrative of Bob's life and the continued work of Nuala and now her daughter Carol, board member, in the current development of An Cosán gives witness to enduring love.

3 Principles – Ethical Signposts

The art of social change always involves efforts to win 'hearts and minds'. Offering people good reasons to do the right thing is as important as touching the heart and evoking an affective response. Practising change requires deep thinking alongside planning strategy and tactics and finding ways to measure results. Our intellect – traditionally understood as a faculty of the human soul – is supported by reference to principles or what we call 'ethical signposts' in order to make the right choices about what needs to change.

The language of principles is experiencing a revival of sorts today, particularly within the arena of equality and human-rights work. We need intellectual benchmarks to help us decide the detail of what to fight for, to support decision-making processes that are rooted in ideas fundamental to promoting the well-being of individuals within the systems of society. Consideration of principles takes us beyond an individualistic path of discerning what is right for me and supports the hard work of making good choices for the benefit of all. We have found that such discernment happens best within an ongoing dialogue between people of different social backgrounds, different ethnicities and identities and experiences. This is as true for our work in Tallaght West as it has been for our work at national level in education and human rights and, indeed, in our own judicial journey.

JUSTICE The first signpost is justice. This prompts us to ask a number of questions: what is needed so that every person receives her or his due, or so that each individual's inalienable rights and responsibilities can unfold without harm or with least harm to any other? As we review different aspects of Irish society, how well are we doing so that the burdens and the benefits of our prosperity are shared? Are there laws or policies that need to change so that the rights of some groups of people receive greater protection?

RELATIONALITY We have found that the principle of justice works best in tandem with the principle of relationality. We inhabit this earth together, we are essentially connected and so our actions necessarily impact on the lives of others and nature. This perspective provokes ethical thinking grounded in a growing awareness of our interdependence. Social, physical or material power can often lead to a false sense of independence and can blind us from seeing our vulnerability and deep interconnectedness. Alternatively, if our capacities or dignity have been damaged or disregarded because of our status or identity, this too can lead to a sense of disconnection and exacerbate a felt isolation. This is why principles are so helpful: they point to the ways things ought to be and offer intellectual resources to act towards the ideal.

FREEDOM One of our favourite signposts signals freedom. We might venture to say that this is a principle best understood by those who, for whatever reason, are restricted in their freedom to realise their own path or potential. Choosing to be free, to live our sexual identity authentically and with integrity, has allowed us the freedom to marry each other. Hopefully the exercise of this freedom will open up spaces for others to make similar choices. Recently, our friend Anne Motherway told us that she had cut out an article that we wrote for the *Irish Times* wherein we described our reasons for marrying each other and for taking a case against the Irish State. She remarked that she wanted to read it to her three daughters, aged between ten and eighteen, as a way of supporting them to feel free in shaping their own choices when the time comes. What a remarkable example of acting upon the basis of the ethical principle of freedom.

EQUALITY, **DIVERSITY** and **MUTUAL RESPECT** Three further principles furnish indispensable mind resources for practising social change. We have found that equality, diversity and mutual respect are best utilised as principles when we bring them to mind together.

Equality refers primarily to the full participation and inclusion of everyone in society's major institutions, which obviously enhances the common good. The most fundamental justification for equality between human beings has been described often as our equal moral worth to one another. But in an inclusive definition of equality, we are of equal intrinsic worth by virtue of being the humans we are.

Our equal worth is not dependent exclusively on capacities or characteristics that we may hold in common; it is dependent also on the reality of diverse ways of being human. So, we are inherently equal to one another in and through our differences, as well as in and through the common essence we share in our humanity.

The signpost of mutual respect demands that we equally value the other regardless of her or his social status, and this is dependent to a large extent on our willingness to come to know the difference of the other on her or his own terms. While this may entail conflict, it requires the resolution of conflict in a way that no one is denigrated, or oppressed. Therefore it becomes apparent that the practice of mutual respect is interdependent with action towards creating societal conditions that support it.

SOCIAL PRACTICES IN PUBLIC

A vibrant civil society – the public activity of voluntary civic and social organisations as distinct from those of the State – is vital for a healthy democracy. Civil society helps to create a free and independent space where citizens gather to debate and to offer critical commentary on how laws, policies and social institutions support or restrict the flourishing of all members of society. Civic groups often move beyond commentary and establish services – such as education, health or housing – where there are gaps in what the State provides, usually to those who experience some form of discrimination, disadvantage or lack of equal access. This is what we have tried to do with The Shanty and An Cosán. It is simply one example among thousands of voluntary efforts to build up the social fabric of how we live together. What we want to emphasise here, however, is that social transformation does not result simply from charitable acts of 'looking after' those who cannot look after themselves. Social transformation is the product of critical debate and creative activity so that more and more people have the proper conditions and social supports to freely choose the lives they want to lead. Social movements, civic actors, voluntary organisations and philanthropy play a crucial role to provide corrective or complimentary activities to the State in this regard.

As we stand back and reflect on our own involvement in this public space, we want to make the case that paying attention to soul, practising virtues and referring regularly to ethical principles supports the effectiveness of social practices for radical change. We have also learned that social change calls for a number of interlinked public activities, as outlined below.

IDENTIFY YOUR STARTING POINT Perhaps the most strategic way to begin is to identify a social issue which, if positively addressed, could have a cascading effect and impact other social ills. To sustain the energy and commitment it takes to remedy the inequality, it is also important to choose an area of engagement that evokes in oneself a sense of moral outrage at the current injustice. We still remember how shocked we felt when we first discovered that there were only three thousand third-level State university places for a population of three million in the early eighties. Though we both lectured in university at the time, both of us had few students who came from geographic regions of disadvantage. And when we started our work in Tallaght West, we did not meet one person with a university degree. Though the State was proud of its investment in education, it was not paying off for a lot of the people we knew. Eventually, academics, other community groups and the national adult-education associaton, AONTAS, built up a body of knowledge about how social class and geographic location create barriers for educational achievement, and they began to communicate this to the country at large. There was little public consciousness of these social problems prior to the engagement of civil society in analysing the causes and offering a critical voice. There was virtually no educational policy on 'second chance' adult education and no finanical support. Our first government grant came through the Department of Social Welfare, not Education, a strong indication of how the State viewed the 'problem'. All of this information and analysis was vital to our work – with so many other individuals and groups – to shift public policy and awareness towards an acceptance of adult community education as a key mechanism for the eradication of poverty.

IMAGINE THE CHANGE As a young girl, Ann Louise was often caught 'daydreaming' at school. Considered to be improper behaviour for the learning environment, the class teacher would chide her and tell her to 'pay attention'. Undeterred, Ann Louise would quietly divert her gaze back to wonder at the activity of nature in the quadrangle outside the classroom window or plan imaginative adventures for her pals after school hours. This persistent exercise of her own imagination and love for all expressions of creativity led later to a study of the philosophy and psychology of the creative imagination and eventually to the development of our practices to imagine social change. As described in an earlier chapter, when we started the Shanty project, Tallaght West comprised of rows and rows of local-authority houses with a few local convenience shops, a couple of pubs, churches and schools. No other social or community infrastructure existed, and we still carry in our memories stark images of a lone 'chipper' van travelling from one community to the next. Often during Shanty classes we invited the people to imagine what they would like their communities to look like in ten years' time. Working with other community groups, class participants brought their ideas to the politicians and county councils, and, eventually, the Government produced a plan to create four 'village cores' – comprised of medical, community and enterprise centres – to each of the four communities of Tallaght West. An Cosán was built in the midst of the Jobstown village core. Today, resulting from ongoing imaginative exercises and countless negotiations with government and the local authority, a wide array of community leaders and organisations have supported the development of a vastly changed infrastructural environ.

ANALYSE HOW OTHERS HAVE DONE IT. In the wake of immense positive public reaction to news that we were granted judicial permission to argue our case for equal treatment as a married couple in the High Court, we were approached by Brian Kearney-Grieve, the Human Rights Programme Executive of Atlantic Philanthropies. Brian watched Irish public response with the eyes of one who was also witnessing change on this issue around the world. As a member of a global philanthropy, he was in touch with those who supported efforts towards marriage equality in other jurisdictions, particularly in the United States and in South Africa. GLAD, the Boston-based Gay and Lesbian Advocates and Defenders, had filed in 2001 a 'freedom to marry' case in Massachusetts on behalf of seven same-sex couples, with a historic win in the state's Supreme Court in 2003. A lesbian South African couple, Marie Fourie and Cecilia Bonthuys, had a 2002 win in their High Court with a ruling that denying same-sex couples the right to marry is discriminatory and thus unconstitutional. They, along with civic organisations like the South African Gay and Lesbian Equality Project, generated further fundamental change when South Africa's Supreme Court defined marriage as 'the union of two persons to the exclusion of all others' and gave law-makers one year to amend the country's Marriage Act. With Brian's expert assistance, Atlantic Philanthropies put Irish civic lesbian and gay groups in contact with change-makers in these and other countries. Reviewing international models of effective social-change practice and how they can inform Ireland (with appropriate cultural amendments) has been a prime factor in provoking government response to the call for equal rights for lesbian and gay couples here.

REVIEW RELEVANT LAW AND POLICY. In March 2006, the Irish Minister for Justice, Equality and Law Reform, Michael McDowell, established a working group of lawyers, civil servants, an economist and the Director of Policy Change from GLEN (the Gay and Lesbian Equality Network) to examine law and policy in Ireland and other countries in order to identify legal options for recognising domestic partnerships of both same-sex and opposite sex couples in Ireland. (There was no such Irish legislation then, and, at the time of this writing, there are still no laws enacted.) The establishment of this group resulted from pressure being brought to bear on government by GLEN, the KAL Advocacy Initiative (the group providing public support for our case) and the National Lesbian and Gay Federation of Ireland, particularly through its publication of the *Gay Community News* under the editorship of Brian Finnegan. Eventually known as 'the Colley Group' (because solicitor Anne Colley was its chairperson), it met for a number of months in order to review numerous research reports from statutory and voluntary bodies as well as submissions from the public. Towards the end of our first week in the High Court, word came through that the report would include a statement about marriage for same-sex couples, even though the group's terms of reference did not explicitly cover this issue. Eoin Collins, GLEN's representative on the group, tirelessly advocated for the positive statement that resulted:

> The introduction of civil marriage for same-sex couples would achieve equality of status with opposite-sex couples and such recognition that would underpin a wider equality for gay and lesbian people.

While the *Colley Report* did not go on to recommend this as an option to government because, in their view, 'introducing civil marriage for same-sex couples is likely to be vulnerable to constitutional challenge', we felt hugely supported by the earlier principled statement of the group. What makes it particularly remarkable is that it emerged from within a government-established group and through a process of dialogue and debate that incorporated civic as well as statutory voices. Radical change usually requires this kind of intensive, systematic and comprehensive analysis, and the *Colley Report*'s conclusion that civil marriage is *the* equality option for same-sex couples continues to be a forceful tool for change in the current climate.

ASK THE QUESTION: IS IT FOR THE LAW-MAKERS, THE PEOPLE OR THE COURTS? In our memoir, there is reference to the lengthy discernment about the most appropriate route to seek change so that Irish law would recognise our life partnership. We witnessed efforts by civic advocates to develop a 'domestic partnership' Bill that could be placed before the law-makers, aware that little appetite existed by the elected representatives for even this type of minimal legal change. Still, we waited and thought it best to seek legal advice through the Equality Authority. The core issue in this instance – as it is for many other fundamental equality or human-rights issues – is, what is the correct path of seeking change? In a democracy, should the rights of minorities be decided directly by 'the people' through a referendum, by the law-makers through negotiating legislation in the midst of various interest groups or by the courts through the highest court of the land? In the midst of this discernment, the miraculous possibility to get married in Canada opened up. This focused our minds and hearts on the most fundamental issue at stake: as members of a minority group, do we have the human right to marry? And where, in a democracy, ought that right be decided? Obviously we judged that, in this case, it was for the courts.

SPARK THE PUBLIC ETHICAL IMAGINATION. 'Something has to be done': these are words spoken by Margaret A Gill, a County Offaly grandmother, mother and wife, as she concluded her interview on Irish national television, telling the story of her lesbian daughter who had been tragically killed as she rode her bicycle to work one morning in early 2008. Barbara Gill had lived a thirteen-year committed relationship with her partner Ruth, and eight weeks prior Ruth had given birth to their son, Stephen. Margaret characterised her daughter as experiencing 'supreme happiness' prior to her death. The last time Margaret spoke with Barbara, she told her by telephone: 'Mum, I'm the happiest person in the world. I have just bathed Stephen and put him to bed.' Twenty-four hours later, Margaret and her husband were called back to Dublin from a fiftieth-wedding anniversary trip, to find Barbara in a coma. When Pat Kenny, the interviewer, asked Margaret how she felt when her daughter had told her years earlier that she was a lesbian, Margaret replied: 'It didn't make any difference, Pat. She was my daughter; she was just different. Your daughter is your daughter.' Margaret went on to describe how Barbara and Ruth had wanted to marry and hoped for the day when that would be possible. They had recently made wills together prior to the birth of their son – waiting for his arrival before putting the final details in order so that they could sign the wills. In those first eight weeks after his arrival, they just hadn't found the time to finish the paperwork. Barbara owned the house that Ruth, Barbara and Stephen lived in, and, in a previous will, she had left it to her parents. Ruth had made the decision to be the 'stay-at-home' parent, and Barbara held the pensionable job. With Barbara's untimely death, her parents inherited the house, and her pension was gone because the couple's legal status was 'strangers in law'. That is the situation still, as it stands at the time of this writing.

Margaret Gill's courageous and dignified words, spoken in public, offer exceptional moral wisdom to the nation. She sparks our desire to live in a modern, enlightened, liberated country.

SPLIT THE PUBLIC CONSCIOUSNESS. As mentioned, Paulo Freire, one of our mentors during doctoral studies, often talked about activities of 'splitting consciousness' in order to get the wider public to awake to the reality of social inequalities and oppression. The voices of prophets, change agents, storytellers and poets can split public apathy and raise critical consciousness. One summer afternoon in 1984 we witnessed the beginnings of such an activity on Henry Street in Dublin, outside the doors of Dunnes Stores. Earlier in the week, Mary Manning, a young cashier, had been presented by one of the customers with two South African oranges to check out. The previous Easter, Mary's union passed a resolution saying that members should not handle South African goods because of apartheid. So Mary politely told the customer that she couldn't handle the fruit because it was South African. Within minutes, Mary was whisked upstairs to management, and they told her that she had five minutes to reconsider her position. Mary said, 'No, I'm sticking by my position', and the Dunnes Stores strike began. Ten workers followed Mary on to the picket line with little awareness that the strike would gain worldwide attention, last for almost three years, or that it would ultimately result in the government banning South African goods from Irish stores. What caught our attention that summer day was the placard held by one of our friends, Chris Mulvey, who had joined the strikers in solidarity. It read: 'Apartheid is too high a price to pay for South African goods.' Though we had been teaching about South African liberation theology in our universities, this was the first time we became truly aware of how our own actions, in Ireland, could block or support black South Africans' march towards freedom. For the next two years, as part of our lectures on black liberation theologies, we encouraged our students to go and talk to the Dunnes Stores strikers and witness at first hand the immense social power of a very ordinary group of citizens.

TELL STORIES. Story carries the power to capture people's hearts and to create a readiness for them to think about things in a new way. Telling stories, in public, can subvert minds from acquiescing to the status quo. Social change does not happen unless many, many people are willing to tell their stories, out loud. During the past couple of years, the Irish public have heard a number of stories told by people who share our sexual identity, offering new meaning to traditional understandings of parenthood, and even some of their children are beginning to speak.

Our friends Denise Charlton and Paula Fagan have written eloquently about their experience as lesbian mothers of their son. They say: 'We are two mothers doing very ordinary things. We change nappies, suffer through *Barney*, cut up carrots, make sure that we always have a spare bib in our handbag, just like thousands of other mothers every day. We both feel that it is the greatest gift to be a parent and to be part of a family living in Ireland. However, in the eyes of the same country we are committed to and have worked hard for, we are not a family. Legally, we are not both recognised as parents to the son we dote on. Because of this, *his rights to his family are not recognised either.* If the Government does not open the institution of civil marriage to us, it will be telling our son (and other children in gay and lesbian families) that they're not the same as their classmates and that their parents are lesser citizens.' Clare Courtney, the thirteen-year-old daughter of Grainne Courtney and Orla Howard, told her story to the papers a few weeks earlier. Claire said: 'We want to be able to say we have a real family; we don't want anyone to be able to question that. We want people to see that children of lesbian parents aren't all messed up, we are normal, we deserve the same rights as anyone else.'

MOBILISE THE PEOPLE. Over the years of our own engagement in practising change, one of the key lessons we have learned is that nobody arrives at the goal alone. When we state clearly that, for example, the achievement of An Cosán must not be attributed to us but to all the people involved over the years, this is not any false humility, this is actually the fact. As we narrated in an earlier part of this memoir, the ultimate success in getting government agreement for the building of An Cosán, and the subsequent growth and development of that organisation is due entirely to all the many people both within the community and outside of it who believed in and continue to believe in this dream. It is hugely important to understand that the truth about any social-change achievement is that many, many people have joined the vision and acted for a positive outcome.

How do you mobilise the people? Perhaps the most important thing to say is, begin the work, however small that beginning may be. The Shanty started with twelve people in a sitting room and today has over seven hundred women and men in adult education, a hundred children in early childhood education and four franchises in a social enterprise for early years education and childcare. Furthermore, ensure that the voices of those who are living with injustice shape the development and growth of practising change in a dialogical and respectful manner. Towards the beginning of our work in Tallaght West, a hundred residents formed a stakeholders association and, as their first public act, held a seminar with elected representatives to find out where they stood on the lack of community facilities and educational opportunities for themselves, their children and young people. The outcome of this meeting resulted in a positive response from local politicians. It also laid the foundation for the supportive relationship that exists to this day between An Cosán and our public representatives. Clearly, the list of methods to mobilise goes on and on, as the work goes on.

We hope that our story and method provide encouragement and offer intimations of the possible.

ACKNOWLEDGEMENTS

The invitation to write our memoir came as an unanticipated surprise. The request to place the narrative of our lives in dialogue with aspects of social history over the period added a distinctive challenge. Once we found a methodology to write a 'joint memoir', a rather unusual genre, we set about the task with verve, finding it an enriching experience; indeed, we would now name it as a privileged opportunity in our lives together. So we wish to begin by acknowledging The O'Brien Press and Mairéad Ashe FitzGerald who suggested that we write this book. Michael O'Brien, publisher, provided genuine encouragement and support throughout the writing process. His own passion for justice is contagious. Grateful acknowledgement is made also to our senior editor Ide ní Laoghaire, who offered key suggestions, insights and editorial advice that greatly improved the final text.

As indicated in the dedication, our deepest gratitude is extended to our parents, whose own stories shaped and influenced our lives in foundational ways. Our happiness is rooted in the seeds of their love. Warmest thanks to our families, especially our sisters and brothers – June Kelly, Suzanne Hoover, Arthur Gilligan, Bob, Philip and Mark Zappone – and to our friends, whose love and support throughout our lives has been indispensable.

Boston College will always hold a special place in our memories. It is where we first met each other and we continue to remember with deep appreciation those who were so significant during that initial period of study; they remain our friends and revered colleagues to this day, especially Tom Groome, Claire Lowery, Ann Morgan, John McDargh and Francine Cardman. Our abiding friendship with Rosemary Haughton and Nancy Schwoyer of Wellspring House in Gloucester, Massachusetts, shaped our story in countless ways.

We are indebted to all those who have walked the path with us from the creation of The Shanty Educational Project to the current organisation, An Cosán: the Centre for Learning, Leadership and Enterprise, located in the heart of Jobstown, Tallaght West. It is no exaggeration to say that thousands of people have contributed in a multiplicity of ways to the growth and success of this organisation – and to the belief that education is the key to the transformation of poverty. In particular, we want to thank the people who have been part of management, fund-raising and development committees over the years, and those who have served as members of our Board, past and present. With gratitude, we acknowledge the able leadership of the current Chair, Dorothy McCann, CEO Liz Waters, and all the staff, community leaders and volunteers. In founding this organisation, little did we ever anticipate that we were forming a community of friends who embrace our lives with love and unbelievable support.

Our professional colleagues have always enriched our lives. Ann Louise is particularly grateful to those in St Patrick's College, Drumcondra – the President, Pauric Travers, and academic and support staff – who have offered much inspiration and kindness over the years. Mark Morgan, Head of the Education Department, deserves particular mention for his gracious facilitation of a six-month sabbatical that enabled Ann Louise to commence work on this book. Katherine wishes to thank most warmly her colleagues, past and present, on the Irish Human Rights Commission, including Donal Barrington and Maurice Manning, its first and current president respectively. They have provided much wisdom and solidarity in their pursuit of justice. Many other academics and leaders in the sectors of civil society, community, equality and human rights have blessed us with friendship and assisted us in our journey as narrated in these memoirs.

Since 2002, when we started to pursue legal recognition of our life partnership in Ireland, many, many people have been instrumental in sustaining us. This includes, first and foremost, our legal team: Phil O'Hehir and Kevin Brophy of Brophy's Solicitors, and Gerard Hogan SC, Michael Collins SC, and Ivana Bacik BL.

Our expert witnesses for the case gave most willingly and generously of their time: Denis Cremins, Daniel Maguire, Harry Kennedy, Andrew Koppleman, Evelyn Mahon, Robert Wintemute, Kenneth Smith, Richard Hynes and Melissa Green. We are also grateful for the support of our accountants Frank McCormack and Máire Ní Shéalaigh. Others who supported us during this time in different ways include: Edel Hackett, Niall Crowley, Shelagh Day, Gwen Brodsky, Melanie Verwoerd, David Norris, Gerard Quinn, Anne Motherway, Rachel Matthews-McKay, Richie Keane, Gary Buseck, Mary Bonauto, and Lee

Swislow of Gay and Lesbian Advocates and Defenders in Massachusetts, and all who contributed to the fund-raising efforts.

We want to say a particular word of thanks to members and staff of MarriagEquality, ably co-chaired by Denise Charlton and Gráinne Healy. They, along with all those who previously supported the KAL Advocacy Initiative – especially the civil society organisations of the National Lesbian and Gay Federation, the Gay and Lesbian Equality Network, LGBT Noise, Dublin Pride, the Irish Council for Civil Liberties, and FLAC – are advancing the cause of justice and equality in Ireland.

We wish to express our heartfelt gratitude to all who have accompanied us during the writing of this book. We acknowledge those in Seattle University, especially Vice-President Tim Leary, Erin Swezey, and Dean Kellye Testy, who afforded us the wonderful opportunity to spend the summer of 2007 in the Law School and placed at our disposal the resources of the university. Due for particular mention is the librarian, Stephanie Wilson. Atlantic Philanthropies provided a grant to enable Katherine to take a sabbatical from other professional work. We honour the generosity and kindness of John R Healy, Colin McCrea and Brian Kearney-Grieve, and we deeply appreciate their commitment to this project.

Finally, we are graced and humbled by the foreword to our memoir by Archbishop Emeritus Desmond Tutu, a holy and courageous man who continues to inspire our lives.

PERMISSIONS

The authors and publisher thank the following for permission to quote copyright material:
The lines from 'Living Memory', from TIME'S POWER: *Poems 1985-1988* by Adrienne Rich.
Copyright © W.W. Norton & Company Inc. Used by permission of the author and W. W.
Norton & Company Inc.
The lines cfrom 'Phantasia for Elvira Shatayev', from THE DREAM OF A COMMON LANGUAGE:
Poems 1974-1977 by Adrienne Rich; copyright © 1978 by W.W. Norton & Com[any Inc; used
by permission of the author and W.W. Norton & Company Inc.
'A Lover's Song', copyright © 1968 by Audre Lorde, 'Love Poem', copyright © 1975 by
Audre Lorde, from *The Collected Poems of Audre Lorde* by Audre Lorde; used by permission of
W.W. Norton & Company Inc.
We have made every effort to contact copyright holders; however, if any infringement has
occurred we ask the holder of such copyright to contact the publishers.